MW01701778

Practice and Problem Solving Workbook

PEARSON

Boston, Massachusetts • Chandler, Arizona • Glenview, Illinois • Upper Saddle River, New Jersey

PEARSON

ISBN-13: 978-0-7854-7033-5
ISBN-10: 0-7854-7033-6
1 2 3 4 5 6 7 8 9 10 V084 13 12 11 10 09

Contents

Chapter 4

Chapter 5

Name ______________________________ Class ____________ Date ____________

1-1 Think About a Plan

Variables and Expressions

Volunteering Serena and Tyler are wrapping gift boxes at the same pace. Serena starts first, as shown in the diagram. Write an algebraic expression that represents the number of boxes Tyler will have wrapped when Serena has wrapped *x* boxes.

Think

1. Since Serena started first she will always have more boxes than Tyler. How many boxes did Serena wrap before Tyler started?

Plan

2. Examine the situation. What phrase in the situation could be rewritten as an algebraic symbol? What is the associated symbol?

Solve

3. When Serena has wrapped *x* boxes, how many boxes has Tyler wrapped?

4. Could this situation be expressed in another manner? Explain and give an example to prove your point.

Name ______________________ Class ____________ Date ____________

1-1 Practice

Form K

Variables and Expressions

Write an algebraic expression for each word phrase.

1. 11 more than *y*

2. 5 less than *n*

3. the sum of 15 and *w*

4. 22 minus *k*

5. a number *b* divided by 8

6. *q* multiplied by 2

7. the product of 3.3 and a number *x*

8. one third of a number *m*

Write a word phrase for each algebraic expression.

9. $8 - a$

10. $v + 9$

11. $\frac{y}{5} - 10$

12. $1.9 + n$

13. $5h + 3k$

14. $2x + 1$

Write a rule in words and as an algebraic expression to model the relationship.

15. The cost of beverages in a vending machine is shown.

Beverages	Cost
1	$1.25
2	$2.50
3	$3.75

1-1 Practice (continued) Form K

Variables and Expressions

16. Jordan gets paid to mow his neighbor's lawn. For every week that he mows the lawn, he earns \$20. Write a rule as an algebraic expression to model the relationship.

Write an algebraic expression for each word phrase.

17. 14 minus the quotient of 25 and p

18. a number w tripled plus t quadrupled

19. the product of 13 and m plus the product of 2.7 and n

20. the product of 2 times a and 5 times b

21. Error Analysis A student writes *the sum of 7 times a number n plus 5* to describe the expression $7(n + 5)$. Explain the error.

22. Sarah is going to pay for an item using gift cards. The clerk tells her that she will need 2 gift cards and an additional \$3 to pay for the item. Write an algebraic expression to model the situation using the variable g for the number of gift cards to pay her total bill, t.

Name ________________ Class ________ Date ________

1-1 Standardized Test Prep

Variables and Expressions

Multiple Choice

For Exercises 1–7, choose the correct letter.

1. The word *minus* corresponds to which symbol?

   A. $+$ B. $-$ C. $\div$ D. $\times$

2. The phrase *product* corresponds to which symbol?

   F. $\times$ G. $+$ H. $-$ I. $\div$

3. The word *plus* corresponds to which symbol?

   A. $-$ B. $+$ C. $<$ D. $\div$

4. What is an algebraic expression for the word phrase *10 more than a number f?*

   F. $10 - f$ G. $\frac{10}{f}$ H. $10 \times f$ I. $f + 10$

5. What is an algebraic expression for the word phrase *the product of 11 and a number s*?

   A. $\frac{11}{s}$ B. $11 \times s$ C. $11 + s$ D. $11 - s$

6. Hannah and Tim collect stamps. Tim is bringing his stamps to Hannah's house so that they can compare. Hannah has 60 stamps. Which expression represents the total number of stamps that they will have if t represents the number of stamps Tim has?

   F. $60 \times t$ G. $60 \div t$ H. $60 + t$ I. $60 - t$

7. Hershel's bakery sells donuts by the box. There are d donuts in each box. Beverly is going to buy 10 boxes for a class field trip. Which expression represents the total number of donuts that Beverly is going to get for her field trip?

   A. $10 \times d$ B. $10 \div d$ C. $10 - d$ D. $10 + d$

Short Response

8. There are 200 people interested in playing in a basketball league. The leaders of the league are going to divide all of the people into n teams. What algebraic expression represents the number of players on each team?

Name ______________________ Class ____________ Date ____________

1-2 Think About a Plan

Order of Operations and Evaluating Expressions

Salary You earn $10 for each hour you work for a canoe rental shop. Write an expression for your salary for working *h* hours. Make a table to find how much you earn for working 10, 20, 30, and 40 hours.

Think

1. What word or phrase indicates the operation that should be used to help you solve this problem?

Plan

2. Using your response from Exercise 1, write an expression that will tell you how much you earn for every *h* hours you work.

Solve

3. Use your expression from Exercise 2 to find the amount that you will earn for working 10, 20, 30, and 40 hours.

4. Make a table summarizing your results.

Name ______________________ Class ____________ Date ____________

1-2 Practice

Form K

Order of Operations and Evaluating Expressions

Simplify each expression.

1. 9^2

2. 8^3

3. $\left(\frac{7}{8}\right)^2$

4. $(4 + 3)^2$

5. $8 + 5(7)$

6. $\left(\frac{21}{3}\right) - 2(3)$

7. $11(3) - 3^2$

8. $\left(\frac{15}{5}\right)^3 - 6(2)^2$

9. $(3(4))^3$

10. $3^4 - 2^4 \div 2^2$

Evaluate each expression for $x = 3$ and $y = 2$.

11. $x + 7$

12. $8 - y$

13. $\frac{x^3}{3} - 8$

14. $5(y)^3 - 6$

15. $-6(x)^2 + y^3 - 8$

16. $\left(\frac{x + 1}{y^2}\right)^2$

1-2 Practice (continued)

Form K

Order of Operations and Evaluating Expressions

17. George is driving at an average speed of 62 miles per hour. Write an expression that would give his distance traveled for h hours. Make a table that records his distance for 3, 5.5, 7, and 8.5 hours.

Simplify each expression.

18. $5[(4 + 8) - 3^3]$

19. $2[(7 - 10)^2 + 5]^2$

20. $[(32 \div 4)^3 - 500]^3$

21. $\left(\frac{2(-2)(4)}{12 - 4(2)}\right)^3$

22. The cost to rent a car is \$30 per day. Write an expression for the cost of renting a car for d days. Make a table to find how much it will cost to rent a car for 3, 5, 7, and 10 days.

Evaluate each expression for the given values of the variables.

23. $2(m + 1) - n^3$; $m = -2, n = 3$

24. $-3[(a - 3)^2 + b]^2$; $a = 4, b = 6$

25. $-1\left[x^3 - \left(\frac{2y}{4}\right)^2\right]$; $x = 5, y = -2$

26. $t[v^2 - (23 - v^2) + 3]$; $t = -2, v = 2$

27. Reasoning Show that the expressions $3m^2n^2$ and $5m^3 + 13m^2n$ are equal when $m = 2$ and $n = 5$.

Name ______________________ Class __________ Date __________

1-2 Standardized Test Prep

Order of Operations and Evaluating Expressions

Gridded Response

Solve each exercise and enter your answer on the grid provided.
Round your answers to the nearest hundredth if necessary.

1. What is the simplified form of $(3.2)^4$?

2. What is the simplified form of $(6^2 + 4) - 15$?

3. What is the simplified form of $4 \times 6^2 \div 3 + 7$?

4. What is the value of $-4d^2 + 15d^2 \div 5$ for $d = 1$?

5. What is the value of $(5x^2)^3 + 16y \div 4y$ for $x = 2$ and $y = 3$?

1.
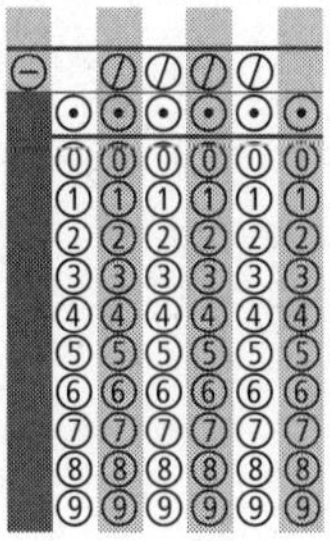

2.
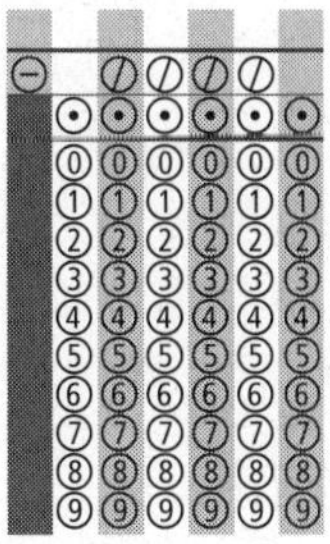

3.
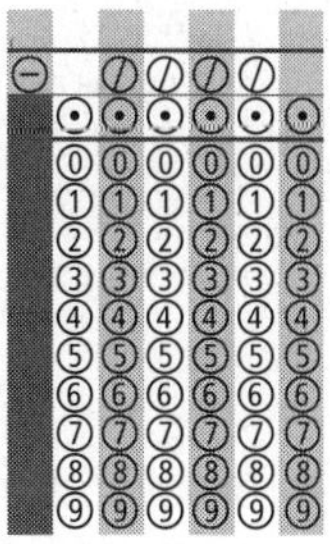

4.
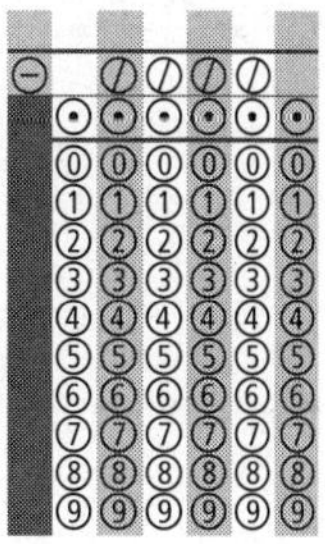

5.
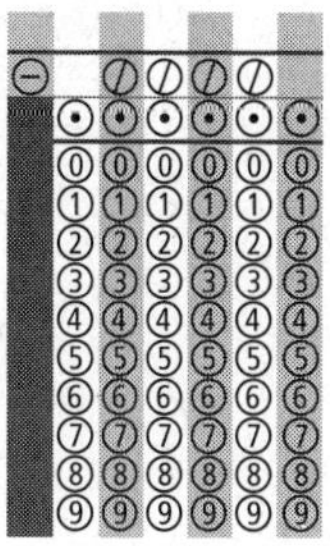

Name ______________________ Class ____________ Date ____________

1-3 Think About a Plan

Real Numbers and the Number Line

Home Improvement If you lean a ladder against a wall, the length of the ladder should be $\sqrt{(x)^2 + (4x)^2}$ ft to be considered safe. The distance x is how far the ladder's base is from the wall. Estimate the desired length of the ladder when the base is positioned 5 ft from the wall. Round your answer to the nearest tenth.

Think

1. What does x represent in the given expression? What value is given for x?

Plan

2. What is the expression when the given value is substituted for x?

3. How do you simplify the expression under the square root symbol?

4. What is the value of the expression under the square root symbol? Is this number a perfect square?

Solve

5. What is an estimate for the desired length of the ladder? Round your answer to the nearest tenth.

Name ______________________ Class ____________ Date ____________

1-3 Practice

Form K

Real Numbers and the Number Line

Simplify each expression.

1. $\sqrt{144}$

2. $\sqrt{25}$

3. $\sqrt{169}$

4. $\sqrt{49}$

5. $\sqrt{256}$

6. $\sqrt{400}$

7. $\sqrt{\frac{9}{49}}$

8. $\sqrt{\frac{196}{144}}$

9. $\sqrt{0.01}$

10. $\sqrt{0.49}$

Estimate the square root. Round to the nearest integer.

11. $\sqrt{38}$

12. $\sqrt{65}$

13. $\sqrt{99}$

14. $\sqrt{145.5}$

15. $\sqrt{23.75}$

16. $\sqrt{64.36}$

Find the approximate side length of each square figure to the nearest whole unit.

17. a tabletop with an area 25 ft^2

18. a wall that is 105 m^2

1-3 Practice (continued)

Form K

Real Numbers and the Number Line

Name the subset(s) of the real numbers to which each number belongs.

19. $\frac{3}{4}$

20. -8

21. 2π

22. 45,368

23. $\sqrt{11}$

24. $-\frac{2}{3}$

Compare the numbers in each exercise using an inequality symbol.

25. $\sqrt{36}, \sqrt{49}$

26. $\frac{1}{3}, \sqrt{1.25}$

27. $\sqrt{100}, -\sqrt{169}$

28. $\frac{34}{19}, 1.8$

Order the numbers in each exercise from least to greatest.

29. $2.75, \sqrt{25}, -\sqrt{36}$

30. $1.25, -\frac{1}{3}, \sqrt{1.25}$

31. $\frac{3}{5}, -0.6, \sqrt{1}$

32. $\frac{80}{25}, \sqrt{9}, \frac{30}{9}$

33. Kate, Kevin, and Levi are comparing how fast they can run. Kate was able to run 5 miles in 47.5 minutes. Kevin was able to run 8 miles in 74 minutes. Levi was able to run 4 miles in 32 minutes. Order the friends from the fastest to the slowest.

1-3 Standardized Test Prep

Real Numbers and the Number Line

Multiple Choice

For Exercises 1–6, choose the correct letter.

1. To which subset of the real numbers does −18 not belong?
   A. irrational **B.** rational **C.** integer **D.** negative integers

2. To which subset of the real numbers does $\sqrt{2}$ belong?
   F. irrational **G.** rational **H.** integer **I.** whole

3. You can tell that π is an irrational number because it has a what?
   A. non-repeating decimal
   B. non-terminating decimal
   C. repeating decimal
   D. non-repeating and a non-terminating decimal

4. What is $\sqrt{324}$?
   F. 15 **G.** 18 **H.** 19 **I.** 24

5. What is $\sqrt{196}$?
   A. −14 **B.** 0 **C.** 4 **D.** 19

6. What is $\sqrt{36x^6y^4}$?
   F. $6x^6y^4$ **G.** $6x^3y^2$ **H.** $18x^3y^2$ **I.** $24x^6y^4$

Short Response

7. Why is 8.8 classified as a rational number?

Name ______________________ Class ____________ Date ____________

1-4 Think About a Plan

Properties of Real Numbers

Travel It is 235 mi from Tulsa to Dallas. It is 390 mi from Dallas to Houston.

a. What is the total distance of a trip from Tulsa to Dallas to Houston?

b. What is the total distance from Houston to Dallas to Tulsa?

c. Explain how you can tell whether the distances described in parts (a) and (b) are equal by using reasoning.

Think

1. What operation(s) will you use to solve the problem?

2. Which of the properties of real numbers involve the operations identified in part (a)?

Plan

3. Write expressions that can be simplified to solve parts (a) and (b).

4. How are the two expressions similar? How are those similarities related to the situation as described?

5. How are the expressions different? How are those differences related to the situation as described?

Solve

6. Find the total distances asked for in parts (a) and (b). What do you notice about the answers?

7. Which of the properties of real numbers best explains your results?

8. Discuss how that property explains your results.

Name ______________________ Class __________ Date __________

1-4 Practice

Form K

Properties of Real Numbers

Match statements 1–8 with the property, a – h, that the statement illustrates.

a **Commutative Property of Addition:** $a + b = b + a$
b. **Commutative Property of Multiplication:** $a \cdot b = b \cdot a$
c. **Additive Identity:** $a + 0 = a$
d. **Multiplicative Identity:** $a \cdot 1 = a$
e. **Associative Property of Addition:** $(a + b) + c = a + (b + c)$
f. **Associative Property of Multiplication:** $(a \cdot b) \cdot c = a \cdot (b \cdot c)$
g. **Zero Property of Multiplication:** $a \cdot 0 = 0$
h. **Multiplicative Property of −1:** $-1 \cdot a = -a$

1. $12 + 917 = 917 + 12$

2. $5 \cdot 0 = 0$

3. $35 \cdot x = x \cdot 35$

4. $(x \cdot 3) \cdot 4 = x \cdot (3 \cdot 4)$

5. $m + 0 = m$

6. $25 \cdot 1 = 25$

7. $(15 + 9) + 11 = 15 + (9 + 11)$

8. $-1 \cdot 6 = -6$

Simplify each expression. Justify each step that has not been justified.

9. $5 + (3x + 2) = 5 + (2 + 3x)$ Commutative Property of Addition
$= (5 + 2) + 3x$ ______________________
$= 7 + 3x$ Combine like terms.

10. $3 \cdot (x \cdot 6) = 3 \cdot (6 \cdot x)$ ______________________
$= (3 \cdot 6) \cdot x$ Associative Property of Multiplication
$= 18x$ Multiply.

1-4 Practice (continued)

Form K

Properties of Real Numbers

Simplify each expression. Justify each step.

11. $(2 + 7m) + 5$

12. $9 \cdot (r \cdot 21)$

Tell whether the expressions in each pair are equivalent.

13. $2x$ and $2x \cdot 1$

14. $(5 - 2) \cdot x$ and $3x$

15. $8 + 6 + b$ and $8 + 6b$

16. $5 \cdot (4 - 4)$ and 0

17. You have prepared 40 mL of vanilla, 20 mL of chocolate, and 50 mL of milk for a milkshake.

a. How many milliliters of milkshake will you have if you first pour the vanilla, then the chocolate, and finally the milk into your glass?

b. How many milliliters of milkshake will you have if you first pour the chocolate, then the vanilla, and finally the milk into your glass?

c. Explain how you can tell whether the amounts of milkshake described in parts (a) and (b) are equal.

Use deductive reasoning to tell whether each statement is *true* or *false*. If it is false, give a counterexample.

18. For all real numbers a and b, $a - b = b - a$.

19. For all real numbers p, q, and r, $p - q - r = p - r - q$.

20. For all real numbers x, y, and z, $(x + y) + z = z + (x + y)$.

21. For all real numbers n, $n + 1 = n$.

22. Writing Explain why the commutative and associative properties do not hold true for subtraction and division.

Name ______________________ Class ____________ Date ____________

1-4 Standardized Test Prep

Properties of Real Numbers

Multiple Choice

For Exercises 1–5, choose the correct letter.

1. Which of the following statements is *not* always true?

   A. $a + (-b) = -b + a$
   B. $a - (-b) = (-b) - a$
   C. $(a + b) + (-c) = a + [b + (-c)]$
   D. $-(-a) = a$

2. Which pair of expressions are equivalent?

   F. $18m \cdot 0$ and 1
   G. $6 + r + 11$ and $6 \cdot r \cdot 11$
   H. $(12 - 5) + \pi$ and 7π
   I. $x(3 - 3)$ and 0

3. What property is illustrated by the equation $(8 + 2) + 7 = (2 + 8) + 7$?

   A. Commutative Property of Addition
   B. Associative Property of Addition
   C. Distributive Property
   D. Identity Property of Addition

4. Which expression is equivalent to $-a \cdot b$?

   F. $a \cdot (-b)$
   G. $b - a$
   H. $(-a)(-b)$
   I. $-a + b$

5. Which is an example of an identity property?

   A. $a \cdot 0 = 0$
   B. $x \cdot 1 = x$
   C. $(-1)x = -x$
   D. $a + b = b + a$

Short Response

6. The fact that changing the grouping of addends does not change the sum is the basis of what property of real numbers?

Name ______________________ Class ______________ Date ______________

1-5 Think About a Plan

Adding and Subtracting Real Numbers

Meteorology Weather forecasters use a barometer to measure air pressure and make weather predictions. Suppose a standard mercury barometer reads 29.8 in. The mercury rises 0.02 in. and then falls 0.09 in. The mercury falls again 0.18 in. before rising 0.07 in. What is the final reading on the barometer?

Think

1. What operation does "rise" suggest? ______________

2. What operation does "fall" suggest? ______________

Plan

3. Write either *plus* or *minus* in each box so that the following represents the problem.

29.8 [ ] 0.02 [ ] 0.09 [ ] 0.18 [ ] 0.07

4. Write an expression to represent the problem.

____

Solve

5. What is the value of the expression you wrote in Exercise 4? ______________

6. What is the final reading on the barometer? ______________

Name ______________________ Class ____________ Date ____________

1-5 Practice

Form K

Adding and Subtracting Real Numbers

Use a number line to find each sum.

1. $2 + 5$

2. $-4 + 6$

3. $7 + (-3)$

4. $-5 + (-1)$

5. $-4 + 2$

6. $5 + (-8)$

7. Is the sum of two negative numbers *positive* or *negative*?

8. Writing Is the sum $-4 + 2$ *positive* or *negative*? How do you know?

Find each sum.

9. $12 + (-4)$

10. $-22 + (-10)$

11. $-25 + 27$

12. $21 + 43$

13. $15 + (-20)$

14. $-25 + (-25)$

15. $-1.5 + 3.6$

16. $-2.2 + (-16.7)$

17. $-\frac{1}{7} + \left(-\frac{4}{7}\right)$

Name ______________________ Class ____________ Date ____________

1-5 Practice (continued) Form K

Adding and Subtracting Real Numbers

18. Which addition problem is equivalent to $-5 - (-8)$?

A. $5 + 8$

B. $-5 + 8$

C. $5 + (-8)$

D. $-5 + (-8)$

Find each difference.

19. $6 - 12$

20. $-5 - 6$

21. $-7 - (-10)$

22. $26 - (-14)$

23. $30 - 50$

24. $-13 - (-13)$

25. $1.2 - (-1.3)$

26. $-\frac{7}{9} - \left(-\frac{2}{9}\right)$

27. $\frac{1}{2} - \frac{1}{4}$

28. A football team gained 5 yards and then lost 7 yards. What real number represents the team's position relative to its original position?

29. The temperature at 6:00 P.M. was 3°C. At midnight, the temperature was −2°C. What real number represents the change in temperature?

30. Rose had $60 in her checking account. She deposited a check for $20 that she received from her grandfather. Then she wrote a check for $35. What is the balance in her checking account?

Name ______________________ Class ____________ Date ____________

1-5 Standardized Test Prep

Adding and Subtracting Real Numbers

Multiple Choice

For Exercises 1–5, choose the correct letter.

1. Which expression is equivalent to $17 + (-15)$?

A. $-17 + 15$ **C.** $17 - 15$

B. $-17 - 15$ **D.** $17 + 15$

2. Which number could be placed in the square to make the equation true?

$$-5 - \square = 14$$

F. -19 **G.** -9 **H.** 9 **I.** 19

3. Which expression has the greatest value?

A. $-14 - (-5)$ **C.** $-14 - 5$

B. $-5 - (-14)$ **D.** $-5 - 14$

4. The wheel was invented about 2500 BC. The gasoline automobile was invented in AD 1885. How many years passed between the invention of the wheel and the invention of the automobile?

F. 1615 years **H.** 1725 years

G. 4385 years **I.** 5385 years

5. If $r = -18$, $s = 27$, and $t = -15$, what is the value of $r - s - t$?

A. -60 **B.** -30 **C.** -6 **D.** 6

Short Response

6. In golf, there is a number of strokes assigned to each hole, called the par for that hole. If you get the ball in the hole in fewer strokes than par, you are under par for the hole. If it takes you more strokes than the par, you are over par for the hole. On the first 9 holes of golf, Avery had a par, 1 over par, 2 under par, another par, 1 under par, 1 over par, 3 over par, 2 under par, and 1 under par.

a. What addition expression would represent all 9 holes?

b. What is Avery's score relative to par?

Name ______________________ Class ____________ Date ____________

1-6 Think About a Plan

Multiplying and Dividing Real Numbers

Farmer's Market A farmer has 120 bushels of beans for sale at a farmer's market. He sells an average of $15\frac{3}{4}$ bushels each day. After 6 days, what is the change in the total number of bushels the farmer has for sale at the farmer's market?

Understanding the Problem

1. How does the number of bushels the farmer has change each day?

2. Should the change be a positive or a negative number? How do you know?

Planning the Solution

3. What expression represents the total number of bushels sold in 6 days?

Getting an Answer

4. Evaluate your expression in Exercise 3 to determine the change in the total number of bushels the farmer has for sale at the farmer's market.

5. Is your answer reasonable? Explain.

Name ______________________ Class ____________ Date ____________

1-6 Practice

Form K

Multiplying and Dividing Real Numbers

1. **Writing** Is the product $-8 \times (-5)$ *positive* or *negative*? How do you know?

2. **Open-Ended** Write a multiplication problem with a negative product. How do you know the product will be negative?

Find each product. Simplify, if necessary.

3. $-2(-3)$

4. $4(-7)$

5. $5 \cdot 10$

6. $(-5)^2$

7. -3×7

8. $-4(-6)$

9. $-3(1.2)$

10. $-\frac{1}{2} \cdot \frac{1}{3}$

11. $-\frac{2}{5}\left(-\frac{1}{4}\right)$

12. A scuba diver descends in the water at the rate of 40 feet per minute. What real number describes the diver's location with respect to the water level after the first 3 minutes of his dive?

13. A football team has three 15-yard penalties. What real number describes the change in yardage from these penalties?

Name ______________________ Class ____________ Date ____________

1-6 Practice (continued)

Form K

Multiplying and Dividing Real Numbers

Simplify each expression.

14. $\sqrt{16}$

15. $-\sqrt{25}$

16. $\pm\sqrt{100}$

17. $-\sqrt{36}$

18. $\pm\sqrt{0.64}$

19. $\pm\sqrt{\frac{4}{25}}$

20. Writing Explain the differences among $\sqrt{4}$, $-\sqrt{4}$, and $\pm\sqrt{4}$.

Find each quotient. Simplify, if necessary.

21. $-12 \div 3$

22. $-25 \div (-5)$

23. $18 \div 2$

24. $24 \div (-8)$

25. $-27 \div (-3)$

26. $\frac{-35}{5}$

27. $4.4 \div (-2)$

28. $-\frac{1}{8} \div \left(-\frac{1}{2}\right)$

29. $-\frac{3}{4} \div \frac{1}{5}$

30. The population of Centerville has decreased by 500 people in the last 5 years. What real number describes the average change in population per year?

Name ______________________ Class __________ Date __________

1-6 Standardized Test Prep

Multiplying and Dividing Real Numbers

Multiple Choice

For Exercises 1-5, choose the correct letter.

1. Which expression has a negative value?

A. $(-2)^2$ **B.** $(-5)(-7)$ **C.** $(-3)^3$ **D.** $0 \times (-5)$

2. If $x = -\frac{3}{4}$ and $y = \frac{1}{6}$, what is the value of $-2xy$?

F. $-\frac{1}{4}$ **G.** $-\frac{1}{6}$ **H.** $\frac{1}{6}$ **I.** $\frac{1}{4}$

3. Which expression has the same value as $-\frac{1}{7} \div \left(-\frac{2}{3}\right)$?

A. $\frac{1}{7} \times \frac{3}{2}$ **B.** $-\left(\frac{1}{7} \times \frac{3}{2}\right)$ **C.** $\frac{7}{1} \times \frac{2}{3}$ **D.** $-\left(\frac{7}{1} \times \frac{2}{3}\right)$

4. ABC stock sold for $64.50. Four days later, the same stock sold for $47.10. What is the average change per day?

F. -$4.35 **G.** -$3.48 **H.** $3.48 **I.** $4.35

5. The formula $C = \frac{5}{9}(F - 32)$ converts a temperature reading from the Fahrenheit scale F to the Celsius scale C. What is the temperature 5°F measured in Celsius?

A. $\left(-20\frac{5}{9}\right)^\circ$ C **B.** −15°C **C.** 15°C **D.** $\left(20\frac{5}{9}\right)^\circ$ C

Short Response

6. A clock loses 2 minutes every 6 hours. At 3:00 P.M., the clock is set to the correct time and allowed to run without interference.

a. What integer would describe the time loss after exactly 3 days?

b. What would the clock read at 3:00 P.M. three days later?

Name ______________________ Class ____________ Date ____________

1-7 Think About a Plan

The Distributive Property

Exercise The recommended heart rate for exercise, in beats per minute, is given by the expression $0.8(200 - y)$ where y is a person's age in years. Rewrite this expression using the Distributive Property. What is the recommended heart rate for a 20-year-old person? For a 50-year-old person? Use mental math.

Understanding the Problem

1. What relationship does the given expression represent? What does the variable in the expression represent?

____

____

2. What does it mean to rewrite the expression using the Distributive Property?

____

____

3. What does it mean to use mental math?

____

Planning the Solution

4. How do you determine the recommended heart rate for people of different ages?

____

____

Getting an Answer

5. Rewrite the expression using the Distributive Property.

____

6. What is the recommended heart rate for a 20-year-old person? Show your work.

____

____

7. What is the recommended heart rate for a 50-year-old person? Show your work.

____

____

Name ______________________ Class ____________ Date ____________

1-8 Practice

Form K

An Introduction to Equations

Tell whether each equation is true, false, or open. Explain.

1. $13 + (-12) - 3 = -2$
2. $7 - 8x = -15$
3. $-72 \div 12 + 6 = 14 - 8$
4. $6(-5) \div (-2) = -3(-5)$
5. $(10 + 5)(-4) - 10 = -80 - 10$
6. $-9(-5 + 8) = \frac{1}{3}(-9)(9)$

Tell whether the given number is a solution of each equation.

7. $5x + 10 = -35; -9$
   $5(-9) + 10 = -35$
8. $8p - 3 = 13; -2$
9. $-16 - h = 20; 4$
10. $-24 = -6m + 6; 5$
11. $-49 + 7t = 21; -10$
12. $32 = 7z - 10; 6$
13. The distance in miles a family has traveled so far on their trip can be modeled by the equation $y = 0.6x - 75$, where x is the number of minutes of driving today. How many minutes has the family been traveling today when they have traveled 201 miles?
14. There are 325 students that need to take Algebra 1 this year. Each class is limited to at most 30 students. How many classes need to be offered?

Use mental math to find the solution of each equation.

15. $n + 9 = 15$
16. $20 = 12 - a$
17. $44 + v = 22$
18. $14 - y = 16$

Name ______________________ Class ____________ Date ____________

1-8 Practice (continued)

Form K

An Introduction to Equations

Write an equation for each sentence.

19. The sum of a number and 11 is −12.

20. −4 times the sum of 6 times a number and 3 is 15

21. Sara is 5 years younger than Geoff. What is an equation that relates the age of Sara *S* and the age of Geoff *G*?

22. Open-Ended Write four equations that all have a solution of 6. The equations should consist of one multiplication, one division, one addition, and one subtraction equation.

Use a table to find the solution of each equation.

23. $2d - 4 = -8$

24. $12 - 5x = -13$

25. $18 = -w + 14$

26. $6z - 14 = -8$

Use a table to find two consecutive integers between which the solution lies.

27. $4k - 13 = 12$

28. $24.1 = 15q - 32.5$

Find the solution of each equation using mental math or a table. If the solution lies between two consecutive integers, identify these integers.

29. $j - 18 = 2$

30. $6y + 5 = 36$

31. $2.2 - 2n = 12.2$

32. $-7b + 15 = -6$

33. Writing Explain how you can determine if a number is a solution of an equation.

Name ______________________ Class ____________ Date ____________

1-8 Standardized Test Prep

An Introduction to Equations

Multiple Choice

For Exercises 1–5, choose the correct letter.

1. Which equation is true?
   A. $25 - (-18) = 7$
   B. $\frac{1}{3}(-9) - 6 = -9$
   C. $25(-2) + 7 = -39 + 4$
   D. $-19 + 8(-2) = -7(-5)$

2. Which equation has a solution of -6?
   F. $15x - 20 = 70$ G. $14 = 6x - 22$ H. $3x - 8 = -10$ I. $\frac{1}{2}x - 8 = -11$

3. Which equation has a solution of $\frac{1}{2}$?
   A. $13x - 12 = 14$ B. $9x + 15 = 20$ C. $-6x - 18 = -21$ D. $-11x = 12x + 12$

4. The money a company received from sales of their product is represented by the equation $y = 45x - 120$, where y is the money in dollars and x is the number of products sold. How many products does the company need to sell in order to receive $3705?
   F. 42 G. 85 H. 105 I. 166,605

5. Mrs. Decker walks for 30 minutes each day as often as possible. What is an equation that relates the number of days d that Mrs. Decker walks and the number of minutes m that she spends walking?
   A. $m = 30d$ B. $d = 30m$ C. $d = m + 30$ D. $m = d + 30$

Short Response

6. There are 450 people travelling to watch a playoff football game. Each bus can seat up to 55 people. Write an equation that represents the number of buses it will take to transport the fans. Use a table to find a solution.

Name ______________________ Class ____________ Date ____________

1-9 Think About a Plan

Patterns, Equations, and Graphs

Air Travel Use the table below. How long will the jet take to travel 5390 miles?

Passenger Jet Travel

Hours, h	1	2	3	4
Miles, m	490	980	1470	1960

Understanding the Problem

1. What does the information in the table represent?

____

____

2. What is the pattern in each row of numbers?

____

Planning the Solution

3. What is a general equation that represents the relationship between hours and miles?

____

4. How can you determine the number of hours it will take for the jet to travel 5390 miles?

____

____

Getting an Answer

5. How long will the jet take to travel 5390 miles? Show your work.

____

____

6. Besides the distance the jet travels and the time it is in flight, what else could be determined from the information in the table?

____

____

Name ______________________ Class ____________ Date ____________

1-9 Practice

Form K

Patterns, Equations, and Graphs

Tell whether the given ordered pair is a solution of the equation.

1. $y = x + 8; (-3, 5)$
$5 = -3 + 8$

2. $y = x - 6; (4, -2)$

3. $y = x - 12; (3, 15)$

4. $y = -7x; (-3, -21)$

5. $y = x + 8; (-1, 7)$

6. $y = -x + 4; (-5, -1)$

Use a table, an equation, and a graph to represent each relationship.

7. Zachary sells pencils for $0.15 each.

8. Jerry earns $40 per hour.

9. Stanton can mow 3 more lawns per day than Farah.

10. Beth has been with the company 6 years longer than Paco.

11. The table shows the height in inches of a stack of lumber. Draw a graph of the situation. What is the height of a stack of 25 pieces of lumber?

Pieces	Height (in.)
2	3
3	4.5
5	7.5
7	10.5
8	12

1-9 Practice (continued) *Form K*

Patterns, Equations, and Graphs

Use the table to write an equation and answer the question.

12. The table shows the cost of staying at a certain hotel. How much does 30 nights cost?

Nights	Cost ($)
3	237
6	474
9	711
12	948

13. The table shows the number of words a secretary types in terms of minutes. How many words can he type in 60 minutes?

Minutes	Words
5	310
10	620
15	930
20	1240
25	1550

Tell whether the given ordered pair is a solution of the equation.

14. $y = -6x + 1; (-1, -5)$

15. $y = -\frac{1}{2}x + 4; (-8, 8)$

16. $y = -0.1x + 5; (10, 4)$

17. $y = 0.25 + 5.5x; (-1, -5.75)$

18. $\frac{2}{5}x + 5 = y; (-15, -1)$

19. $y = 12 - \frac{3x}{4}; (-8, 6)$

20. Writing Explain how you can use an equation to make predictions about a particular relationship.

Name ______________________ Class ____________ Date ____________

2-1 Practice

Form K

Solving One-Step Equations

Solve each equation using addition or subtraction. Check your answer.

1. $6 = p - 8$

2. $z + 5 = 4$

3. $m - 4 = 12$

4. $-10 = h - 4$

5. $n + 14 = -5$

6. $2 = a + 7$

Solve each equation using multiplication or division. Check your answer.

7. $4t = -32$

8. $-25 = -5x$

9. $-3.2k = 16$

10. $2.8r = 16.8$

11. $\frac{m}{7} = 4$

12. $25 = \frac{z}{-4}$

Solve each equation. Check your answer.

13. $\frac{3}{4}b = 15$

14. $-8 = \frac{2}{5}t$

15. $\frac{9}{10}y = -36$

16. $\frac{1}{2}m = \frac{6}{11}$

Name ______________________ Class ____________ Date ____________

2-1 Practice (continued)

Form K

Solving One-Step Equations

Define a variable and write an equation for each situation. Then solve.

17. Bradley has a goal to work 28 hours each week at the pizza shop. So far he has worked 12 hours. How many more hours does he need to work to meet his goal?

18. Sheree is 4 times as old as Benjamin. If Sheree is 72 years old, how old is Benjamin?

Solve each equation. Check your answer.

19. $-8h = 26$

20. $-\frac{3}{5} = \frac{1}{10} + q$

21. $n + 3\frac{2}{3} = 5\frac{7}{9}$

22. $-9w = 6.3$

23. $5.8 = -4.5 + z$

24. $\frac{d}{5} = -\frac{3}{10}$

25. A youth club is taking a field trip to a community farm. 27 members attended the trip. The total cost for the club was $148.50.

a. Write and solve an equation to determine the cost for each person.

b. The farm brought in $1512.50 that day including what they received from the youth club. Write and solve an equation to find the number of people that visited the community farm that day.

Name ______________________ Class ____________ Date ____________

2-1 Standardized Test Prep

Solving One-Step Equations

Multiple Choice

For Exercises 1–6, choose the correct letter.

1. What is the solution of $-3 = x + 5$?

A. -15 **B.** -8 **C.** 2 **D.** 8

2. What operation should you use to solve $-6x = -24$?

F. addition **G.** subtraction **H.** multiplication **I.** division

3. Which of the following solutions is true for $\frac{x}{3} = \frac{1}{4}$?

A. $-2\frac{3}{4}$ **B.** $\frac{1}{12}$ **C.** $\frac{3}{4}$ **D.** $3\frac{1}{4}$

4. There are 37 more cats c than dogs d in an animal shelter. If there are 78 cats at the shelter, which equation represents the relationship between the number of cats and dogs?

F. $d + 37 = 78$ **G.** $d - 37 = 78$ **H.** $c + 37 = 78$ **I.** $c - 37 = 78$

5. Which property of equality should you use to solve $6x = 48$?

A. Addition Property of Equality
B. Subtraction Property of Equality
C. Multiplication Property of Equality
D. Division Property of Equality

6. Shelly completed 10 problems of her homework in study hall. This is $\frac{2}{7}$ of the total assignment. How many problems does she have left to complete?

F. 20 **G.** 25 **H.** 30 **I.** 35

Short Response

7. A high school marching band has 55 male members. It is determined that five-eighths of the band members are male.

a. What equation represents the total number of members in the band?
b. How many members are in the band?

Name ________________ Class ________ Date ________

2-2 Think About a Plan

Solving Two-Step Equations

Earth Science The temperature beneath Earth's surface increases by 10°C per kilometer. The surface temperature and the temperature at the bottom of a mine are shown. How many kilometers below Earth's surface is the bottom of the mine?

Understanding the Problem

1. What happens to the temperature as the distance below Earth's surface increases?

   ____

2. What do you need to determine?

   ____

3. What is the change in temperature from Earth's surface to the bottom of the mine?

   ____

Planning the Solution

4. Write an expression for how much the temperature increases *x* kilometers below the surface.

   ____

5. Write an equation that relates the change in temperature, from 18°C at Earth's surface to 38°C at the bottom of the mine, to the expression for how much the temperature increases *x* kilometers below the surface.

   ____

Getting an Answer

6. Solve the equation.

7. Is your answer reasonable? Explain.

   ____

   ____

Name ______________________ Class ____________ Date ____________

2-2 Practice

Form K

Solving Two-Step Equations

Solve each equation. Check your answer.

1. $4x + 5 = 13$

2. $-8 + 3h = 1$

3. $2j - 13 = 25$

4. $\frac{n}{5} - 1 = 7$

5. $-5 = -8 + \frac{y}{10}$

6. $7 = -6m + 7$

7. $\frac{n}{-8} - 5 = -2$

8. $-14 = -6 + 4w$

9. $15 - 3t = -12$

10. $13 + \frac{a}{11} = 7$

Define a variable and write an equation for each situation. Then solve.

11. A fair charges $7.25 for admission and $5.50 for a ride pass. Ten friends visited the fair. Not all of the friends purchased ride passes. If their total cost was $105.50, how many friends purchased ride passes?

12. A cafeteria sells entrées and additional items. An entrée costs $4.75, and each additional item costs $1.25. A customer pays $9.75 for one entree and some additional items. How many additional items were ordered?

Name ______________________ Class ____________ Date ____________

2-2 Practice (continued) *Form K*

Solving Two-Step Equations

Solve each equation. Check your answer.

13. $\frac{f+4}{2} = 5$

14. $\frac{p-6}{3} = -15$

15. $\frac{c+5}{-6} = -4$

16. $\frac{1}{4}z + 9 = -1$

17. $\frac{1}{2} = \frac{1}{2}t + 3$

18. $4.52 - 5h = 2.8$

19. Jasmine is 23 years old. Jasmine is 3 years less than half of George's age. Write and solve an equation to find George's age.

20. An appliance repair person charges $55 per trip plus $15 per hour for her labor. The cost of fixing a stove was $92.50. Write and solve an equation to find how many hours it took to repair the stove.

21. Shelly has a cell phone plan that costs $9.99 per month plus $0.05 per minute. Her total bill for the month is $25.59. Write and solve an equation to find how many minutes she used for the month.

22. **Writing** Describe using words how to solve the equation $3 - 5n = -22$. Describe the properties utilized in the solution.

2-2 Standardized Test Prep

Solving Two-Step Equations

Gridded Response

Solve each exercise and enter your answer on the grid provided.

1. What is the solution of $-28 = 22 - 5x$?

2. What is the solution of $\frac{m}{4} - 3 = 7$?

3. The amount of money that Pamela p has and Julie j has are related by the equation $3p + 5 = j$. If Julie has \$83, how much money does Pamela have?

4. An ice cream sundae costs \$1.75 plus an additional \$0.35 for each topping. If the total cost is \$2.80, how many toppings did the sundae have?

5. The cost of a gallon of gasoline g is \$3.25 less than 2 times the cost of a gallon of diesel d. If a gallon of gasoline costs \$3.95, what is the cost of a gallon of diesel?

1.
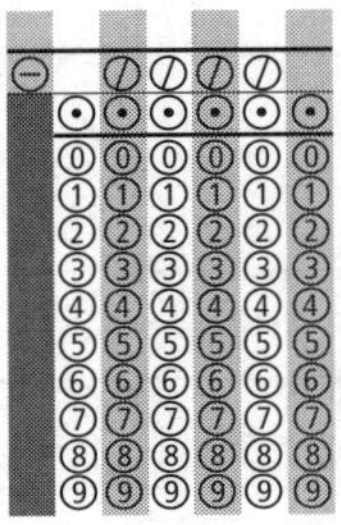

2.
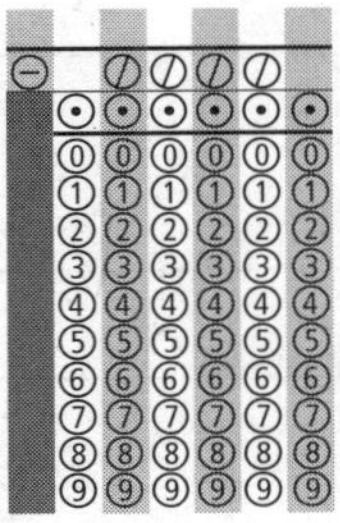

3.
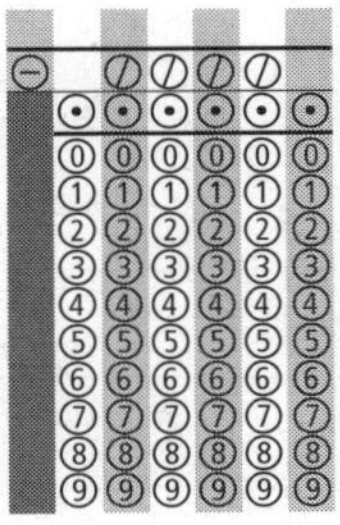

4.
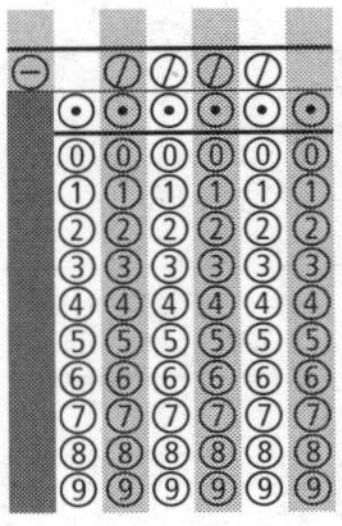

5.
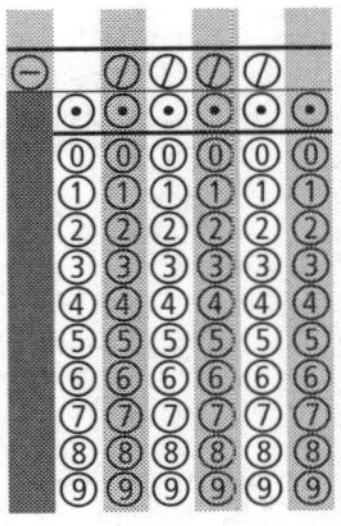

Name ______________________ Class ____________ Date ____________

2-3 Think About a Plan

Solving Multi-Step Equations

Online Video Games Angie and Kenny play online video games. Angie buys 1 software package and 3 months of game play. Kenny buys 1 software package and 2 months of game play. Each software package costs $20. If their total cost is $115, what is the cost of one month of game play?

Know

1. What values are you given?

____

____

Need

2. What do you need to find?

____

Plan

3. What equation can you use to solve the problem?

____

4. Solve the equation. Show your work and justify each step.

____

____

____

____

____

____

5. Check your answer.

____

____

____

6. Is your answer reasonable? Explain.

____

Name ________________________ Class ____________ Date ____________

2-3 Practice

Form K

Solving Multi-Step Equations

Solve each equation. Check your answer.

1. $20 + g + g = 14$

2. $7 + 4x - 9 = -6$

3. $-12 = -5 - 6n + 11$

4. $t + 10 - 4t = -11$

5. $8 = 8p + 13 - 3p$

6. $4y - 16 + 8y = -4$

Write an equation to model each situation. Then solve the equation.

7. A plumber finished three jobs on Tuesday. The first two only cost the owner the \$45 trip fee because they took very little time to complete. For the third job, the plumber charged the trip fee plus 6 times his hourly rate. If the plumber received a total of \$303 for the day, what is the hourly rate?

8. Three times a number plus 12 minus 5 times the same number is 22. What is the number?

Solve each equation. Check your answer.

9. $4(-2d - 3) = 12$

10. $5(5t - 2) = -35$

11. $-2(a + 6) = -22$

12. $60 = 6(6 - 2n)$

13. $-14 = -4(9x - 1)$

14. $-(5z + 12) = 18$

Name ______________________ Class ____________ Date ____________

2-3 Practice (continued) — Form K

Solving Multi-Step Equations

15. Eli took the fleet of 8 vans for oil changes. All of the vans needed windshield wipers which cost \$24 per van. The total bill was \$432. Write an equation to find out what each oil change cost. Solve the equation.

Solve each equation. Choose the method you prefer. Check your answer.

16. $\frac{m}{3} + \frac{1}{3} = \frac{2}{3}$

17. $5r - \frac{1}{5} = \frac{4}{5}$

18. $\frac{w}{9} - 6 = \frac{7}{9}$

19. $1.75t - 4.5 = 7.75$

20. $6z + 0.36 = 24.72$

21. $7.85 - 2.15c = 20.75$

22. Writing Describe the first step you would take in solving $12 = 7 - 3x + 5x$. Explain.

23. Writing Describe how you would solve $-8 = \frac{1}{9}(-9t + 27)$.

Solve each equation. Round to the nearest hundredth if necessary.

24. $11 + \frac{4x}{-5} = \frac{2}{3}$

25. $\frac{5}{7}(k + 5) = -7$

26. Reasoning Can you solve the equation $\frac{3}{4}(6x + 9) = 14$ by using the Division Property of Equality? Explain.

Name ______________________ Class ____________ Date ____________

2-3 Standardized Test Prep

Solving Multi-Step Equations

Multiple Choice

For Exercises 1–5, choose the correct letter.

1. What is the solution of $-17 = -2n + 13 - 8n$?

A. -3 **B.** $-\frac{2}{3}$ **C.** 3 **D.** 5

2. What is the solution of $-4(-3m - 2) = 32$?

F. -2 **G.** 2 **H.** 4 **I.** 6

3. What is the solution of $\frac{x}{3} + \frac{3}{5} = -\frac{1}{15}$?

A. -2 **B.** $\frac{8}{5}$ **C.** 2 **D.** $\frac{16}{3}$

4. When the sum of a number and 7 is multiplied by 4, the result is 16. What is the original number?

F. -12 **G.** -3 **H.** 3 **I.** 11

5. A merchant is selling wind chimes from a booth at a flea market. He rents his space for $125 per day. The profit from each wind chime sold is $12. His goal is to make $3500 in a five day work week. Which equation represents how many chimes he needs to sell in a week to meet his goal?

A. $12c - 625 = 3500$

B. $5(12c) - 125 = 3500$

C. $5(12c + 125) = 3500$

D. $5(12c - 125) = 3500$

Short Response

6. Four friends are planning to play 18 holes of golf. Two of them need to rent clubs at $5 per set. Cart rental is $10. The total cost of the golf outing, including green fees, is $92.

a. Write an equation to represent the total cost of the golf outing per player.

b. How much did the friends pay in green fees?

Name ______________________ Class ____________ Date ____________

2-4 Think About a Plan

Solving Equations With Variables on Both Sides

Skiing A skier is trying to decide whether or not to buy a season ski pass. A daily pass costs $67. A season ski pass costs $350. The skier would have to rent skis with either pass for $25 per day. How many days would the skier have to go skiing in order to make the season pass less expensive than daily passes?

Understanding the Problem

1. What do you know about the costs associated with buying a daily pass?

____

2. What do you know about the costs associated with buying a season pass?

____

Planning the Solution

3. Write an expression using words to represent the cost of a daily pass. Write the algebraic expression.

____

4. Write an expression using words to represent the cost of a season pass. Write the algebraic expression.

____

____

5. How can you compare the cost of a daily pass with the cost of a season pass algebraically? What is the equation?

____

____

Getting an Answer

6. Solve the equation you wrote in Step 5. Show your work.

____

____

7. Explain what this solution means.

____

Name ______________________ Class ____________ Date ____________

2-4 Practice

Form K

Solving Equations With Variables on Both Sides

Solve each equation. Check your answer.

1. $4y + 15 = 6y - 11$

2. $5p + 6 = -4p - 8$

3. $13k + 5 = k - 7$

4. $6q - 1 = -q + 20$

5. $25h + 40 = -15h - 80$

6. $-2m + 13 = 2m - 3$

Write and solve an equation for each situation. Check your solution.

7. Suzanne is going to rent a car while she is out of town. One car rental company offers a flat rate of $35 per day plus $0.10 per mile. Another car rental company offers the same car for $25 per day plus $0.25 per mile. She will need the car for 5 days. How many miles would she need to drive for the first rental company to be the better deal?

8. Jeremy is looking at two different lawncare companies to weed and mulch his flower beds. Greenscape Lawncare offers to charge $100 for the mulch plus $12 per hr for the labor. D & J Landscape offers to charge $23 per hr for the job including the mulch. What is the minimum number of hours the job could be for D & J Landscape to have the better deal?

Solve each equation. Check your answer.

9. $4(h + 2) = 3(h - 2)$

10. $-(3b - 15) = 6(2b + 5)$

11. $5x + 7 + 3x = -8 + 3x$

12. $18 - 6a = 4a - 4(a + 3)$

2-4 Practice (continued) Form K

Solving Equations With Variables on Both Sides

Solve each equation. If the equation is an identity, write *identity*. If it has no solution, write *no solution*.

13. $6(4z + 2) = 3(8z + 4)$

14. $-8t - 3t + 2 = -5t - 6t$

15. $-(8m + 4) = 4m - 2(6m + 2)$

16. $-5(x + 7) = -5x + 35$

17. $5.5 - 3b = 2b - 6.25$

18. $\frac{3}{4} + \frac{1}{4}m = \frac{3}{4}m - \frac{1}{4}$

19. $-5(5.25 + 3.1x) = -6.2(2.5x + 1.9)$

20. $\frac{2}{3}h - 9 = 6 - \frac{2}{3}h$

21. $0.2f + 0.6(f + 20) = -8 + 0.4f$

22. $-2(-w + 11) = -13 + 2w - 9$

23. Six times the sum of a number and 3 is 12 less than 12 times the number. Write and solve an equation to find the number.

24. A triangle with equal sides and a square have the same perimeters. The length of a side of the triangle is $2x + 2$. The length of a side of the square is $x + 8$. Write and solve an equation to find x.

25. Open-Ended Give one example of an equation with variables on both sides that is an identity and one equation with variables on both sides that has no solution. Justify your examples by solving the equations.

Name ______________________ Class ____________ Date ____________

2-4 Standardized Test Prep

Solving Equations With Variables on Both Sides

Multiple Choice

For Exercises 1–5, choose the correct letter.

1. What is the solution of $-8x - 5 + 3x = 7 + 4x - 9$?

A. -3 **B.** $-\frac{1}{3}$ **C.** $\frac{1}{3}$ **D.** 3

2. What is the solution of $-(-5 - 6x) = 4(5x + 3)$?

F. -2 **G.** $-\frac{1}{2}$ **H.** $\frac{1}{2}$ **I.** 2

3. What is the solution of $2n - 3(4n + 5) = -6(n - 3) - 1$?

A. -8 **B.** -6 **C.** $-\frac{1}{2}$ **D.** 4

4. Negative one times the sum of twice a number and 3 is equal to two times the difference of -4 times the number and 3. What is the number?

F. -4 **G.** -2 **H.** $-\frac{1}{2}$ **I.** 2

5. Jacob is saving for a new bicycle which costs $175. He has already saved $35. His goal is to have enough money saved in six weeks to pay for the bicycle. Which equation represents how much money he needs to save each week to meet his goal?

A. $35 + 6d = 175$

B. $35 + 12d = 175$

C. $6(35 + 2d) = 175$

D. $2(35 + 6d) = 175$

Short Response

6. Admission for a water park is $17.50 per day. A season pass costs $125. A locker rental costs $3.50 per day.

a. What is an equation that represents the relationship between the cost of a daily pass and the cost of a season pass?

b. How many days would you have to go to the water park for the season pass to save you money?

Name ______________________ Class ____________ Date ____________

2-5 Think About a Plan

Literal Equations and Formulas

Density The density of an object is calculated using the formula $D = \frac{m}{V}$, where m is the object's mass and V is its volume. Gold has a density of 19.3 g/cm^3. What is the volume of an amount of gold that has a mass of 96.5 g?

KNOW

1. What is the formula you are given for the density of an object?

____

2. What values are you given in the problem?

____

____

NEED

3. What measurement are you asked to determine?

____

4. Solve $D = \frac{m}{V}$ for the variable V. Show your work.

____

____

____

PLAN

5. Write your new formula. Substitute the values you are given into the formula.

____

6. What is the volume of 96.5 g of gold?

____

7. In what units is your answer? Do these units make sense? Explain.

____

____

Name ______________________ Class ____________ Date ____________

2-5 Practice

Form K

Literal Equations and Formulas

Solve each equation for *y*. Then find the value of *y* for each value of *x*.

1. $y + 5x = 6; x = -1, 0, 1$

2. $8x - 4y = -12; x = -3, -1, 1$

3. $-3y = 2x - 9; x = -3, 0, 3$

4. $5x = -y + 6; x = 1, 2, 3$

5. $6y = -3x + 12; x = -4, -2, 0$

6. $-5y + 10x = 5; x = -2, 0, 2$

Solve each equation for *p*.

7. $xp + yp = z$

8. $n = \frac{p - k}{j}$

9. $a = b + cp$

10. $\frac{p + 3}{m} = -1$

Solve each problem. Round to the nearest tenth, if necessary. Use 3.14 for π.

11. What is the width of a rectangle with length 25 in. and area 375 in.^{2}?

12. What is the radius of a circle with circumference 5 cm?

13. A triangle has base 15 ft and area 60 ft^2. What is the height?

2-5 Practice (continued) Form K

Literal Equations and Formulas

Solve each problem. Round to the nearest tenth, if necessary.

14. In baseball, a player's batting average is calculated by using the formula $\text{Average} = \frac{\text{Hits}}{\text{At Bats}}$. Find the number of times a player has batted if he has 24 hits and a batting average of approximately 0.320.

15. Dan drove 512 miles in 8 hours. What was his average speed for the trip?

Solve each equation for the given variable.

16. $-2z - xy = x + 7$ for x

17. $\frac{a}{b} - 8 = \frac{c}{d}$ for a

18. $6qr + 7rs - 2st = -9$ for r

19. $p = \left(\frac{m + n}{-5}\right)$ for n

20. A large box shaped like a rectangular prism needs to be painted.

a. Write a formula for the area A to paint in terms of length l, width w, and height h.

b. Rewrite the formula to find l in terms of A, h, and w.

c. If h is 36 in., w is 28 in. and A is 6112 in.^{2}, what is the length of the prism?

Name ______________________ Class ____________ Date ____________

2-5 Standardized Test Prep

Literal Equations and Formulas

Multiple Choice

For Exercises 1–5, choose the correct letter.

1. What is the value of the expression $-2(3x - 2) + x + 9$ when $x = -3$?

A. -16 **B.** -2 **C.** 28 **D.** 34

2. What is the value of the expression $6m + m - 4(-2m + 1 - m)$ when $m = -8$?

F. -156 **G.** -92 **H.** -44 **I.** 36

3. What is the solution of $2d = \frac{a - b}{b - c}$ when you solve for a?

A. $2d - b + c + b$

B. $\frac{2d + b}{b - c}$

C. $\frac{2d}{b - c} + b$

D. $2d(b - c) + b$

4. A triangle has area 49.5 cm^2. If the base of the triangle is 9 cm, what is the height of the triangle?

F. 5.5 cm **G.** 11 cm **H.** 222.75 cm **I.** 445.5 cm

5. A circle has circumference 10.99 yd. What is the radius of the circle? Round to the nearest tenth if necessary. (Use 3.14 for π.)

A. 1.8 yd **B.** 3.5 yd **C.** 7 yd **D.** 34.5 yd

Short Response

6. The formula for the circumference of a circle is $C = 2\pi r$, where r is the radius of the circle.

a. What is the formula when solved for r?

b. What is the radius of a circle with a circumference of 37.7 m? Round to the nearest tenth if necessary.

Name ______________________ Class ____________ Date ____________

2-6 Think About a Plan

Ratios, Rates, and Conversions

Reasoning A traveler changed $300 to euros for a trip to Germany, but the trip was canceled. Three months later, the traveler changed the euros back to dollars. Would you expect that the traveler got exactly $300 back? Explain.

Know

1. What facts do you know about the situation?

____

____

2. What circumstances would affect whether or not the traveler would receive exactly $300 back?

____

____

Need

3. What would you need to know to determine the amount of dollars the traveler would receive after three months?

____

____

4. How do you convert the amount in euros to dollars?

____

Plan

5. Once you have the information you need to answer the question, explain how you would determine the amount of dollars the traveler would receive in exchange for the euros.

____

____

____

6. Would this process change over time? Explain.

____

____

Name ______________________ Class ____________ Date ____________

2-6 Practice *Form K*

Ratios, Rates, and Conversions

Convert the given amount to the given unit.

1. 12 in.; cm

2. 528 cm; yd

3. 9 hr; min

4. 12 meters; cm

5. 8 liters; qt

6. 7 days; hours

7. 10 pounds; grams

8. 45 ft; yd

9. 10 meters; ft

10. A plumber needs to replace 20 feet of copper piping. When he gets to the supply store, the lengths are given in meters. How many meters of piping does he need to purchase?

11. An athletic director is laying out a rectangular soccer field to be 60 m wide and 95 m long. What are the dimensions of the field to the nearest whole yard?

Complete each statement.

12. 9 gal/s = _______ qt/min

13. 5.5 days = _______ min

14. 50 yd = _______ m

15. 10 mi/hr = _______ m/min

16. 25 mi/gal = _______ km/L

17. 5 m/s = _______ ft/s

2-6 Practice (continued) — Form K

Ratios, Rates, and Conversions

18. Which weighs more, 5 ounces or 150 grams?

19. Which is longer, 5 miles or 10 kilometers?

20. Which is the better buy, 3 pounds for $8.31 or 5 pounds for $12.95? Explain.

21. A cyclist is riding 18 miles per hour.

a. What conversion factors should be used to convert 18 mi/hr to ft/sec?

b. How many feet per second is the cyclist riding?

Determine if each rate is a unit rate. Explain.

22. 3 liters per 60 seconds **23.** 55 miles per hour **24.** $15 per hour

Find each unit rate.

25. 5 pounds of apples cost $9.95.

26. The tub filled with 12 gallons of water in 5 minutes.

27. Rocky earned $102 in 8 hours.

28. Writing Suppose you want to convert pounds to kilograms. What conversion factors would you choose to use? How did you determine which units should go in the numerators and the denominators of the conversion factors?

Name ______________________ Class ____________ Date ____________

2-6 Standardized Test Prep

Ratios, Rates, and Conversions

Multiple Choice

For Exercises 1–6, choose the correct letter.

1. Which of the following rates is a unit rate?

   A. $\frac{24\text{ in.}}{1\text{ yd}}$ **B.** $\frac{24\text{ in.}}{2\text{ ft}}$ **C.** $\frac{3\text{ ft}}{1\text{ yd}}$ **D.** $\frac{1\text{ ft}}{12\text{ in.}}$

2. How many centimeters are in 1 kilometer?

   F. 0.000001 **G.** 0.00001 **H.** 10,000 **I.** 100,000

3. How many inches are in 3 yd 2 ft?

   A. 60 **B.** 72 **C.** 132 **D.** 180

4. To convert miles per hour to feet per second, which conversion factor would not be used?

   F. $\frac{1\text{ hr}}{60\text{ min}}$ **G.** $\frac{1\text{ min}}{60\text{ sec}}$ **H.** $\frac{5280\text{ ft}}{1\text{ mi}}$ **I.** $\frac{1\text{ mi}}{5280\text{ ft}}$

5. A healthy, adult cheetah can run 110 feet per second. How fast can a cheetah run in miles per hour?

   A. 55 **B.** 75 **C.** 87 **D.** 161.3

6. Emmanuel was speaking with a friend from another country. His friend told him that the speed limit on most highways is 100 kilometers per hour in her country. This speed sounded fast to Emmanuel. Approximately what speed is this in miles per hour?

   F. 62 mph **G.** 65 mph **H.** 70 mph **I.** 100 mph

Short Response

7. Samantha earns $22 per hour as a plumbing apprentice. How much does she earn per minute in cents?

   a. What conversion factors would she use?

   b. What amount does she earn per minute in cents?

Name ______________________ Class ____________ Date ____________

2-7 Think About a Plan

Solving Proportions

Video Downloads A particular computer takes 15 min to download a 45-min TV show. How long will it take the computer to download a 2-hour movie?

Understanding the Problem

1. What facts do you know about the situation?

____

____

____

2. Are the units given in such a way that the numerators and the denominators of the proportion have the same units? If so, what are the units? If not, which units need to be converted?

____

____

____

Planning the Solution

3. If unit conversions are necessary, use conversion factors to convert the units. Show your work.

____

____

4. Write a proportion that can be used to determine the length of time necessary for the computer to download the movie.

____

Getting an Answer

5. Solve the proportion you wrote in Step 4 to find how long it will take the computer to download the movie.

Name ______________________ Class ____________ Date ____________

2-7 Practice

Form K

Solving Proportions

Solve each proportion using the Multiplication Property of Equality.

1. $\frac{3}{4} = \frac{a}{12}$

2. $\frac{1}{3} = \frac{m}{21}$

3. $\frac{x}{5} = \frac{2}{3}$

4. $\frac{f}{24} = \frac{3}{8}$

5. $\frac{9}{7} = \frac{z}{126}$

6. $\frac{3}{10} = \frac{b}{14}$

Solve each proportion using the Cross Products Property.

7. $\frac{2}{5} = \frac{k}{18}$

8. $\frac{4}{n} = \frac{6}{7}$

9. $\frac{q}{-15} = \frac{1}{3}$

10. $\frac{4}{d} = \frac{-1}{4}$

11. $\frac{-13}{15} = \frac{k}{-5}$

12. $\frac{-14}{h} = \frac{-2}{5}$

13. On a scale drawing of a park, the length of a trail is 12 cm from the playground to the pond and 15 cm from the pond to the parking lot. If the actual length of the trail from the pond to the parking lot is 60 m, what is the actual length of the trail between the playground and the pond?

14. Jennifer is ordering cake for her wedding reception. If one cake will feed 18 people, how many cakes does she need to order for 150 people?

2-7 Practice (continued)

Form K

Solving Proportions

15. Julie is drawing a map of the town. She knows that City Hall is 3 miles down Main St. from the fire station. If the scale for the map is 0.25 in.: 0.5 miles, how long should Main St. be between City Hall and the fire station on the map?

Solve each proportion using any method.

16. $\frac{2}{j + 3} = \frac{4}{5}$

17. $\frac{p + 1}{6} = \frac{6}{11}$

18. $\frac{-4}{5} = \frac{3}{z - 5}$

19. $\frac{15 - b}{6} = \frac{-2}{3}$

20. A furniture factory makes 5 recliners for every 2 couches. If the factory makes a total of 154 recliners and couches in a day, how many recliners were made?

21. On the football team, two out of every seven players are seniors. If the team has 84 players, how many of the players are not seniors?

Solve each proportion.

22. $\frac{5}{n - 12} = \frac{-1}{n}$

23. $\frac{4v - 2}{8v} = \frac{2}{3}$

24. **Writing** Describe two different ways to solve $\frac{5}{6} = \frac{x}{24}$. Demonstrate both methods.

Name ______________________ Class __________ Date __________

2-7 Standardized Test Prep

Solving Proportions

Multiple Choice

For Exercises 1–5, choose the correct letter.

1. What is the solution to the proportion $\frac{3}{5} = \frac{x}{10}$?

A. $\frac{10}{3}$ **B.** 6 **C.** 10 **D.** 150

2. What is the solution to the proportion $\frac{x-1}{x} = \frac{2}{3}$?

F. −2 **G.** 0 **H.** 2 **I.** 3

3. There are 105 members of the high school marching band. For every 3 boys there are 4 girls. Which proportion represents how many boys are in the marching band?

A. $\frac{3}{7} = \frac{b}{105}$ **B.** $\frac{3}{4} = \frac{b}{105}$ **C.** $\frac{4}{7} = \frac{b}{105}$ **D.** $\frac{7}{3} = \frac{b}{105}$

4. A baker is making bread dough. He uses 3 cups of flour for every 8 ounces of water. How many cups of flour will he use if he uses 96 ounces of water?

F. 4 **G.** 12 **H.** 32 **I.** 36

5. Mr. Carter offered to stay after school for an extra help session, and $\frac{2}{11}$ of his students stayed for the session. If there were 24 students that stayed for the help session, how many students does Mr. Carter teach throughout the day?

A. 100 **B.** 121 **C.** 132 **D.** 144

Extended Response

6. Elisabeth goes on a 5 mile run each Saturday. Her run typically takes her 45 minutes. She wants to increase this distance to 7 miles. Determine the proportion you use to find the time it would take her to run 7 miles. Solve the proportion. What proportion can be used to determine the time it takes for her to run a marathon, which is approximately 26 miles? What is her time?

Name ______________________ Class ____________ Date ____________

2-8 Think About a Plan

Proportions and Similar Figures

Trucks A model of a trailer is shaped like a rectangular prism and has a width of 2 in., a length of 9 in., and a height of 4 in. The scale of the model is 1 : 34. How many times the volume of the model of the trailer is the volume of the actual trailer?

Understanding the Problem

1. What is the formula you use to find the volume of a rectangular prism?

____

2. Using the scale, how can we find the dimensions of the actual trailer?

____

____

Planning the Solution

3. What is the volume of the model?

____

____

4. Write three proportions that can be used to determine the actual length, height, and width of the trailer. Solve the proportions.

____

____

____

____

5. What is the volume of the actual trailer?

____

____

Getting an Answer

6. How many times the volume of the model of the trailer is the volume of the actual trailer? Justify your answer.

____

____

Name ________________________ Class ____________ Date ____________

2-8 Practice

Form K

Proportions and Similar Figures

The figures in each pair are similar. Identify the corresponding sides and angles.

1. $ABCD \sim EFGH$

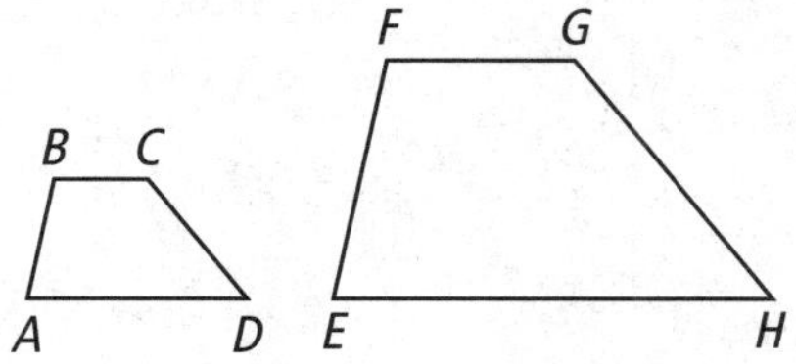

2. $\triangle MNO \sim \triangle PQR$

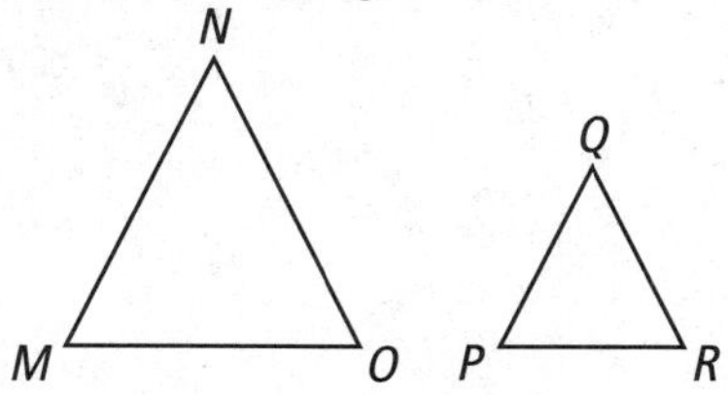

The figures in each pair are similar. Find the missing length.

3.

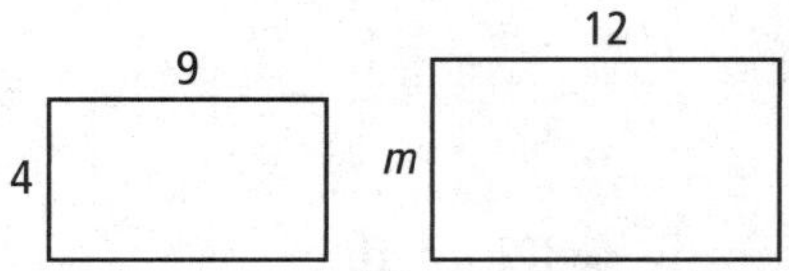

4.

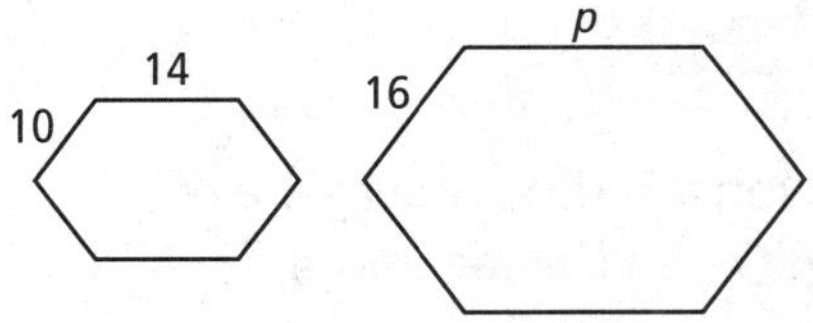

5.

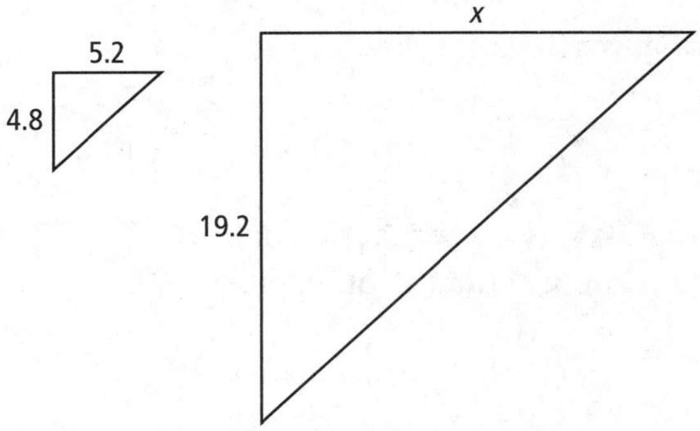

2-8 Practice (continued) *Form K*

Proportions and Similar Figures

The scale of a map is 0.25 cm : 15 km. Find the actual distance corresponding to each map distance.

6. 0.75 cm

7. 2 cm

8. 3.5 cm

9. 5.25 cm

10. For a celebration a town is going to pass out miniature replicas of the town's bell. The replicas are 9 in. tall. If the scale of the replica is 1 in. : 0.5 ft, how tall is the actual bell?

11. An architect created a scale model of what a college campus will look like once construction is finished. The scale for the model is 2 in. : 25 ft. The tallest building in the model is 10 in. tall. How tall is the actual building?

12. A model of a golf course says that hole #9 is 175 yards long. If the scale of the model is 2 in. : 20 yards, how many inches are there between the tee and the hole on the model?

13. Open-Ended Give an example of similar figures in your school.

14. Reasoning You are given two similar triangles. You know that one pair of corresponding sides is equal. What do you know about the other sides? Explain.

Name ______________________ Class __________ Date __________

2-8 Standardized Test Prep

Proportions and Similar Figures

Multiple Choice

For Exercises 1–4, choose the correct letter.

1. The distance between Capeton and Jonesville is 80 miles. The scale on the map is 0.75 in. : 10 miles. How far apart are the cities on the map?

A. 6 in. **B.** 60 in. **C.** 600 in. **D.** 1067 in.

2. The floor plan of a room has a scale of 2.5 in.: 35 ft. In the drawing, the length of the room is 8 in. and the width of the room is 6 in. What is the perimeter of the actual room?

F. 84 ft **G.** 112 ft **H.** 196 ft **I.** 392 ft

3. The figures are similar. What is the missing length?

A. 9.33 cm
B. 5.4 cm
C. 6 cm
D. 21 cm

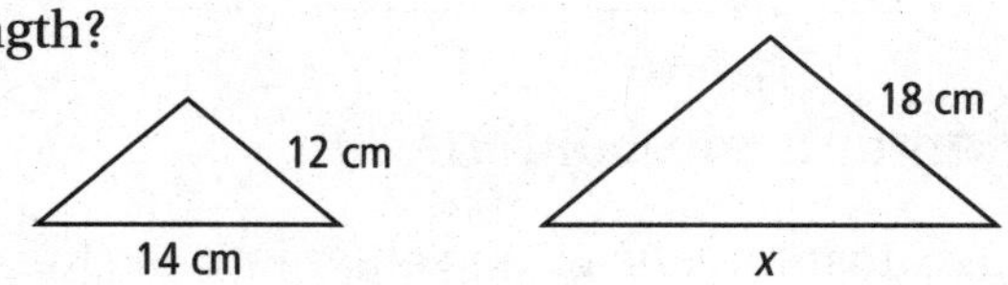

4. A model car is constructed with a scale of 1 : 15. If the actual car is 12 feet long, which proportion represents the length x of the model car?

F. $\frac{1}{15} = \frac{x}{12}$ **G.** $\frac{1}{15} = \frac{12}{x}$ **H.** $\frac{12}{15} = \frac{1}{x}$ **I.** $\frac{1}{12} = \frac{15}{x}$

Short Response

5. The scale of a map is 0.5 in. : 25 mi. The actual distance between two cities is 725 mi. Write a proportion that represents the relationship. How far apart will the cities be on the map?

Name ______________________ Class ____________ Date ____________

2-9 Think About a Plan

Percents

Finance A savings account earns simple interest at a rate of 6% per year. Last year the account earned $10.86 in interest. What was the balance in the account at the beginning of last year?

Understanding the Problem

1. What is the formula for finding simple interest?

____

2. What values are given in terms of the formula you wrote in Step 1?

____

____

Planning the Solution

3. Substitute the given values into the formula for simple interest.

____

Getting an Answer

4. Solve for the unknown value.

____

____

5. Is your answer reasonable? Explain.

____

____

6. What does your solution mean?

____

____

Name ______________________ Class ____________ Date ____________

2-9 Practice

Form K

Percents

Find each percent.

1. What percent of 58 is 18?

2. What percent of 36 is 27?

3. What percent of 65 is 115?

4. What percent of 45 is 42?

Find each part.

5. What is 40% of 120?

6. What is 62% of 500?

7. What is 150% of 84?

8. What is 33% of 171?

9. A pair of pants that regularly costs $55 are on sale for 35% off the regular price. What is the sale price of the pants?

10. A friend purchases items from a wholesale website and resells them on her own website. She typically marks up her merchandise 40%. If she purchased an item for $15, what price should she set for the item?

Find each base.

11. 70% of what number is 63?

12. 55% of what number is 231?

13. 165% of what number is 132?

14. 8% of what number is 1.2?

Name ______________________ Class ____________ Date ____________

2-9 Practice (continued)

Form K

Percents

15. \$13,000 is deposited into a savings account that earns simple interest at a rate of 6.5% per year. How much interest will the money have earned after 3 years?

16. Erma has \$175,000 in a retirement account that earns simple interest at a rate of 9% per year. How much interest will the money have earned after 25 years?

17. A family deposited \$8000 into an account six years ago. The account earned simple interest at a yearly rate. So far the total interest earned is \$1200. What is the rate for the account?

Tell whether you are finding a *percent*, a *part*, or a *base*. Then solve.

18. 112 is 20% of what number?

19. What is 126% of 50?

20. What percent of 88 is 36.96?

21. What percent of 22 is 33?

22. What is 268% of 150?

23. What is 50% of 1175?

Name ______________________ Class ____________ Date ____________

2-9 Standardized Test Prep

Percents

Multiple Choice

For Exercises 1–5, choose the correct letter.

1. What percent of 92 is 23?

A. 0.25% **B.** 4% **C.** 25% **D.** 400%

2. 60% of a number is 66. Which proportion best represents this relationship?

F. $\frac{66}{b} = \frac{60}{100}$ **G.** $\frac{a}{66} = \frac{60}{100}$ **H.** $\frac{60}{b} = \frac{66}{100}$ **I.** $\frac{60}{66} = \frac{b}{100}$

3. A store is having an after Christmas clearance sale where merchandise on the sales racks is reduced by 80% from the original price. If a jacket was originally priced at $76, what is the sale price?

A. $15.20 **B.** $24.20 **C.** $60.80 **D.** $72.40

4. If you deposit $3000 in a savings account that earns simple interest at a rate of 2.5% per year, how much interest will you have earned after 4 years?

F. $30 **G.** $300 **H.** $3000 **I.** $30,000

5. Five years ago you deposited a sum of money into a savings account which has earned $150 in interest. The interest rate for the account is 3% simple interest per year. How much money was originally deposited in the account?

A. $22.50 **B.** $100 **C.** $1000 **D.** $10,000

Short Response

6. There are 3200 students at Martinsville High School. There are 575 students involved in athletics during the spring athletic seasons. What proportion represents the percent of students not involved in athletics during the spring season? What percent of students is not involved in athletics?

Name ______________________ Class ____________ Date ____________

2-10 Think About a Plan

Change Expressed as a Percent

Student Discounts You show your student identification at a local restaurant in order to receive a 5% discount. You spend $12 for your meal at the restaurant. How much would your meal cost without the discount?

Understanding the Problem

1. What information are you given in the problem? What are you looking to find?

2. Does this question represent an amount of increase or an amount of decrease? In general, how is the amount of increase or decrease determined?

Planning the Solution

3. What formula can you use to determine the solution?

4. Substitute values from the problem into your formula using x for the unknown value.

Getting an Answer

5. Solve for the unknown value.

6. Check your answer.

7. Is your answer reasonable? Explain.

Name ______________________ Class ____________ Date ____________

2-10 Practice

Form K

Change Expressed as a Percent

Tell whether each percent change is an increase or decrease. Then find the percent change. Round to the nearest percent.

1. Original amount: 25
New amount: 18

2. Original amount: 48
New amount: 72

3. Original amount: 178
New amount: 136

4. Original amount: 17
New amount: 15

5. Original amount: 45
New amount: 60

6. Original amount: 95
New amount: 90

7. A store sells a running suit for $35. Joey found the same suit online for $29. What is the percent decrease to the nearest percent?

8. An online auction store started the bid on an item at $19. The item sold for $49. What was the percent increase to the nearest percent?

9. The original price for a motorcycle was $11,000. The sale price this week is $9799. What is the percent decrease to the nearest percent?

Find the percent error in each estimation. Round to the nearest percent.

10. You estimate that a tree is 45 ft tall. It is actually 58 ft tall.

11. A carpenter estimates the wall is 20 ft tall. The wall is actually 18 ft tall.

Name ______________________ Class ____________ Date ____________

2-10 Practice (continued) *Form K*

Change Expressed as a Percent

A measurement is given. Find the minimum and maximum possible measurements.

12. A patient weighs 178 lb to the nearest quarter pound.

13. A board is cut to 28 in. to the nearest half in.

Find the percent change. Round to the nearest percent.

14. $158.49 to $149.99

15. $29\frac{1}{2}$ oz to $23\frac{1}{4}$ oz

16. $12\frac{1}{4}$ hr to $13\frac{1}{2}$ hr

17. 7 in. to $12\frac{1}{2}$ in.

The measured dimensions of a rectangle are given to the nearest whole unit. Find the minimum and maximum possible areas of each rectangle.

18. 25 in. by 22 in.

19. 5 m by 7 m

The measured dimensions of a shape are given to the nearest whole unit. Find the greatest percent error of each shape.

20. The perimeter of a rectangle with length 15 cm and width 21 cm.

21. The area of a triangle with base length 32 in. and height 25 in.

Name ______________________ Class ____________ Date ____________

2-10 Standardized Test Prep

Change Expressed as a Percent

Multiple Choice

For Exercises 1–5, choose the correct letter.

1. Sam ran 3.5 miles on Saturday. On Wednesday, he ran 5.2 miles. What was his percent increase to the nearest percent?

A. 33% **B.** 42% **C.** 49% **D.** 67%

2. A department store purchases sweaters wholesale for $16. The sweaters sell retail for $35. What is the percent increase to the nearest percent?

F. 19% **G.** 46% **H.** 54% **I.** 119%

3. Josephine measured the room to be 125 ft wide and 225 ft long. What is the maximum possible area of the room?

A. 700 ft^2 **B.** 27,950.25 ft^2 **C.** 28,125 ft^2 **D.** 28,300.25 ft^2

4. You estimate the height of the flagpole to be 16 ft tall. The actual height of the flagpole is 18 ft. Which equation can be used to determine your percent error in the estimated height?

F. $\frac{16 - 18}{18}$ **G.** $\frac{|16 - 18|}{18}$ **H.** $\frac{|16 - 18|}{16}$ **I.** $\frac{16 - 18}{16}$

5. You estimate that a box can hold 1152 in^3. The box is actually 10.5 in. long, 10.5 in. wide, and 8 in. tall. What is the percent error in your estimation? Round to the nearest percent.

A. 23% **B.** 31% **C.** 42% **D.** 77%

Short Response

6. You measure a tub shaped as a rectangular prism to be 3 ft wide, 4 ft long, and 2.5 feet tall to the nearest half foot. What are the minimum and maximum volumes of the tub? What is the greatest possible percent error in calculating the volume of the tub?

Name ______________________ Class ____________ Date ____________

3-1 Think About a Plan

Inequalities and Their Graphs

Class Party You are making muffins for a class party. You need 2 cups of flour to make a pan of 12 muffins. You have a 5-lb bag of flour, which contains 20 cups. Write an inequality that represents the possible numbers of muffins you can make.

What do you know?

1. [ ] cups make [ ] muffins.

2. The maximum number of cups in a 5-lb bag of flour is [ ] cups.

What do you need to solve the problem?

3. What is the greatest number of muffins you can make with a 5-lb bag of flour?

How do you solve the problem?

4. What inequality can you use to show the possible number of muffins you can make with 2 cups of flour?

5. What number can you multiply by both sides to represent 20 cups? Write the new inequality.

6. What are two solutions to the inequality for 20 cups?

7. What is the greatest possible solution?

8. Are these solutions to the inequality reasonable? Explain.

____

____

____

Name ______________________ Class ____________ Date ____________

3-1 Practice

Form K

Inequalities and Their Graphs

Write an inequality that represents each verbal expression.

1. a is greater 4.

$a \square 4$

2. c is less than or equal to -2.

$c \square -2$

3. m is greater or equal to 1.

$m \square 1$

4. f is less than 2.

$f \square 2$

Determine whether each number is a solution of the given inequality. The first step is shown.

5. $2x + 4 < 20$

a. 2

Substitute 2 for x. $2(2) + 4 \overset{?}{<} 20$

b. 10

Substitute 10 for x. $2(10) + 4 \overset{?}{<} 20$

3-1 Practice (continued) — Form K

Inequalities and Their Graphs

Graph each inequality.

6. $m < 1$

7. $n \geq 5$

8. $j > -4$

9. $k \leq 10$

Write an inequality for each graph.

10. 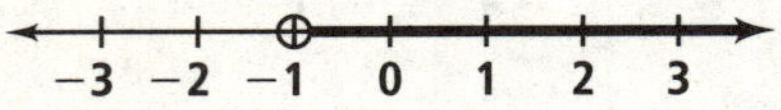

11. 

Define a variable and write an inequality to model each situation.

12. No more than 10 people may use the treadmills at any time in the gym.

Let n =

n ☐ 10

13. To train for a marathon, a runner decides that she must run at least 12 miles each day.

Let d =

d ☐ 12

Name ______________________ Class __________ Date __________

3-1 Standardized Test Prep

Inequalities and Their Graphs

Multiple Choice

For Exercises 1–6, choose the correct letter.

1. A student will study French for at least 3 years. Which inequality describes the situation?

A. $y < 3$ **B.** $y \leq 3$ **C.** $y > 3$ **D.** $y \geq 3$

2. All employees of a company work less than 40 hours. Which inequality describes the situation?

F. $h < 40$ **G.** $h \leq 40$ **H.** $h > 40$ **I.** $h \geq 40$

3. Which inequality has the same solutions as $d < -5$?

A. $d < 5$ **B.** $-5 > d$ **C.** $-d < -5$ **D.** $-d < 5$

4. Which value of n makes the inequality $-3 + (-n) \leq n$ false?

F. -3 **G.** -1 **H.** 0 **I.** 1

5. Which number is a solution of the inequality $7x - 5 \geq -2$?

A. -3 **B.** -1 **C.** 0 **D.** 1

6. Which inequality represents the graph shown below?

F. $x < -2$ **G.** $x \leq -2$ **H.** $x > -2$ **I.** $x \geq -2$

Short Response

7. The chess club is seeking to raise at least $150 in a fundraiser.

a. What inequality represents this situation?

b. What is the graph of the inequality?

Name ______________________ Class ____________ Date ____________

3-2 Think About a Plan

Solving Inequalities Using Addition or Subtraction

Government The U.S. Senate is composed of 2 senators from each of the 50 states. In order for a treaty to be ratified, at least two thirds of the senators present must approve the treaty. Suppose all senators are present and 48 of them have voted in favor of a treaty. What are the possible numbers of additional senators who must vote in favor of the treaty in order to ratify it?

What do you know?

1. How many senators make up the U.S. Senate? __________

2. How many senators already have voted in favor of a treaty? __________

3. What words make you think of an inequality? ______________________

What do you need to solve the problem?

4. What inequality can you use to describe the number of senators needed to ratify a treaty?

____

5. What inequality can you use to find the possible number of senators needed to ratify a treaty, if 48 of them already approve?

____

6. Does your answer need to be a whole number? Why?

____

____

How do you solve the problem?

7. What inequality is the solution to the number of additional senators needed?

Name ______________________ Class ____________ Date ____________

3-2 Practice

Form K

Solving Inequalities Using Addition or Subtraction

State what number you would add to or subtract from each side of the inequality to solve the inequality.

1. $x - 3 < 0$

2. $3 > -\frac{1}{5} + a$

3. $6.2 \leq c - 3.1$

4. $w + \frac{1}{3} \geq \frac{7}{3}$

5. $m + 2 \geq 0$

6. $2 \leq \frac{1}{4} + s$

Solve each inequality. Graph and check your solutions. The first step is started for you.

7. $y - 3 < 0$

$y - 3 \square 3 < 0 \square 3$

8. $4 \geq c + 2$

$4 \square 2 \geq c + 2 \square 2$

9. $\frac{1}{3} + f > -\frac{2}{3}$

$\frac{1}{3} \square \frac{1}{3} + f > -\frac{2}{3} \square \frac{1}{3}$

Name ______________________ Class ____________ Date ____________

3-2 Practice (continued)

Form K

Solving Inequalities Using Addition or Subtraction

Solve each inequality. Justify each step.

10. $-g - 2 + 2g > 4$

11. $j + 1.1 \geq 2.3$

12. A local television station sponsors a food drive. The goal is to donate more than 1000 canned goods. The station already has collected 400 canned goods. How many more canned goods does the television station need to meet its goal? Write and solve an inequality to find the number of canned goods needed.

Let f be how many more canned goods will come.

$f + 400 \,\square\, 1000$

13. A family earns at most \$2500 a month. The family's monthly expenses are \$2000. Write and solve an inequality to find the possible amounts of money the family could save each month.

Name ______________________ Class ____________ Date ____________

3-2 Standardized Test Prep

Solving Inequalities Using Addition or Subtraction

Multiple Choice

For Exercises 1–6, choose the correct letter.

1. What is the solution of $p - 12 > -18$?

A. $p < -30$ **B.** $p < -6$ **C.** $p > -6$ **D.** $p > -30$

2. What is the solution of $x + 5 \leq 29$?

F. $x < 24$ **G.** $x \leq 24$ **H.** $x > 24$ **I.** $x \geq 24$

3. Which graph represents all of the solutions of $z - 7 \leq -3$?

A.

C.
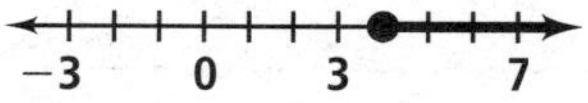

B.
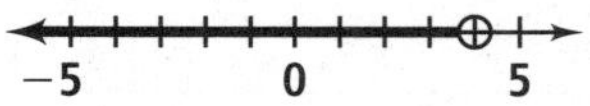

D.
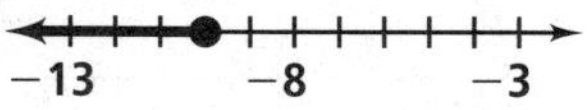

4. Which graph represents all of the solutions of $n - 2 > 0$?

F.
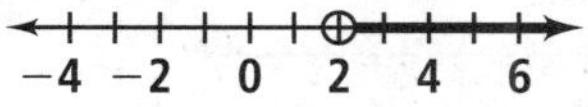

H.
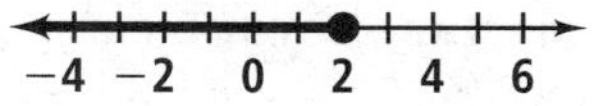

G.
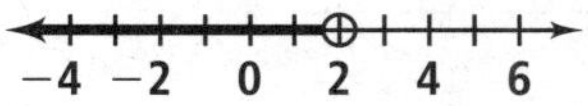

I.
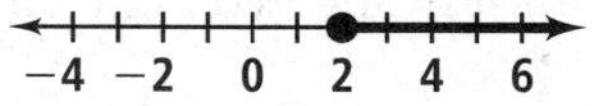

5. Which inequality is equivalent to $-1 \geq m + 4$?

A. $m < -5$ **B.** $m \leq -5$ **C.** $m \geq -5$ **D.** $m \leq 3$

6. Your goal in training for the race is to run more than 50 miles per week. So far this week you have run 32 miles. Which inequality represents the situation?

F. $d \geq 18$ **G.** $d - 32 > 50$ **H.** $d + 32 \geq 50$ **I.** $d + 32 > 50$

Short Response

7. In order to earn an A in a class, your test scores must average at least 92%. On the first 6 tests, you have an average of 91%. What score do you need to get on the last test to earn an A? Show your work.

Name ______________________ Class ____________ Date ____________

3-3 Think About a Plan

Solving Inequalities Using Multiplication or Division

Lunch You have $30 and would like to buy a sandwich and a drink for yourself and two friends from the menu at the right. What is the least number of snacks you can afford? What is the greatest number of snacks? Explain.

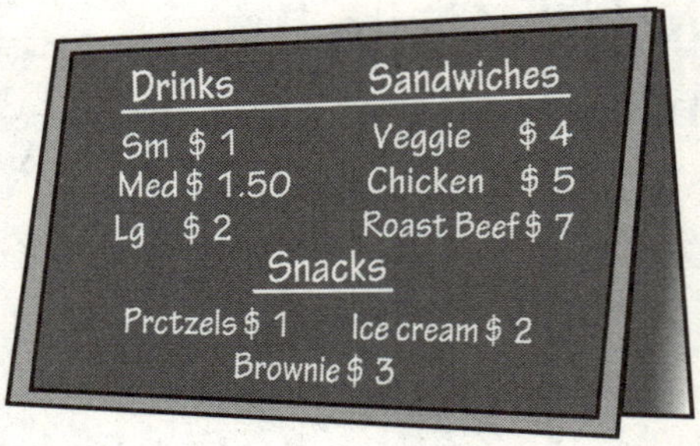

What do you know?

1. What combinations of items can you buy?

____

____

____

____

How do you plan to solve the problem?

2. What is the most money you can spend on sandwiches? ____________

3. What is the least money you can spend on sandwiches? ____________

4. What is the most money you can spend on drinks? ____________

5. What is the least money you can spend on drinks? ____________

6. How can you have the most money to buy snacks? ____________

How do you solve the problem?

7. What is the least number of snacks you can afford? Explain.

____

____

8. What is the greatest number of snacks you can afford? Explain.

____

____

Name ______________________ Class ____________ Date ____________

3-3 Practice

Form K

Solving Inequalities Using Multiplication or Division

State what number you would multiply or divide each side of the inequality by to solve the inequality.

1. $2x < 2$
2. $3 > -3a$
3. $6.2 \leq 3.1c$
4. $\frac{w}{3} \geq \frac{7}{3}$
5. $\frac{i}{5} \geq -3$
6. $2 \leq \frac{s}{4}$

Solve each inequality. Graph and check your solution. The first step is started for you.

7. $\frac{x}{3} > -1$

   $\square\left(\frac{x}{3}\right) > \square(-1)$

8. $1 \leq -\frac{2}{3}y$

   $\square(1)\ \square\ \square\left(-\frac{2}{3}y\right)$

9. $3m > 6$

   $\frac{3m}{\square} > \frac{6}{\square}$

10. $-4t < -16$

   $\frac{-4t}{\square}\ \square\ \frac{-16}{\square}$

3-3 Practice (continued) — Form K

Solving Inequalities Using Multiplication or Division

Write four solutions of each inequality.

11. $-3.0 > 6p$

12. $0.25 < \frac{1}{4}r$

13. A company sells parts in both the United States and in Europe. The company must report its product's size in both the metric system and in inches. If a product is reported to be no more than 12 inches long, how long is it in centimeters? Assume 1 inch $=$ 2.54 cm.

Let $x =$ the length of a product in inches.

14. You want to see if you are really saving money each month by exclusively using your cell phone for all long distance calls. Long distance calls cost $.03 per minute on your cell phone. The basic plan for your cell phone is $30 each month. The cost of regular phone service with unlimited long distance is $40. Write an inequality that will help you find the number of long-distance call minutes you may make and still save money.

Name ______________________ Class ____________ Date ____________

3-3 Standardized Test Prep

Solving Inequalities Using Multiplication or Division

Multiple Choice

For Exercises 1–5, choose the correct letter.

1. What is the solution of $\frac{a}{10} < -2$?

A. $a < -20$ **B.** $a > -20$ **C.** $a < -5$ **D.** $a > -5$

2. What is the solution of $-3 \geq -\frac{2}{3}z$?

F. $z \leq -\frac{9}{2}$ **G.** $z \leq \frac{9}{2}$ **H.** $z \geq -\frac{9}{2}$ **I.** $z \geq \frac{9}{2}$

3. What is the solution of $48 < -6h$?

A. $h < -8$ **B.** $h > -8$ **C.** $h \geq -8$ **D.** $h \leq -8$

4. You have budgeted to spend no more than $108 on gasoline for your vehicle this month. It typically takes $27 to fill up your tank. Which inequality represents how many times you can fill your tank this month?

F. $27f = 108$ **G.** $27f > 108$ **H.** $27f \leq 108$ **I.** $27f < 108$

5. Which graph represents all of the solutions of $-15b \leq 45$?

A.
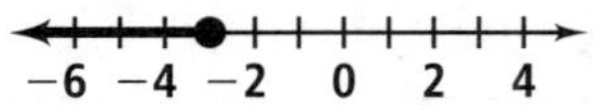

C.
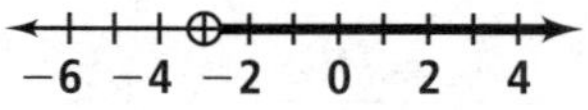

B.
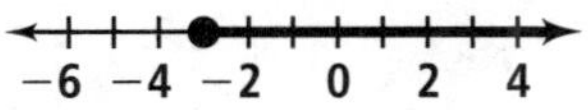

D.
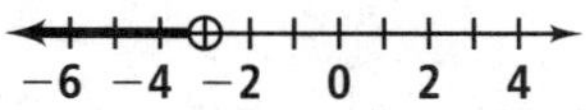

Short Response

6. In a town, there are 170 teenagers that own portable media players. This is at least $\frac{2}{3}$ of all the teenagers in the town. What is the maximum number of teenagers who live in the town? Show your work.

Name ______________________ Class ____________ Date ____________

3-4 Think About a Plan

Solving Multi-Step Inequalities

Commission A sales associate in a shoe store earns $325 each week, plus a commission equal to 4% of her sales. This week her goal is to earn at least $475. At least how many dollars' worth of shoes must the associate sell in order to reach her goal?

What do you know?

1. Write an expression to represent how much a sales associate earns each week. Let $s =$ total sales.

____

2. How much does she want to earn this week?

____

How do you plan to solve the problem?

3. Should you use an equation or an inequality to compare the amount the sales associate earns and her goal? Explain.

____

How do you solve the problem?

4. What inequality can you use to find how many dollars' worth of shoes she must sell this week to reach her goal?

____

5. Solve the inequality. Show your work.

Name ______________________ Class ____________ Date ____________

3-4 Practice

Form K

Solving Multi-Step Inequalities

Solve each inequality. Check your solutions. The first step is started for you.

1. $3m + 12 < 24$

$3m + 12 \square 12 < 24 \square 12$

2. $4w - 3 \geq 33$

$4w - 3 \square 3 \geq 33 \square 3$

3. $-2 + 2p \leq -14$

$-2 \square 2 + 2p \leq -14 \square 2$

4. $12 > 60 - 6t$

$12 \square 60 > 60 \square 60 - 6t$

Solve each inequality.

5. $4(k + 2) - 3k \leq 12$

6. $3(2c - 2) - 2c > 0$

7. $12(j + 1) + 3j < 57$

8. $22 \geq 5(y - 2) - 3y$

Name ______________________ Class ____________ Date ____________

3-4 Practice (contiued) Form K

Solving Multi-Step Inequalities

Solve each inequality, if possible. If the inequality has no solution, write *no solution*. If the solutions are all real numbers, write *all real numbers*.

9. $8w - 5 > 2(4w - 3)$

10. $-3r + 15 \geq 4(r - 2)$

11. A grandmother devises an equation to help her remember the ages of her two grandchildren. She knows her grandson is two years older than her granddaughter and that together, they are at least 12 years old. What are the youngest that her grandson and granddaughter could be?

Let a be the age of the granddaughter. Let $a +$ ☐ be the age of the grandson.

12. A family decides to rent a boat for the day. The boat's rental rate is \$500 for the first two hours and \$50 for each additional half hour. Suppose the family budgeted \$700 to rent the boat. What is the maximum number of additional half hours for which they can rent the boat?

Let $t =$ the time in half hours.

☐ t + \$500 ☐ \$700

13. Suppose a friend is having difficulty solving $-2(q - 5) > -3(q + 1)$. Explain how to solve the inequality, showing all the necessary steps and identifying the properties you would use.

Name ________________________________ Class ______________ Date ______________

3-4 Standardized Test Prep

Solving Multi-Step Inequalities

Multiple Choice

For Exercises 1–6, choose the correct letter.

1. What is the solution of $6w - 8 \geq 22$?

A. $w > \frac{7}{3}$ **B.** $w \geq \frac{7}{3}$ **C.** $w > 5$ **D.** $w \geq 5$

2. What is the solution of $2(y + 5) + 7y \leq 19$?

F. $y < 1$ **G.** $y \leq 1$ **H.** $y > 1$ **I.** $y \geq 1$

3. What is the solution of $25 > -3(4n - 3)$?

A. $n < -\frac{4}{3}$ **B.** $n < \frac{4}{3}$ **C.** $n > -\frac{4}{3}$ **D.** $n > \frac{4}{3}$

4. Which graph represents the solution of $-12 > -k - (3k + 4)$?

F.
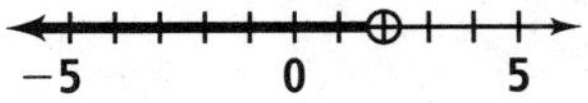

H.
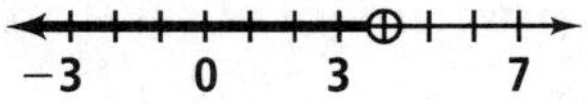

G.
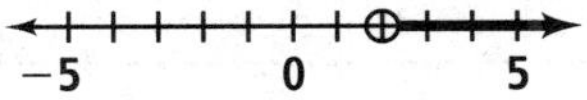

I.
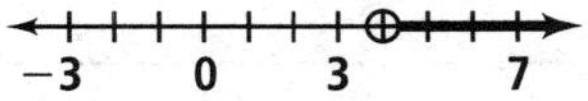

5. You have already saved \$55. You earn \$9 per hour at your job. You are saving for a bicycle that costs \$199. What inequality represents the minimum number of hours you need to work to save for the bicycle?

A. $h < 16$ **B.** $h \leq 16$ **C.** $h \geq 16$ **D.** $h > 16$

6. Admission to the fair costs \$7.75. Each ride costs you \$.50. You have \$15 to spend at the fair including admission. Which inequality represents the number of rides you can ride?

F. $r > 14$ **G.** $r < 14$ **H.** $r \leq 14$ **I.** $r \leq 15$

Short Response

7. The perimeter of a rectangle is at least 32 cm. The length of the rectangle is 9 cm. What are the possible widths of the rectangle? Show your work.

Name ______________________ Class ____________ Date ____________

3-5 Think About a Plan

Working With Sets

Universal set U = {planets in Earth's solar system} and set P = {planets that are farther from the sun than Earth}. What is the complement of set P? Write your answer in roster form.

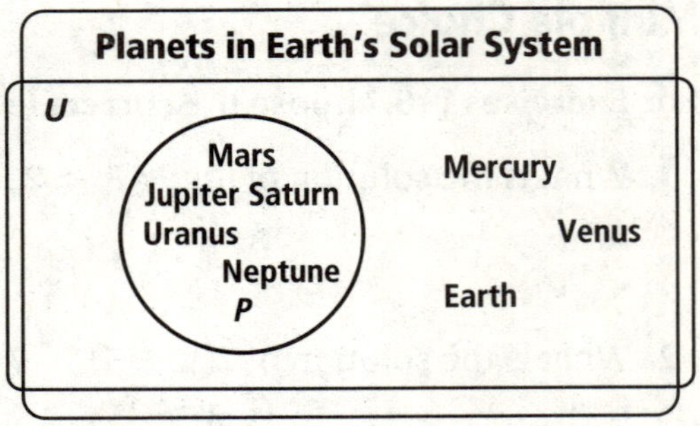

1. What does complement mean?

____

____

2. Where is the complement of set P on the Venn diagram?

____

____

3. What planets belong to the complement of set P?

____

____

4. How do you write your answer in roster form?

____

____

Name ______________________ Class ____________ Date ____________

3-5 Practice

Form K

Working With Sets

Write each set in roster form and in set-builder notation.

1. M is the set of integers that are greater than -5 and less than 2.

2. N is the set of real numbers that are factors of 36.

Write each set in set-builder notation.

3. $B = \{-3, -2, -1, 0, 1, \ldots\}$

$B = \{x \mid x$ is

4. $M = \{2, 4, 6, 8, 10\}$

Solve each inequality. Write the solutions of each inequality in set-builder notation.

5. $2y + 5 < 21$

6. $3r + 3 > 633$

7. $12 - 8m \geq 60$

8. $-(3x + 5) \leq -13$

9. $-2(x - 7) > -10 - 6x$

10. $-2(x + 7) \leq -14 + 2x$

3-5 Practice (continued)

Form K

Working With Sets

List all the subsets of each set.

11. {x, y, z}

12. {0}

13. {car, boat, airplane}

14. {−2, 2}

15. Suppose $U = \{0, 1, 3, 5, 7, 9\}$ is the universal set and $A = \{1, 3, 7\}$. What is A'?

16. Suppose $U = \{-4, -2, 0, 2, 4\}$ is the universal set and $R = \{2, 4\}$. What is R'?

Suppose $U = \{1, 3, 7, 11, 15\}$, $A = \{1, 3, 7\}$, and $B = \{1, 3, 7, 15\}$. Tell whether each statement is *true* or *false*. Explain your reasoning.

17. $A \subseteq U$

18. $U \subseteq B$

19. $B \subseteq A$

20. The universal set U and set A are defined below. What are the elements of the complement of A? Write your answer in roster form and in set-builder notation.

U = {all the days in a week}

A = {all the days in the weekend}

Name ______________________ Class ____________ Date ____________

3-5 Standardized Test Prep

Working With Sets

Multiple Choice

For Exercises 1–6, choose the correct letter.

1. What is the solution of $-(3n - 7) \geq 4$ written in set-builder notation?

A. $n \leq 1$ **B.** $\{1\}$ **C.** $\{n \mid n \geq 1\}$ **D.** $\{n \mid n \leq 1\}$

2. What set represents the solution of $15 < -9j - 3$?

F. $j < -2$ **G.** $\{-2\}$ **H.** $\{j \mid j > -2\}$ **I.** $\{j \mid j < -2\}$

3. Which of the following sets is not a subset of $\{-1, 1, 3\}$?

A. $\{\}$ **B.** $\{0\}$ **C.** $\{-1, 3\}$ **D.** $\{-1, 1, 3\}$

4. Given the universal set $U = $ {dog, cat, fish, gerbil, snake} and set L are all of the pets that have legs, what is the complement of set L?

F. {dog, cat, fish, gerbil, snake}

G. {fish, snake}

H. {dog, cat, gerbil}

I. $\emptyset$

5. Suppose the universal set U is the set of all real numbers and M is the set of all real numbers greater than or equal to 8. Which number is not in M'?

A. -8 **B.** 0 **C.** 5 **D.** 8

6. Suppose $U = \{-2, 0, 2, 4\}$ is the universal set and $A = \{-2, 2\}$. What is A'?

F. $\emptyset$ **G.** $\{-2, 2\}$ **H.** $\{0, 4\}$ **I.** $\{-2, 0, 2, 4\}$

Short Response

7. The width of a soccer field must be between 55 yd and 80 yd.

a. What compound inequality represents the width of a soccer field?

b. List the possible values for the field's width if the width is a multiple of 5.

Name ______________________ Class ____________ Date ____________

3-6 Think About a Plan

Compound Inequalities

Physics The force exerted on a spring is proportional to the distance the spring is stretched from its relaxed position. Suppose you stretch a spring a distance of d inches by applying a force of F pounds. For your spring, $\frac{d}{F} = 0.8$. You apply forces between 25 and 40 lb, inclusive. What inequality describes the distances the spring is stretched? Write the inequality in interval notation.

What do you know?

1. What inequality would you use to describe the forces that are applied to the spring?

____

2. How would you rewrite the proportion $\frac{d}{F} = 0.8$ to solve for d?

____

What do you need to solve the problem?

3. What variable will be in the inequality that solves the problem?

____

4. By what factor will you multiply each part of the compound inequality?

____

How do you solve the problem?

5. How do you write the inequality you found in interval notation?

____

Name ______________________ Class ____________ Date ____________

3-6 Practice

Form K

Compound Inequalities

Write a compound inequality that represents each phrase. Graph the solutions.

1. All real numbers that are less than −3 and greater than or equal to 5.

$x <$ ☐ ☐ $x \geq$ ☐

2. A certain recipe calls for a cake to bake between 25 minutes and 30 minutes, inclusive.

☐ $\leq$ ☐ $\leq$ ☐

Solve each compound inequality. Graph your solutions.

3. $5 < k - 2 < 11$

4. $-4 > y + 2 > -10$

5. $6b - 1 \leq 213$ or $2b + 1 \geq 11$

6. $5 - m < 4$ or $7m > 35$

7. $3 > \frac{11 + k}{4} \geq -3$

8. $4 \leq y + 12 \leq 24$

3-6 Practice (continued) Form K

Compound Inequalities

Write each interval as an inequality. Then graph the solutions.

9. $(-2, 3]$

$-2 \,\square\, x \,\square\, 3$

10. $[-2, 2]$

$-2 \,\square\, y \,\square\, 2$

11. $(-\infty, -1]$ or $(1, \infty)$

12. $[0, \infty)$

Write a compound inequality that each graph could represent.

13. 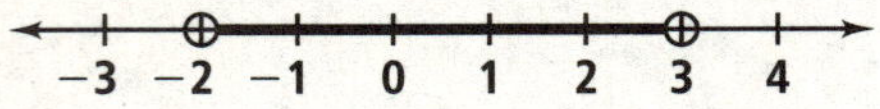

14. 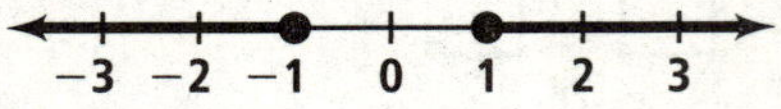

Solve each compound inequality. Justify each step.

15. $3f + 3 < 6$ or $7f - 20 > 50$

16. $3 > -0.5h > -3$

17. $-\frac{1}{2} \leq \frac{5}{6}j - \frac{1}{3} \leq 2$

18. $-\frac{3}{2} \leq \frac{5}{6}k$ or $k - \frac{3}{4} \geq 2$

19. A family is comparing different DVD recorders. One recorder can tape up to eight hours. Another recorder can tape from two to 10 hours. A third recorder can tape up to 12 hours. Model these ranges on a number line. Represent each range of hours using interval notation.

Name ____________________ Class __________ Date __________

3-6 Standardized Test Prep

Compound Inequalities

Multiple Choice

For Exercises 1–5, choose the correct letter.

1. Which inequality represents the phrase all real numbers that are greater than -7 and less than -4?

A. $n > -7$ **B.** $n < -4$ **C.** $-7 < n < -4$ **D.** $n > -7$ or $n < -4$

2. What are the solutions of $8 \le x + 2 < 12$?

F. $x \ge 6$ **G.** $6 \le x < 10$ **H.** $10 \le x < 14$ **I.** $x < 10$

3. What are the solutions of $3d - 4 < -10$ or $2d + 7 \ge 9$?

A. $d > -2$ **B.** $d \le 1$ **C.** $-2 < d \le 1$ **D.** $d < -2$ or $d \ge 1$

4. Which compound inequality represents the graph shown below?

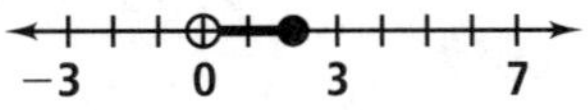

F. $7d + 1 > 0$

G. $7d + 1 < 1$ or $7d + 1 \ge 15$

H. $1 < 7d + 1 \le 15$

I. $1 \le 7d + 1 < 15$

5. A teacher knows that 80% of her students will score within 5 points of the class average, 85%, on the test. Which inequality represents the test scores of 80% of her students?

A. $75 < A < 85$

B. $85 \le A \le 90$

C. $80 < A < 90$

D. $80 \le A \le 90$

Extended Response

6. a. Solve the compound inequality $-4 \le 3p - 7 < 5$. Show your work.

b. Graph your solution.

Name ______________________ Class ____________ Date ____________

3-7 Think About a Plan

Absolute Value Equations and Inequalities

Banking The official weight of a nickel is 5 g, but the actual weight can vary from this amount by up to 0.194 gram. Suppose a bank weighs a roll of 40 nickels. The wrapper weighs 1.5 g.

a. What is the range of possible weights for the roll of nickels?

b. Reasoning If all of the nickels in the roll each weigh the official amount, then the roll's weight is $40(5) + 1.5 = 201.5$ g. Is it possible for a roll to weigh 201.5 g and contain nickels that do not weigh the official amount? Explain.

What do you know?

1. What inequality describes the weight range of a single nickel?

____

What do you need to solve the problem?

2. What inequality would you use to describe the weight range of a roll of nickels?

____

3. Is the weight 201.5 g within the interval you found above? ____________

How do you solve the problem?

4. Is it possible for a roll to weigh 201.5 g and contain nickels that do not weigh the official amount? Explain.

____

____

Name ______________________ Class ____________ Date ____________

3-7 Practice

Form K

Absolute Value Equations and Inequalities

Solve each equation. Graph and check your solutions.

1. $|z| = \frac{1}{4}$

$z = \square\frac{1}{4}$

$z = \square\frac{1}{4}$

2. $12 = |x|$

$x = \square 12$

$x = \square 12$

3. $|n| + 1 = 4$

4. $4 = |l| - 3$

5. $7 = |j| + 2$

6. $10 = |l| - 6$

Solve each equation. If there is no solution, write *no solution*.

7. $|s - 6| = 3$

8. $-2 = \left|m - \frac{1}{5}\right|$

3-7 Practice (continued) *Form K*

Absolute Value Equations and Inequalities

Solve and graph each inequality.

9. $|a| > 2$

10. $|b| < 3$

11. $|c + 4| < 5$

12. $|y - 4| > 8$

13. $|f - 1| \leq 6$

14. $|p + 3| \geq 10$

Solve each equation or inequality. If there is no solution, write *no solution.*

15. $|f| - \frac{2}{5} < \frac{3}{10}$

16. $|w| + 1.2 > 0.8$

17. A particular toddler has an average nap of about two hours and sleeps for 13 hours at night. Nap time and night time sleep can each vary by about 15 minutes. What are the possible time lengths for the child's total nap and night time sleep?

Name ______________________ Class ____________ Date ____________

3-7 Standardized Test Prep

Absolute Value Equations and Inequalities

Multiple Choice

For Exercises 1–5, choose the correct letter.

1. What are the solutions of $|4a| \geq 32$?

A. $a \geq 8$
B. $a \leq -8$ or $a \geq 8$
C. $-8 \leq a \leq 8$
D. $\emptyset$

2. What are the solution(s) of $|n| - 4 = 14$?

F. $n = 10$ **G.** $n = -18, 18$ **H.** $n = 10, 18$ **I.** $\emptyset$

3. What are the solution(s) of $4|2x| + 1 = -3$?

A. $z = -\frac{1}{2}$ **B.** $z = \frac{1}{2}$ **C.** $z = -\frac{1}{2}, \frac{1}{2}$ **D.** $\emptyset$

4. Some people are guessing the number of jelly beans in a jar. Each person who guesses within 15 of the correct number will win a prize. The correct number of jelly beans is 389. What values of n represent the numbers that will win a prize?

F. $n = 389$ or 404
G. $n = 389$ and 404
H. $389 \leq n \leq 404$
I. $374 \leq n \leq 404$

5. A carpenter is cutting a 2 by 4 for the framing of a roof. The length needs to be 5 feet. He allows 0.1 feet possible variation for the length of the cut. What values of l represent the acceptable lengths for the board?

A. $l = 5$
B. $l \leq 5.1$
C. $l \geq 4.9$
D. $4.9 \leq l \leq 5.1$

Short Response

6. A student reads an average of 34 pages per day. The number of pages she reads per day varies by 8.

a. Write an absolute value inequality that represents the range of the number of pages she reads per day.

b. Solve your inequality.

Name ______________________________ Class ____________ Date ____________

3-8 Think About a Plan

Unions and Intersections of Sets

In a survey of students about favorite sports, the results include 22 who like tennis, 25 who like football, 9 who like tennis and football, 17 who like tennis and baseball, 20 who like football and baseball, 6 who like all three sports, and 4 who like none of the sports. How many students like only tennis and football? How many students like only tennis and baseball? How many students like only baseball and football?

1. How can a Venn diagram help you solve the problem?

____

____

2. How many circles will you need in your diagram? ____________

3. What strategies can you use to complete the Venn diagram?

____

____

a. Which parts of the Venn diagram can you complete? ____________

b. Where will you place the students who like all 3 sports? ____________

c. Where will you place the students who like none of the sports? ____________

4. How many students like only tennis and football?

5. How many students like only tennis and baseball?

6. How many students like only baseball and football?

Name ______________________ Class ____________ Date ____________

3-8 Practice

Form K

Unions and Intersections of Sets

Find each union or intersection. Let $A = \{0, 2, 4, 6, 8\}$, $B = \{x \mid x$ is a positive even integer less than 12$\}$, $C = \{1, 2, 4, 7\}$, and $D = \{-3, 2\}$.

1. $A \cup B$

2. $A \cap C$

3. $A \cap D$

4. $B \cup C$

5. $B \cap D$

6. $C \cup D$

7. $A \cap B \cap C$

8. $D \cup C \cup B$

Draw a Venn diagram to represent the union and intersection of these sets.

9. Let $A = \{a, b, c, d, e\}$, $B = \{a, b, c\}$, and $C = \{b, m, n, p\}$.

10. Let $E = \{$all negative even integers$\}$, $F = \{$all negative integers greater than or equal to $-10\}$, and $G = \{-4, -2, 0, 2, 4\}$.

3-8 Practice (continued)

Form K

Unions and Intersections of Sets

11. A child sells lemonade and cookies. Ten customers buy both lemonade and cookies. Fifteen customers buy lemonade. Five customers buy cookies only. There are a total of 20 customers. How many customers only buy lemonade? Draw a Venn diagram to help you solve this problem.

Find each union or intersection.

12. the intersection of $\{\ldots, -2, 0, 2, \ldots\}$ and $\{1, 2, 3, \ldots\}$

13. the union of $\{\ldots, -3, -2, -1\ldots\}$ and $\{1, 2, 3, \ldots\}$

14. the intersection of the set of positive integers and the set of negative integers

15. the intersection of the set of the factors of 36 and the set of factors of 90

16. A salon surveys how many clients use their two additional services—manicures and massages. Thirty-five clients come in for both manicures and massages. Ten clients come in only for massages. Five clients only come in for manicures. How many total clients are represented by the data?

Name ______________________ Class ____________ Date ____________

3-8 Standardized Test Prep

Unions and Intersections of Sets

Gridded Response

Solve each exercise and enter your answer on the grid provided.

1. Let $A = \{1, 3, 5\}$ and $B = \{x \mid x \text{ is an integer less than } 2\}$. Find $A \cap B$.

2. Let $C = \{1, 2, 3, 4, 5\}$ and $D = \{x \mid x \text{ is a positive, even integer less than } 7\}$. How many elements are in $C \cup D$?

3. Let $X = \{8, 10, 12\}$, $Y = \{6, 7, 8\}$, and $Z = \{-4, 4, 8\}$. Find $X \cap Y \cap Z$.

4. Let $M = \{1, 3, 5, 7\}$, $N = \{x \mid x \text{ is an even whole number less than } 12\}$, and $P = \{x \mid x \text{ is an odd whole number less than } 4\}$. How many elements are in $(M \cup N) \cap P$?

5. Let $F = \{-1, 0, 1, 2, 3\}$, $G = \{1, 3, 5, 7\}$, and $H = \{2, 4, 6, 8\}$. What is the difference of the number of elements of $G \cup H$ and the number of elements of $F \cap G$?

1.
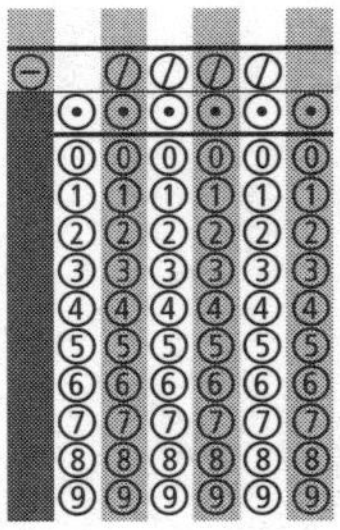

2.
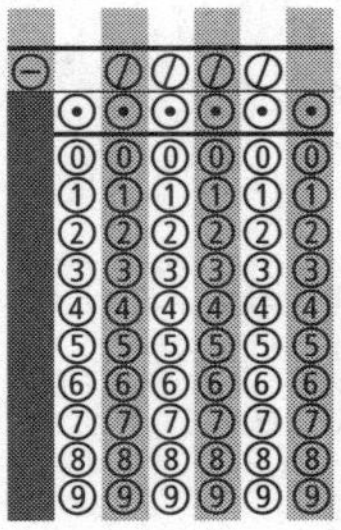

3.
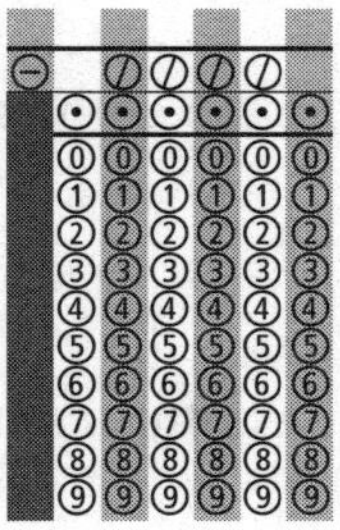

4.
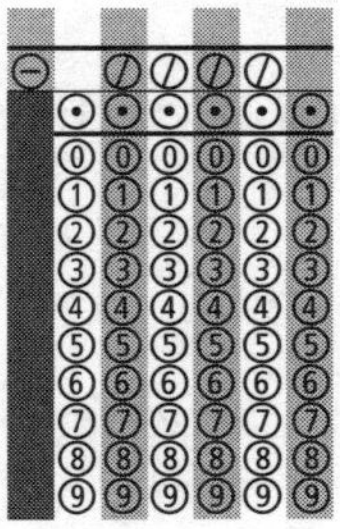

5.
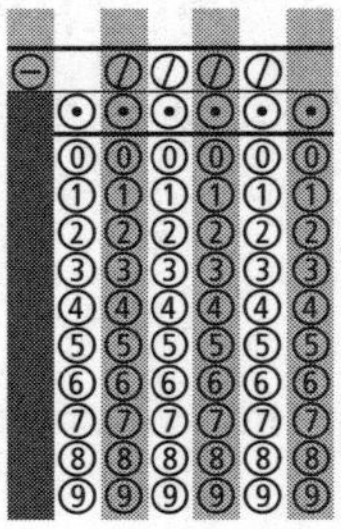

Name ______________________ Class ____________ Date ____________

4-1 Think About a Plan

Using Graphs to Relate Two Quantities

Skiing Sketch a graph of each situation. Are the graphs the same? Explain.

a. your speed as you travel from the bottom of a ski slope to the top

b. your speed as you travel from the top of a ski slope to the bottom

Understanding the Problem

1. What is likely to be true about your speed as you go from the bottom of the ski slope to the top?

____

____

2. What is likely to be true about your speed as you go from the top of the ski slope to the bottom?

____

____

Planning the Solution

3. What will the graph tend to look like relating to your speed as you go up the ski slope?

____

4. What will the graph tend to look like relating to your speed as you go down the ski slope?

____

Getting an Answer

5. Sketch the graph as you travel to the top of the slope.

6. Sketch the graph as you travel to the bottom of the slope.

7. Are the graphs the same? Explain.

____

____

Name ______________________ Class ____________ Date ____________

4-1 Practice

Form K

Using Graphs to Relate Two Quantities

What are the variables in each graph? Describe how the variables are related at various points on the graph.

1.

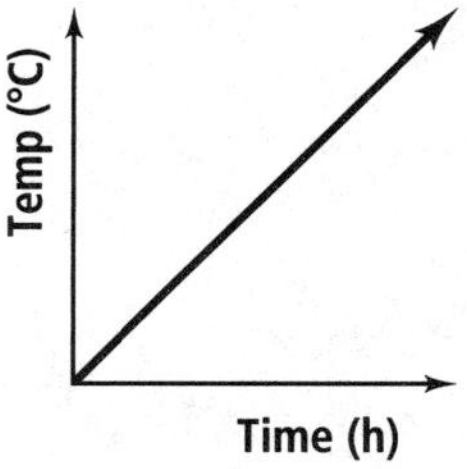

2.

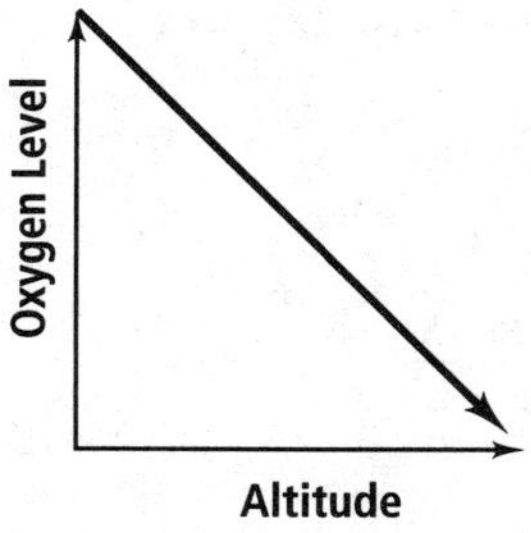

Match each graph with its related table. Explain your answers.

3.

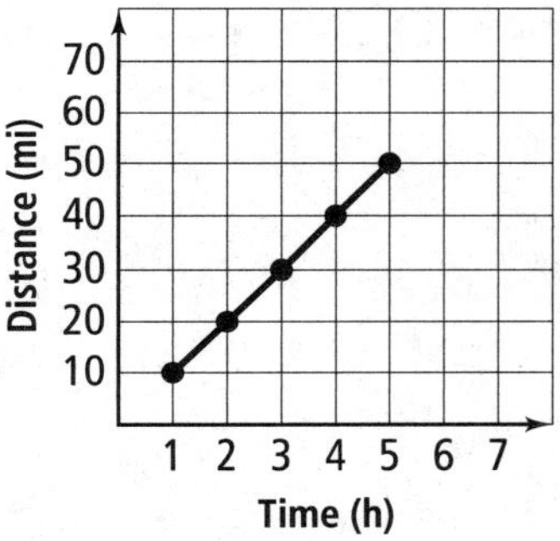

4.

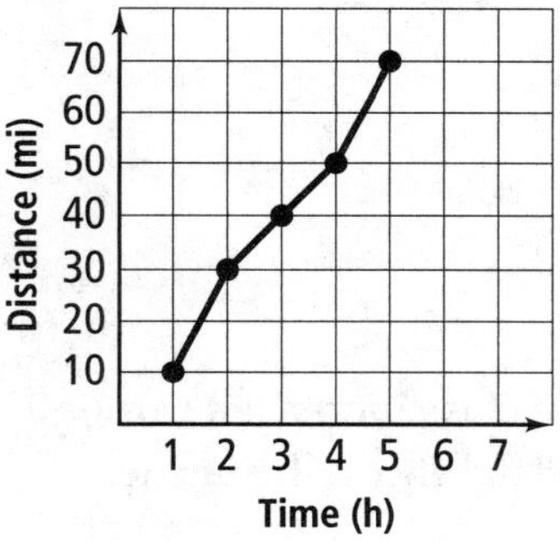

5.

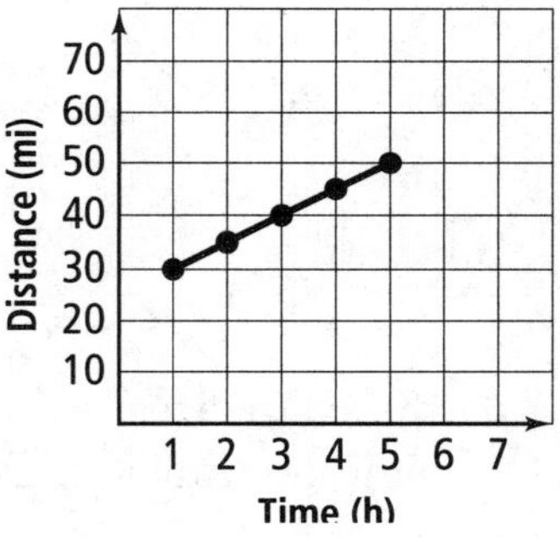

A.

Time (h)	Distance (mi)
1	10
2	20
3	30
4	40
5	50

B.

Time (h)	Distance (mi)
1	30
2	35
3	40
4	45
5	50

C.

Time (h)	Distance (mi)
1	10
2	30
3	40
4	50
5	70

Name ______________________ Class ____________ Date ____________

4-1 Practice (continued)

Form K

Using Graphs to Relate Two Quantities

Sketch a graph to represent the situation. Label each section.

6. During a trip, your speed increases during the first hour and decreases over the next 2 hours.

7. The average temperature steadily decreases over the course of the football season.

8. The average test score of the class increased throughout the semester until it decreased slightly on the last test.

9. Error Analysis During the first 2 weeks of training, Shelly ran 15 miles per week. Then, she increased to 20 miles per week. Describe and correct the error in sketching a graph to represent the relationship between the weeks and the total number of miles she has run.

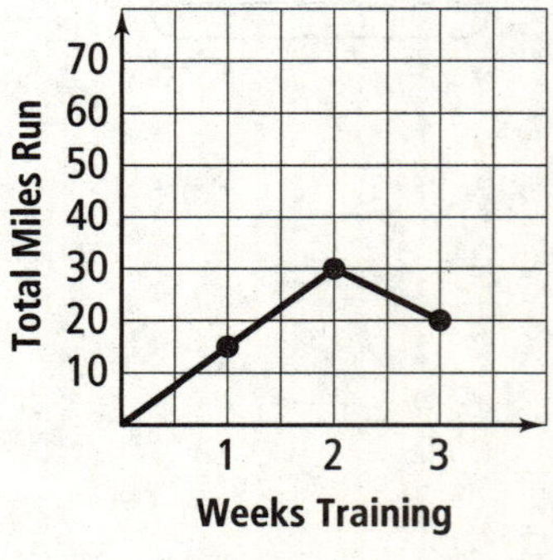

Name ____________________ Class __________ Date __________

4-1 Standardized Test Prep

Using Graphs to Relate Two Quantities

Multiple Choice

For Exercises 1–3, choose the correct letter.

1. The graph shows your distance from the practice field as you go home after practice. You received a ride from a friend back to his house where you ate supper. You then walked home from there. Which point represents a time when you are walking home?

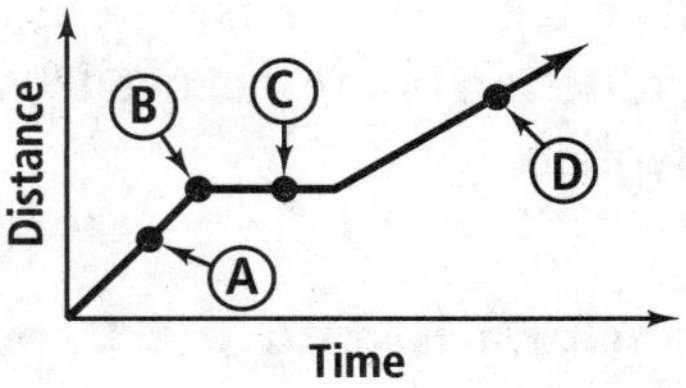

A. A **B.** B **C.** C **D.** D

2. Which table is related to the graph at the right?

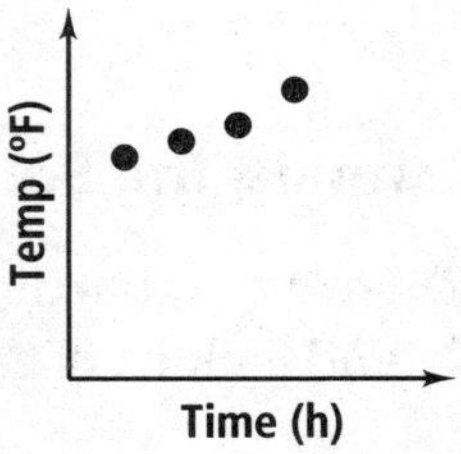

F.

Time (h)	Temp. (°F)
1	68
2	73
3	78
4	85

G.

Temp. (°F)	Time (h)
1	85
2	78
3	73
4	68

H.

Time (h)	Temp. (°F)
68	1
73	2
78	3
85	4

I.

Temp. (°F)	Time (h)
85	1
78	2
73	3
68	4

3. How are the variables related on the graph?

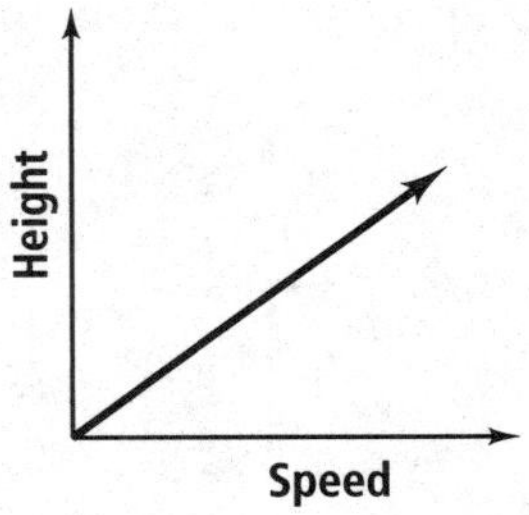

A. as speed decreases, height stay constant
B. as speed decreases, height increases
C. as speed increases, height decreases
D. as speed increases, height increases

Short Response

4. For the race you swim 1 mile, run 10 miles, and bike 25 miles. Sketch a graph to represent the relationship. Label the axes with the related variables. What are the important points on the graph?

Name ______________________ Class ____________ Date ____________

4-2 Think About a Plan

Patterns and Linear Functions

Electric Car An automaker produces a car that can travel 40 mi on its charged battery before it begins to use gas. Then the car travels 50 mi for each gallon of gas used. Represent the relationship between the amount of gas used and the distance traveled using a table, an equation, and a graph. Is total distance traveled a function of the gas used? What are the independent and dependent variables? Explain.

Understanding the Problem

1. Describe the miles that the car can travel on the different types of fuel.

____

Planning the Solution

2. Give a verbal description of the relationship between the miles the car travels and gallons of gas it uses.

____

____

Getting an Answer

3. Represent this relationship with an equation.

____

4. Represent this relationship with a table.

5. Represent this relationship with a graph.

6. Is total distance traveled a function of the gas used? What are the independent and dependent variables? Explain.

____

____

Name ______________________________ Class ____________ Date ____________

4-2 Practice

Form K

Patterns and Linear Functions

1. For the diagram below, find the relationship between the number of shapes and the perimeter of the figure they form. Represent this relationship using a table, words, an equation, and a graph.

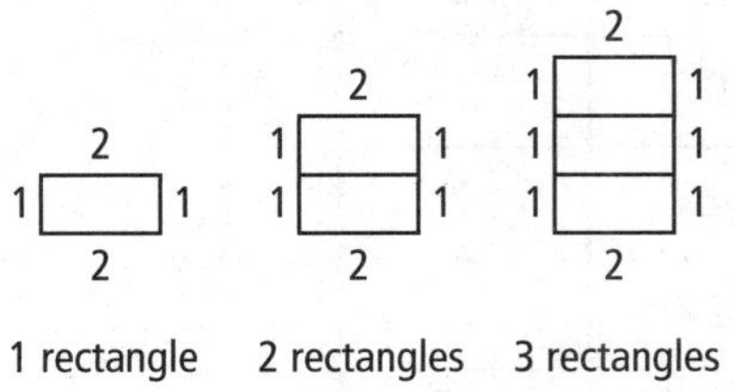

For each table, determine whether the relationship is a function. Then represent the relationship using words, an equation, and a graph.

2.

x	*y*
0	2
1	3
2	4
3	5

3.

x	*y*
0	5
1	10
2	15
3	20

4-2 Practice (continued)

Form K

Patterns and Linear Functions

For each table, identify the dependent and independent variables. Then describe the relationship using words, an equation, and a graph.

4.

x	*y*
0	−2
1	−1
2	0
3	1

5.

n	*m*
0	1
1	−2
2	−5
3	−8

6. Reasoning Graph the set of ordered pairs (0, 6), (1, 4), (2, 2), (3, 0). Determine whether the relationship is a linear function. Explain how you know.

Name ______________________ Class ____________ Date ____________

4-2 Standardized Test Prep

Patterns and Linear Functions

Multiple Choice

For Exercises 1–4, choose the correct letter.

1. Which equation represents the relationship shown in the table at the right?

x	y
0	−3
1	−1
2	1
3	3

A. $y = -x - 3$ **C.** $y = 2x - 3$

B. $y = x - 3$ **D.** $y = -2x + 3$

2. In a relationship between variables, what is the variable called that changes in response to another variable?

F. function **H.** independent variable

G. input function **I.** dependent variable

3. A lawn care company charges a \$10 trip fee plus \$0.15 per square foot of x square feet of lawn for fertilization. Which equation represents the relationship?

A. $x = 0.10y + 15$ **B.** $y = 0.15x + 10$ **C.** $y = 10x + 0.15$ **D.** $x = 10y + 0.15$

4. Which equation represents the relationship shown in the graph?

F. $y = -2x$ **H.** $y = -\frac{1}{2}x$

G. $y = 2x$ **I.** $y = \frac{1}{2}x$

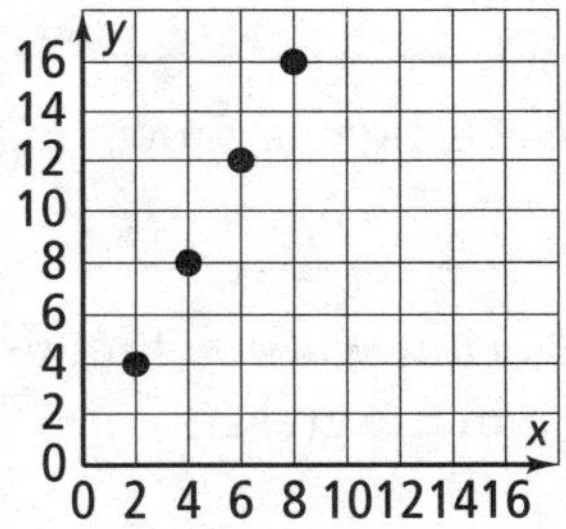

Short Response

5. The table below shows the relationship between the number of teachers and the number of students going on a field trip. How can the relationship be described using words, an equation, and a graph?

Field Trip					
Teachers	2	3	4	5	6
Students	34	51	68	85	102

Name ______________________ Class ____________ Date ____________

4-3 Think About a Plan

Patterns and Nonlinear Functions

Fountain A designer wants to make a circular fountain inside a square of grass as shown at the right. What is a rule for the area A of the grass as a function of r?

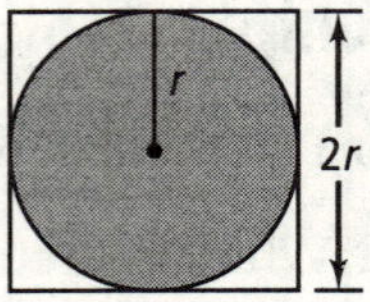

Understanding the Problem

1. What shapes are involved in the areas of grass and the fountain?

____

2. What are the formulas for the areas of these shapes?

____

Planning the Solution

3. Using r as shown in the drawing, what is a rule for the area of the square?

____

4. Using r as shown in the drawing, what is a rule for the area of the circle?

____

5. How will you find the area of the remaining grass after the fountain is placed in the grass?

____

____

Getting an Answer

6. What is a rule for the area A of the grass as a function of r after the fountain is placed in the grass?

____

____

Name ______________________ Class __________ Date __________

4-3 Practice

Form K

Patterns and Nonlinear Functions

1. A worker's wages W, in dollars, is a function of the number h of hours worked. Graph the function shown by the table. Tell whether the function is *linear* or *nonlinear*.

Hours, *h*	2	4	6	8	10
Wages ($), *W*	20	40	60	80	100

Graph the function shown by each table. Tell whether the function is *linear* or *nonlinear*.

2.

x	*y*
0	–1
1	0
2	3
3	8

3.

x	*y*
0	–4
1	2
2	8
3	14

Name ______________________ Class ____________ Date ____________

4-3 Practice (continued)

Form K

Patterns and Nonlinear Functions

Each set of ordered pairs represents a function. Write a rule that represents the function.

4. (0, 0), (1, 1), (2, 4), (3, 9), (4, 16)

5. (0, 1), (1, 5), (2, 9), (3, 13), (4, 17)

6. (0, −1), (1, 0), (2, 7), (3, 26), (4, 63)

7. (0, 2), (1, 1), (2, 0), (3, −1), (4, −2)

8. Writing How can you determine if a function is linear or nonlinear from the graph of the function?

9. Error Analysis A student says that the function shown by the table below can be represented by the rule $y = x^2 - 1$. Describe and correct the error.

x	0	1	2	3	4
y	−1	1	3	5	7

Name ______________________ Class ____________ Date ____________

4-3 Standardized Test Prep

Patterns and Nonlinear Functions

Multiple Choice

For Exercises 1–5, choose the correct letter.

1. Which ordered pair represents a linear function?
   A. (−2, −15), (−1, −9), (0, −3), (1, 3), and (2, 9)
   B. (−2, 4), (−1, 1), (0, 0), (1, 1), and (2, 4)
   C. (−2, −1), (−1, −4), (0, −5), (1, −4) and (2, −1)
   D. (−2, −8), (−1, −1), (0, 0), (1, 1), and (2, 8)

2. The following ordered pairs represent a function: (-2, 10), (-1, 7), (0, 6), (1, 7), and (2, 10). Which equation could represent the function?
   F. $y = -4x + 2$ G. $y = x^2 - 6$ H. $y = 5x$ I. $y = x^2 + 6$

3. Which rule could represent the function shown by the table at the right?
   A. $y = -x^3$
   B. $y = x^2 + 1$
   C. $y = -x^2 + 1$
   D. $y = -x - 1$

x	y
−2	−3
−1	0
0	1
1	0
2	−3

4. The ordered pairs (−1, 1), (0, 2), (1, 1), (2, -2), and (3, −7) represent a function. Which rule could represent the function?
   F. $y = -x^2 - 2$ G. $y = -x^2 + 2$ H. $y = x^2 - 2$ I. $y = x^2 + 2$

5. Which ordered pair represents a nonlinear function?
   A. (0, 0), (1, 1), (2, 2), (3, 3), and (4, 4)
   B. (0, 0), (1, −1), (2, −2), and (4, −4)
   C. (0, −1), (1, 0), (2, 1), (3, 2), and (4, 3)
   D. (0, 0), (1, 1), (2, 8), (3, 27), and (4, 64)

Short Response

6. Graph the function shown in the table below. Is the function *linear* or *nonlinear*?

x	1	2	3	4
y	−9	−8	−5	0

Name ______________________ Class ____________ Date ____________

4-4 Think About a Plan

Graphing a Function Rule

Falling Objects The height h, in feet, of an acorn that falls from a branch 100 ft above the ground depends on the time t, in seconds, since it has fallen. This is represented by the rule $h = 100 - 16t^2$. About how much time does it take for the acorn to hit the ground? Use a graph and estimate your answer between two consecutive whole-number values of t.

Understanding the Problem

1. What do the variables represent in the situation?

____

2. What does h equal when the acorn hits the ground?

____

Planning the Solution

3. How can you determine how much time has elapsed when the acorn hits the ground algebraically?

____

4. How will you use a graph to estimate the time?

____

____

Getting an Answer

5. Graph the function on the grid shown at the right.

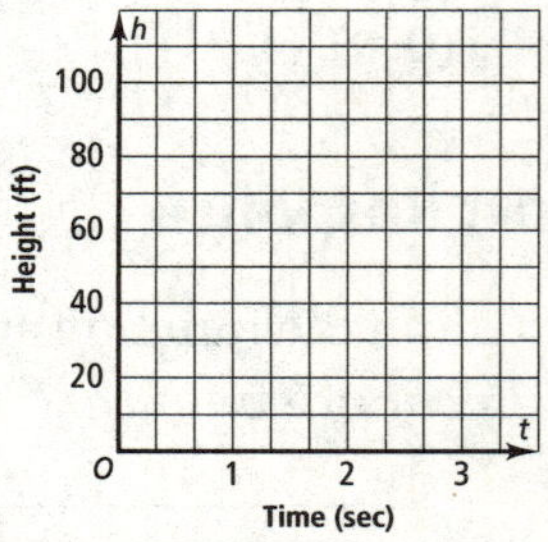

6. What two whole-number values is the answer between? What is your estimate? What does this answer mean?

____

____

7. Check your answer algebraically. Show your work.

Name ______________________ Class ____________ Date ____________

4-4 Practice

Form K

Graphing a Function Rule

Make a table of values for each function. Then graph each function rule.

1. $y = -x + 3$

2. $y = \frac{1}{4}x$

3. $y = 5x - 2$

Graph each function rule. Explain your choice of intervals on the axes of the graph. Tell whether the graph is *continuous* or *discrete*.

4. The cost d, in dollars, for a parking pass depends on the number of whole weeks w you purchase. This situation is represented by the function rule $d = 25w$.

5. The price p, in dollars, for apples depends on the weight p, in pounds, of the apples. This situation is represented by the function rule $p = 1.99w$.

4-4 Practice (continued) Form K

Graphing a Function Rule

Graph each function rule.

6. $y = |x| + 3$

7. $y = -3x^2$

8. $y = |x - 2| + 3$

9. $y = -x^2 - 2$

10. Open-Ended Sketch a graph of a quadratic function. Write the function rule that you graphed.

11. Writing Describe the general shape of the function $y = |x|$.

Name ______________________ Class ______________ Date ______________

4-4 Standardized Test Prep

Graphing a Function Rule

Multiple Choice

For Exercises 1–4, choose the correct letter.

1. Which table of values can be used to graph the function $y = -4x + 3$?

A.

x	y
–1	–1
0	3
1	7
2	11

C.

x	y
0	3
1	–1
2	–5
3	–9

B.

x	y
–3	–9
–1	–1
1	7
3	15

D.

x	y
0	3
1	7
2	11
3	15

2. Which term best describes a function whose graph is composed of isolated points?
   F. continuous   G. linear   H. discrete   I. nonlinear

3. Which relationship is continuous?
   A. the number of cows a farmer has owned over the years
   B. the number of cookies Stan baked for the party
   C. the number of people attending the assembly
   D. the distance a runner ran during training

4. The total cost c a painter charges to paint a house depends on the number h of hours it takes to paint the house. This situation can be represented by the function rule $c = 15h + 245$. What is the total cost if the painter works for 30.25 hours?
   F. \$245   G. \$453.75   H. \$572.75   I. \$698.75

Short Response

5. The profit y on the number x of items a store sells is represented by the rule $y = 2x - 1$. What does a table of values for the function rule and the graph of the function look like?

Name ______________________ Class ____________ Date ____________

4-5 Think About a Plan

Writing a Function Rule

Projectors You consult your new projector's instruction manual before mounting it to the ceiling. The manual says *multiply the desired image width by 1.8 to find the correct distance of the projector lens from the wall.*

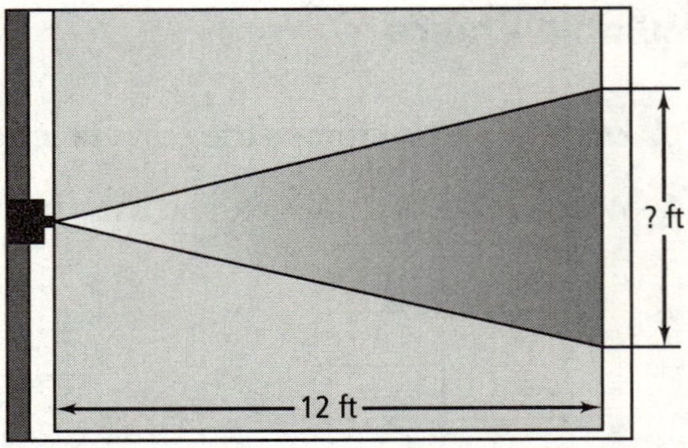

a. Write a rule to describe the distance of the lens from the wall as a function of desired image width.

b. The diagram shows the room in which the projector will be installed. Will you be able to project an image 7 ft wide? Explain.

c. What is the maximum image width you can project in the room?

1. What represents the desired image width in the drawing?

____

2. What variables will you use in writing the rule and what do they represent?

____

3. Write a rule to describe the distance of the lens from the wall as a function of desired image width.

____

4. How can you determine if the room is large enough to project an image that is 7 ft wide?

____

5. Is the room large enough to project an image that is 7 ft wide? Explain.

____

____

6. How can you determine the maximum image width that can be projected in this room?

____

7. What is the maximum image width you can project in the room? Show your work.

____

____

Name ______________________ Class ____________ Date ____________

4-5 Practice

Form K

Writing a Function Rule

Write a function rule that represents each sentence.

1. 8 less than one third of x is y.

2. 12 more than the quotient of a number t and 7 is v.

3. z is 6 more than twice y.

4. 10 more than 8 times a number a is b.

For Exercises 5–7, write a function rule that represents each situation.

5. The price p of a large, cheese pizza is $7.95 plus $0.75 for each topping t on the pizza.

6. Jaquelyn's earnings m are a function of the number of lawns n she mows at a rate of $12 per lawn.

7. The total fees f of a book club membership are $10 per month m and a one-time administrative fee a of $4.75.

8. Eric is 2 years younger than 2 times his sister's age. Write a rule that represents Eric's age a as a function of his sister's age s. How old is Eric if his sister is 11?

4-5 Practice (continued)

Form K

Writing a Function Rule

9. An online music club charges \$5.75 for the first music download and \$2 for each additional download per month. Write a rule for describing the total monthly fees f as a function of additional downloads d. What are the fees for 15 music downloads in a month?

10. Write a function rule for the area of a rectangle whose length is 6 ft more than its width. What is the area of the rectangle when its width is 12 ft?

11. Write a function rule for the area of a rectangle with a length 7 m more than three times its width. What is the area of the rectangle when its width is 3 m?

12. Write a function rule for the area of a triangle with a base 10 cm less than 8 times its height. What is the area of the triangle when its height is 5 cm?

13. Reasoning Is the graph of a function that relates a square's side length to its perimeter *continuous* or *discrete*? Explain.

14. Open-Ended Describe a real-world situation that can be represented by a linear function. Describe a change that could occur in this situation that would change it to a nonlinear function.

Name ______________________________ Class ____________ Date ____________

4-5 Standardized Test Prep

Writing a Function Rule

Multiple Choice

For Exercises 1–5, choose the correct letter.

1. Jill earns $45 per hour. Using p for her pay and h for the hours she works, what function rule represents the situation?

A. $h = 45p$ **B.** $p = 45h$ **C.** $h = p + 45$ **D.** $p = h + 45$

2. What is a function rule for the perimeter P of a building with a rectangular base if the width w is two times the length l?

F. $p = 2l$ **G.** $p = 2w$ **H.** $p = 6l$ **I.** $p = 6w$

3. Which function rule can be used to represent the area of a triangle with a base b 8 in. longer than twice the height h in terms of the height?

A. $A = \frac{1}{2}bh$ **C.** $A = h^2 + 4h$

B. $A = \frac{1}{2}h(h + 8)$ **D.** $A = \frac{1}{2}(2h)(h + 8)$

4. Which equation represents the sentence "d is 17 less than the quotient of n and 4"?

F. $d = \frac{n}{4} - 17$ **H.** $d = 4n - 17$

G. $d = \frac{n}{4} + 17$ **I.** $d - 17 = \frac{n}{4}$

5. The function rule for the profit a company expects to earn is $P = 1500m + 2700$, where P represents profit and m represents the number of months the company has been in business. How much profit should the company earn after 12 months in business?

A. $15,700 **B.** $17,700 **C.** $18,000 **D.** $20,700

Extended Response

6. A plane was flying at an altitude of 30,000 feet when it began the descent toward the airport. The airplane descends at a rate of 850 feet per minute.

a. What is the function rule that describes this situation?

b. What is the altitude of the plane after it has descended for 8 minutes? Show your work.

c. How long will it take for the airplane to land on the ground if it continues to descend at the same rate? Show your work.

Name ______________________ Class ____________ Date ____________

4-6 Think About a Plan

Formalizing Relations and Functions

Car Wash A theater group is having a carwash fundraiser. The liquid soap costs $34 and is enough to wash 40 cars. Each car is charged $5.

a. If c is the total number of cars washed and p is the profit, which is the independent variable and which is the dependent variable?

b. Is the relationship between c and p a function? Explain.

c. Write an equation that shows this relationship.

d. Find a reasonable domain and range for the situation.

Understanding the Problem

1. What are the expenses associated with the car wash?

____

2. If c is the total number of cars washed and p is the profit, which is the independent variable and which is the dependent variable? Explain.

____

Planning the Solution

3. How do you know if a relation is a function?

____

4. How are a reasonable domain and range determined for a function?

____

5. What limitations does the domain of this function have?

____

Getting an Answer

6. Is the relationship between c and p a function? Explain.

____

7. Write an equation that shows this relationship.

____

8. Describe a reasonable domain and range for the situation.

____

4-6 Practice

Form K

Formalizing Relations and Functions

Identify the domain and range of each relation. Use a mapping diagram to determine whether the relation is a function.

1. $\{(2, 4), (8, 11), (9, 1), (4, 2)\}$

2. $\{(5, 2.2), (3, 2.6), (1, 2.6), (0, 2.5)\}$

3. $\{(-4, -6), (1, -2), (-4, 4), (-1, 2)\}$

4. $\{(6, 5), (5, 6), (2, 2), (2, 6)\}$

Use the vertical line test to determine whether the relation is a function.

5.

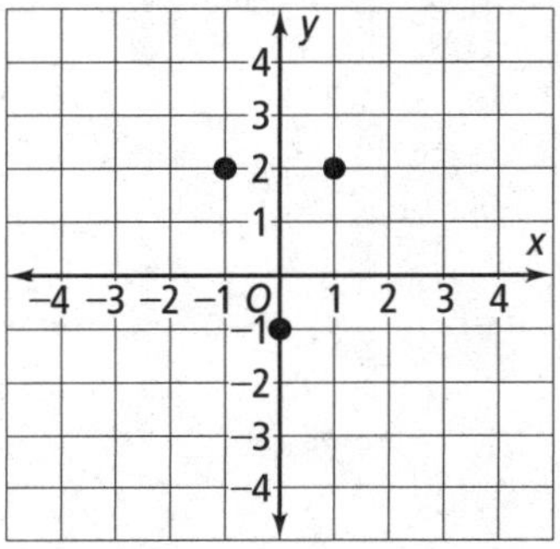

6.

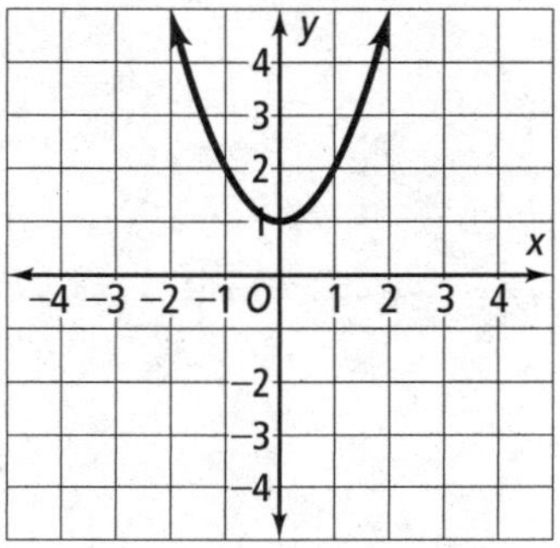

Name ______________________ Class ____________ Date ____________

4-6 Practice (continued)

Form K

Formalizing Relations and Functions

Find the range of each function for the given domain.

7. $f(x) = -4x + 3; \{-1, 0, 1, 2, 3\}$

8. $f(x) = x^3 + 1; \{-2, -1, 0, 1, 2\}$

9. $f(x) = x - 6; \{-5, -3, -1, 1, 3\}$

10. $f(x) = x^2 - 2; \{-4, -2, 0, 1, 3\}$

11. A tenth grade class is selling granola bars for a fundraiser. They earn \$0.75 for every granola bar that they sell. They have ordered 300 granola bars for the sale. The function $P(b) = 0.75b$ represents the profit P the class earns for each bar b they sell. Find a reasonable domain and range for the function.

12. The function $t(x) = 150x$ represents the number of words $t(x)$ you can speak in x minutes. How many words can you speak in 20 minutes?

13. Reasoning If $f(x) = x^2 - 15$ and $f(a) = 49$, what is the value of a? Explain.

14. Open-Ended What is a value of x that makes the relation $\{(3, 5), (2, 5), (9, x)\}$ a function?

4-6 Standardized Test Prep

Formalizing Relations and Functions

Gridded Response

Solve each exercise and enter your answer on the grid provided.

1. What is $f(-3)$ for the function $f(x) = -5x - 7$?

2. You have returned some merchandise to a store and received a store credit of \$23. In the same store, you are purchasing picture frames that cost \$9 each. The function $f(x) = 9x - 23$ represents your total cost $f(x)$ if you purchase x picture frames. How many dollars will you pay if you purchase 7 picture frames?

3. If $f(x) = 12x + 14$, what is the range value for the domain value 3?

4. When Jerome travels on the highway, he sets his cruise control at 65 mi/h. The function $f(x) = 65x$ represents his total distance $f(x)$ when he has traveled x hours. How many miles will he have travelled after 3.5 hours of driving on the highway?

5. For what value of x is the value of $f(x) = 4x - 2$ equal to 18?

1.
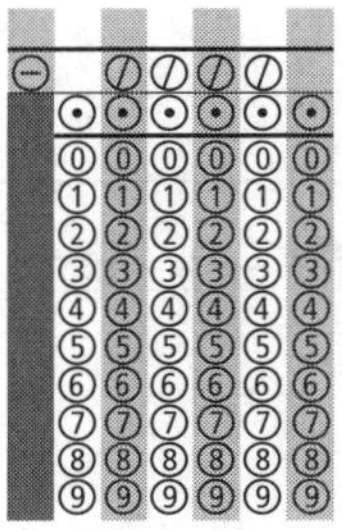

2.
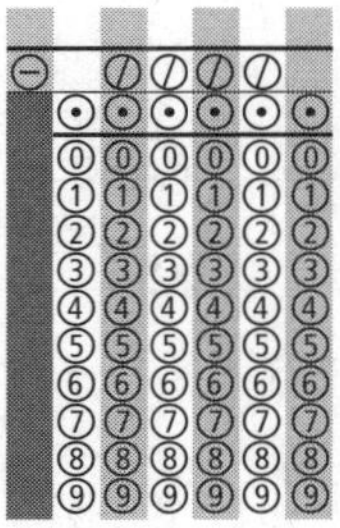

3.
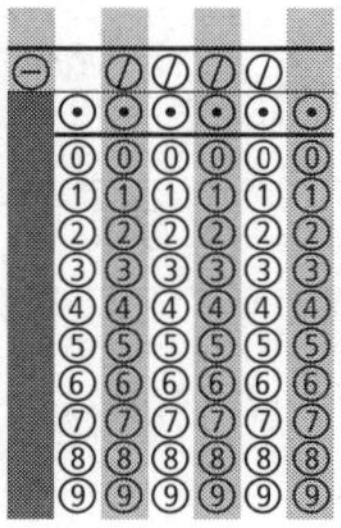

4.
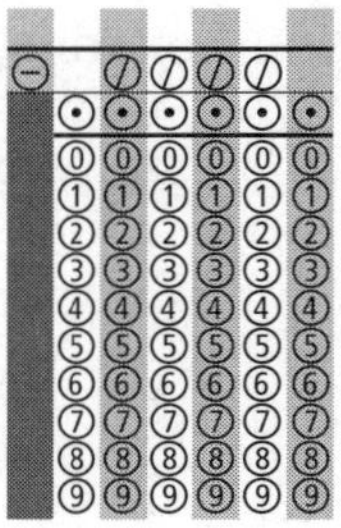

5.
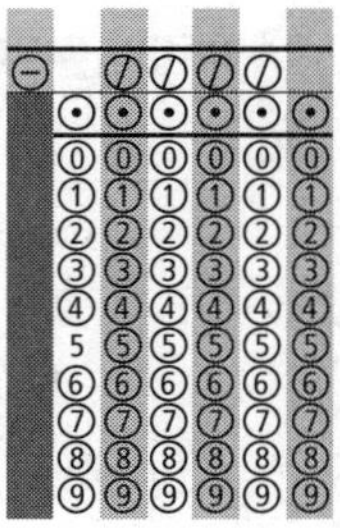

Name ______________________ Class ____________ Date ____________

4-7 Think About a Plan

Sequences and Functions

Transportation Buses on your route run every 9 minutes from 6:00 A.M. to 10:00 A.M. You get to the bus stop at 7:16 A.M. How long will you wait for a bus?

Understanding the Problem

1. What is the maximum amount of time you should have to wait for a bus?

____

2. How many minutes after the buses begin running at 6:00 A.M. do you arrive at the bus stop?

____

3. What time does the first bus of the day arrive at your bus stop?

____

Planning the Solution

4. Fill in the table at the right showing the times a bus will stop at your stop.

5. What is the common difference?

____

6. According to the table, when will the next bus arrive at your bus stop?

____

Getting an Answer

7. How long will you wait for a bus?

____

____

Name ______________________ Class ____________ Date ____________

4-7 Practice

Form K

Sequences and Functions

Describe the pattern in each sequence. Then find the next two terms of the sequence.

1. 15, 11, 7, 3, −1, . . .

2. −2, 2, 6, 10, 14, . . .

3. 1.5, 3, 4.5, 6, . . .

4. 6.8, 5.4, 4, 2.6, . . .

5. 1, 10, 19, 28, . . .

6. −27, −22, −17, −12, . . .

Tell whether the sequence is arithmetic. If it is, identify the common difference.

7. 9, 15, 21, 27, . . .

8. −14, −10, −7, −3, . . .

9. −9, 6, 21, 36, . . .

10. 1, 5, 7, 9, . . .

11. 7, −5, −17, −29, . . .

12. 72, 48.5, 25, 1.5, . . .

13. You budget $100 for parking each month. Each day you use the downtown parking lot, it costs you $5. Write a rule to represent the amount of money left in your monthly budget as an arithmetic sequence. How much money is left in your budget after you have used the downtown parking lot 11 times this month?

14. You start an investment account with $3000 and save $100 each month. Write a rule to represent the total amount of money you invest into your account as an arithmetic sequence. How much money will you have invested after 12 months?

4-7 Practice (continued)

Form K

Sequences and Functions

Find the fourth, sixth, and thirteenth terms of the sequence described by each rule.

15. $A(n) = 6 + (n - 1)(-2)$

16. $A(n) = 12 + (n - 1)(5)$

17. $A(n) = -2.2 + (n - 1)(-1)$

18. $A(n) = 5 + (n - 1)(0.5)$

19. $A(n) = -3 + (n - 1)(6)$

20. $A(n) = -7.6 + (n - 1)(3)$

Tell whether each sequence is arithmetic. Justify your answer. If the sequence is arithmetic, write a function rule to represent it.

21. 22, 16, 10, 4, . . .

22. 6, 12, 24, 48, . . .

23. −18, −9, 0, 9, . . .

24. 1.5, 2.1, 2.7, 3.3, . . .

25. Open-Ended Write an arithmetic sequence whose common difference is −18.

26. Reasoning The initial term of an arithmetic sequence is 5. The eleventh term is 125. What is the common difference of the arithmetic sequence?

27. Writing Explain how you can determine if a sequence is arithmetic.

Name ______________________ Class ____________ Date ____________

4-7 Standardized Test Prep

Sequences and Functions

Multiple Choice

For Exercises 1–5, choose the correct letter.

1. What are the next two terms of the following sequence? $-3, 1, 5, 9, \ldots$

A. $-7, -11$ **B.** $10, 11$ **C.** $12, 15$ **D.** $13, 17$

2. What are the next two terms of the following sequence? $-2, 4, -8, 16, \ldots$

F. $-32, -64$ **G.** $32, -64$ **H.** $-32, 64$ **I.** $32, 64$

3. What is the common difference of the following arithmetic sequence?
$13, -7, -27, -47, \ldots$

A. -20 **B.** -6 **C.** -4 **D.** 20

4. What is the ninth term of the arithmetic sequence defined by the rule
$A(n) = -14 + (n - 1)(2)$?

F. -32 **G.** -30 **H.** 2 **I.** 4

5. Each time a touchdown is scored in a football game, 6 points are added to the score of the scoring team. A team already has 12 points. What rule represents the number of points as an arithmetic sequence?

A. $A(n) = 12 + 6n$
C. $A(n) = 12 + (n - 1)(6)$
B. $A(n)12 - (n - 1)(6)$
D. $A(n) = 12 + (n - 6)$

Short Response

6. A friend opens a savings account by depositing \$1000. He deposits an additional \$75 into the account each month.

a. What is a rule that represents the amount of money in the account as an arithmetic sequence?

b. How much money is in the account after 18 months? Show your work.

Name ______________________ Class ____________ Date ____________

5-1 Think About a Plan

Rate of Change and Slope

Profit John's business made $4500 in January and $8600 in March. What is the rate of change in his profit for this time period?

Understanding the Problem

1. What is the formula for finding rate of change?

____

2. What are the two changing quantities that affect rate of change in this problem? What are the units of each quantity?

____

____

3. Will the rate of change be positive or negative? Explain.

____

____

Planning the Solution

4. Which quantity is the dependent variable? Which quantity is the independent variable? Explain.

____

____

5. What is the general equation that represents the rate of change?

____

Getting an Answer

6. Substitute values into your general equation and simplify. Show your work.

____

____

7. If you were to graph this relationship, what would the rate of change be in relation to your graph?

____

____

Name ______________________ Class ____________ Date ____________

5-1 Practice

Form K

Rate of Change and Slope

Each rate of change is constant. Find the rate of change and explain what it represents.

1. **Fences Painted**

Hours	Fences
3	1
6	2
9	3
12	4

2. **Miles Per Hour**

Hours	Miles
2	70
4	140
6	210
8	280

Find the slope of each line.

3. 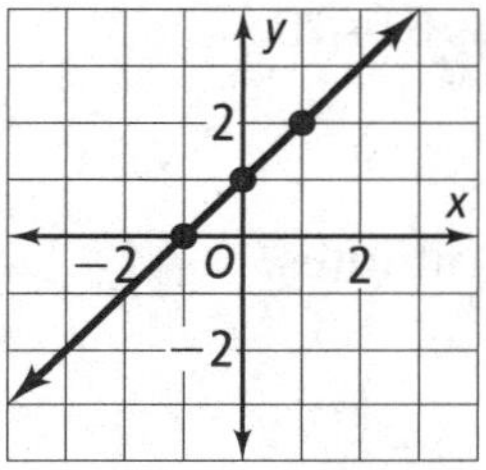

4. 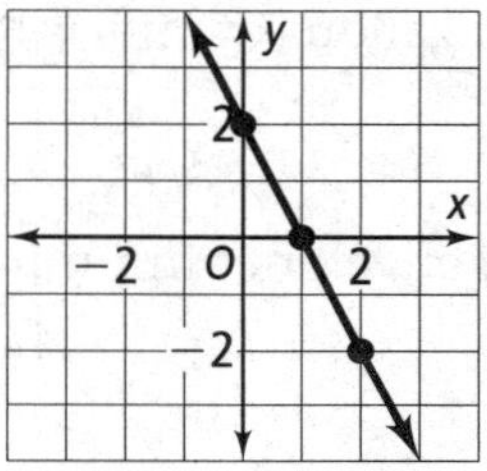

5. 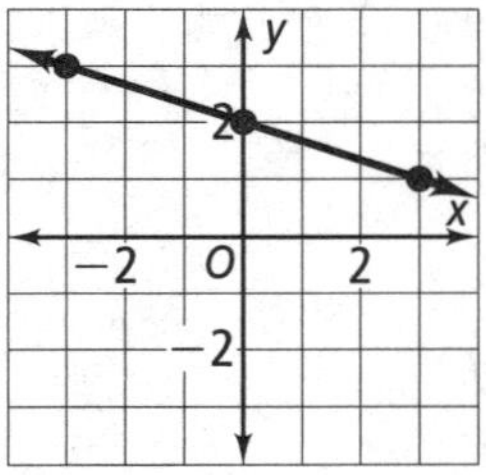

6. 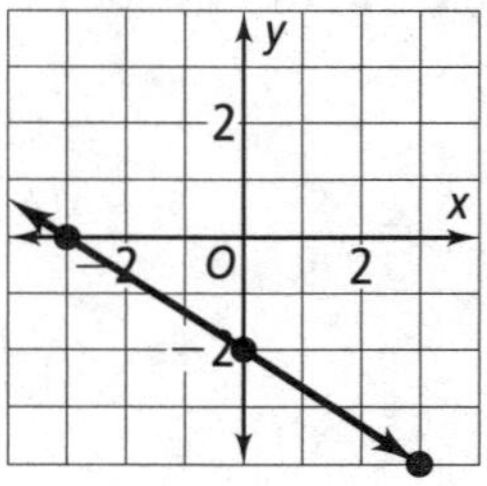

Find the slope of the line that passes through each pair of points.

7. $(-4, 5), (1, 1)$

8. $(0, 0), (-1, 3)$

9. $(2, 2), (3, 4)$

10. $(5, 3), (-2, -4)$

Find the slope of each line.

11. 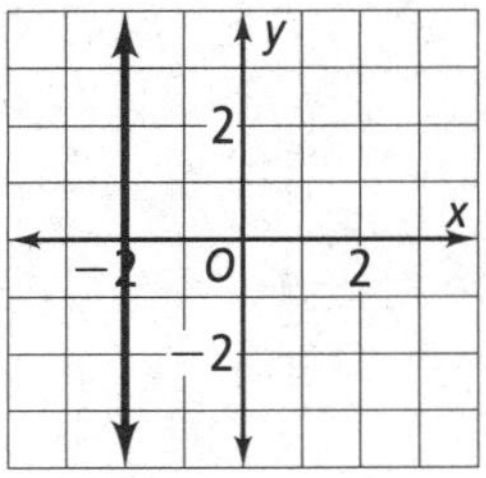

12. 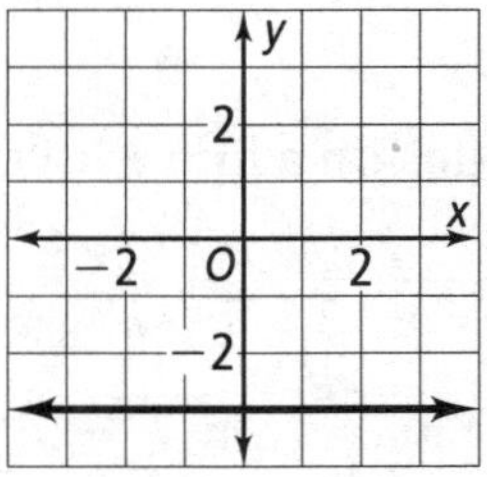

Name ______________________ Class ____________ Date ____________

5-1 Practice (continued)

Form K

Rate of Change and Slope

Without graphing, tell whether the slope of a line that models each linear relationship is *positive, negative, zero,* or *undefined.* Then find the slope.

13. The cost of a pair of jeans is \$22.50 for 1 pair and \$67.50 for 3 pairs.

14. An employee earns \$28.50 after 3 hours and \$237.50 after 25 hours.

State the independent variable and the dependent variable in each situation. Then find the rate of change for each situation.

15. The cost of three gallons of milk is \$8.85 and five gallons of milk is \$14.75.

16. Jacques filled 10 envelopes in 1 minute and 100 envelopes in 10 minutes.

Find the slope of the line that passes through each pair of points.

17. $(7, -1), (7, 1)$

18. $(3, -2), (-2.5, 9)$

19. $\left(\frac{1}{3}, \frac{2}{5}\right), \left(-\frac{1}{3}, \frac{3}{5}\right)$

20. $\left(-\frac{3}{4}, \frac{2}{3}\right), \left(-\frac{3}{4}, \frac{5}{3}\right)$

21. Writing Explain why the slope of a vertical line is always undefined.

22. Writing Describe how to draw a line that passes through the origin and has a slope of $\frac{3}{5}$.

Each pair of points lies on a line with the given slope. Find *x* or *y*.

23. $(2, 2), (5, y)$; slope $= 2$

24. $(9, 4), (x, 6)$; slope $= -\frac{1}{3}$

Name ______________________ Class ____________ Date ____________

5-1 Standardized Test Prep

Rate of Change and Slope

Multiple Choice

For Exercises 1–5, choose the correct letter.

1. What is the slope of the line that passes through the points $(-2, 5)$ and $(1, 4)$?

A. -3 **B.** -1 **C.** $-\frac{1}{3}$ **D.** $\frac{1}{3}$

2. A line has slope $-\frac{5}{3}$. Through which two points could this line pass?

F. (12, 13), (17, 10) **H.** (0, 7), (3, 10)

G. (16, 15), (13, 10) **I.** (11, 13), (8, 18)

3. The pair of points $(6, y)$ and $(10, -1)$ lie on a line with slope $\frac{1}{4}$. What is the value of y?

A. -5 **B.** -2 **C.** 2 **D.** 5

4. What is the slope of a vertical line?

F. -1 **G.** 0 **H.** 1 **I.** undefined

5. Shawn needs to read a book that is 374 pages long. The graph shown at the right shows his progress over the first 5 hours of reading. If he continues to read at the same rate, how many hours total will it take for Shawn to read the entire book?

A. 15 hours **C.** 19 hours

B. 17 hours **D.** 21 hours

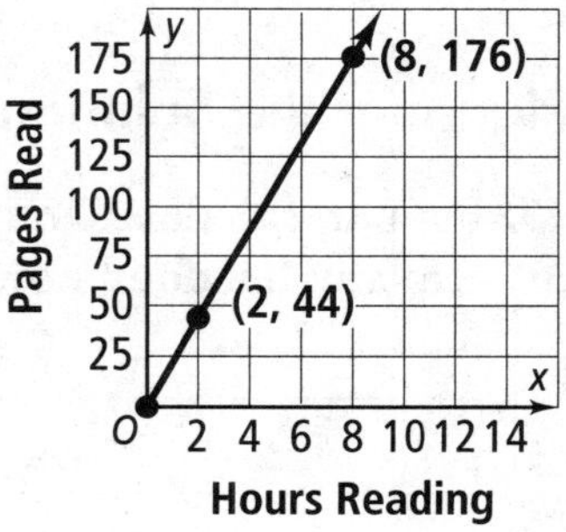

Short Response

6. Robi has run the first 4 miles of a race in 30 minutes. She reached the 6 mile point after 45 minutes. Without graphing, is the slope of the line that represents this situation positive, negative, zero, or undefined? What is the slope?

Name ______________________ Class ____________ Date ____________

5-2 Think About a Plan

Direct Variation

Electricity Ohm's Law $V = I \times R$ relates the voltage, current, and resistance of a circuit. V is the voltage measured in volts. I is the current measured in amperes. R is the resistance measured in ohms.

a. Find the voltage of a circuit with a current of 24 amperes and a resistance of 2 ohms.

b. Find the resistance of a circuit with a current of 24 amperes and a voltage of 18 volts.

Understanding the Problem

1. Does Ohm's Law represent a direct variation? Explain.

____

____

2. If the formula is rearranged to solve for R or I, is it still a direct variation? Explain.

____

____

Planning the Solution

3. For part (a), does Ohm's Law need to be rearranged to answer the question? Explain. If it does, how should the formula be rearranged?

____

____

4. For part (b), does Ohm's Law need to be rearranged to answer the question? Explain. If it does, how should the formula be rearranged?

____

____

Getting an Answer

5. For part (a), substitute the given values into the formula and simplify.

____

6. For part (b), substitute the given values into the formula and simplify.

____

Name ______________________________ Class ____________ Date ____________

5-2 Practice

Form K

Direct Variation

Determine whether each equation represents a direct variation. If it does, find the constant of variation.

1. $3y + 2 = 2x$

2. $2x - 5y = 0$

3. $-7x = -56y$

4. $-2 + 4y + 2 = 8x$

Suppose *y* varies directly with *x*. Write a direct variation equation that relates *x* and *y*. Then find the value of *y* when $x = 8$.

5. $y = 4$ when $x = 8$

6. $y = 15$ when $x = 5$

7. $y = 3$ when $x = 8$

8. $y = 7.92$ when $x = 2.2$

Graph each direct variation equation.

9. $y = 3x$

10. $y = -x$

11. $y = \frac{2}{3}x$

12. The perimeter of a square varies directly with the length of one side. What is an equation that relates the perimeter p and length l of the side? What is the graph of the equation?

5-2 Practice (continued) Form K

Direct Variation

For the data in each table, tell whether *y* varies directly with *x*. If it does, write an equation for the direct variation.

13.

x	y
4	5.4
2	2.7
−2	−2.7

14.

x	y
6	−6.9
10	−11.5
−7	−8.05

Write a direct variation equation that relates *x* and *y*. Then graph the equation.

15. $y = -21$ when $x = 7$

16. $y = \frac{15}{2}$ when $x = -5$

Tell whether the two quantities vary directly. Explain your reasoning.

17. Sara makes $3.50 more per hour than Pasco.

18. The cafeteria provides three meals per day.

19. Jasmine scores 10 points per game.

20. Reasoning How can you tell, by examining the graph, if a line represents a direct variation?

Name ______________________ Class ____________ Date ____________

5-2 Standardized Test Prep

Direct Variation

Gridded Response

Solve each exercise and enter your answer on the grid provided.

1. Suppose y varies directly with x and $y = 14$ when $x = -4$. What is the value of y when $x = -6$?

2. Suppose y varies directly with x and $y = 25$ when $x = 140$. What is the value of x when $y = 36$?

3. The point (12, 9) is included in a direct variation. What is the constant of variation?

4. The equation of the line on the graph at the right is a direct variation equation. What is the constant of variation?

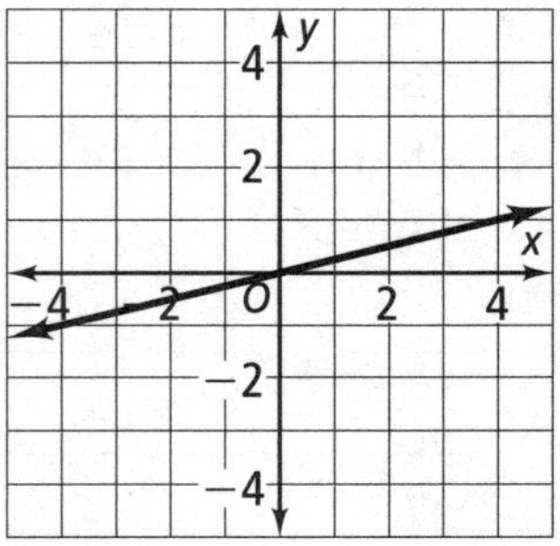

5. The distance d a train travels varies directly with the amount of time t that has elapsed since departure. If the train travels 475 miles in 9.5 hours, how many miles did the train travel after 4 hours?

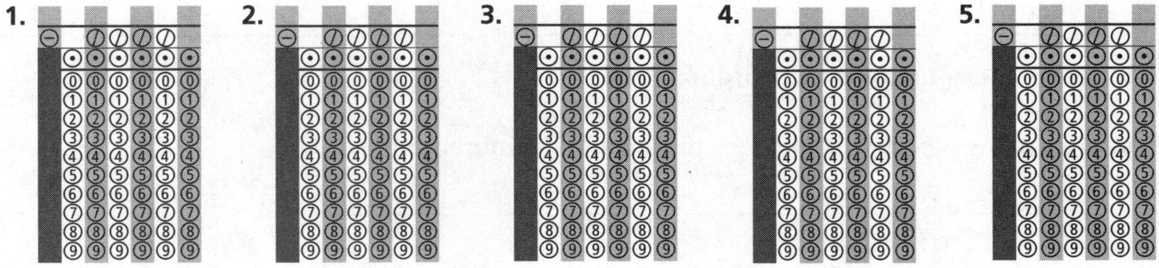

Name ______________________ Class __________ Date __________

5-3 Think About a Plan

Slope-Intercept Form

Hobbies Suppose you are doing a 5000-piece puzzle. You have already placed 175 pieces. Every minute you place 10 more pieces.

a. Write an equation in slope-intercept form to model the number of pieces placed. Graph the equation.

b. After 50 more minutes, how many pieces will you have placed?

Understanding the Problem

1. Is this relationship linear? How do you know?

____

____

Planning the Solution

2. How many pieces have you already placed? What does this represent in the slope-intercept form?

____

____

3. What two quantities are used to find the rate of change or slope? What is the slope of this relationship?

____

____

Getting an Answer

4. Use your answers in Steps 2 and 3 to write an equation in slope-intercept form to model the number of pieces placed.

____

5. Graph the equation on a coordinate grid.

6. How many pieces will you have placed after 50 more minutes?

____

Name ______________________ Class ____________ Date ____________

5-3 Practice

Form K

Slope-Intercept Form

Find the slope and *y*-intercept of the graph of each equation.

1. $y = -2x + 7$

2. $y = 6x + 11$

3. $y = -7x - 8$

4. $y = -2.5x + 3.2$

5. $y = -9$

6. $y = \frac{1}{4}x - \frac{2}{7}$

Write an equation of a line with the given slope *m* and *y*-intercept *b*.

7. $m = -5, b = -6$

8. $m = 1, b = -4$

9. $m = 0.4, b = -9$

10. $m = 0, b = 3$

Write an equation in slope-intercept form of each line.

11.

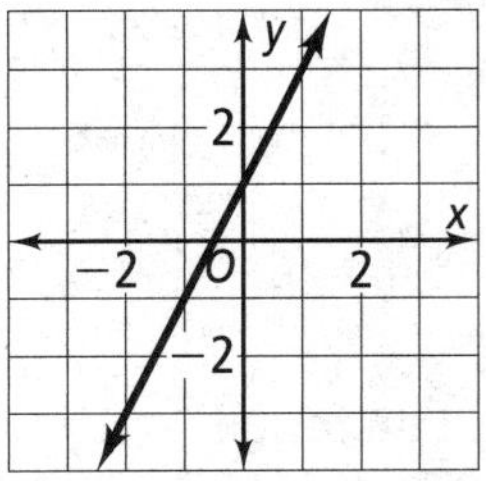

12.

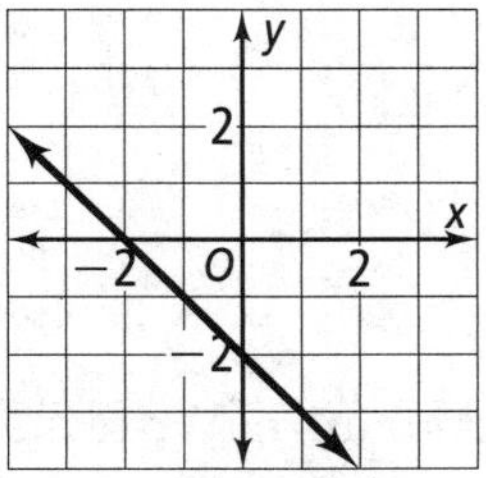

Write an equation in slope-intercept form of the line that passes through the given points.

13. $(-1, 2)$ and $(0, 0)$

14. $(-2, 9)$ and $(1, 6)$

15. $(12, 10)$ and $(16, 8)$

16. $(-4, -1)$ and $(-8, 7)$

Name ______________________ Class ____________ Date ____________

5-3 Practice (continued)

Form K

Slope-Intercept Form

Graph each equation.

17. $y = x - 2$

18. $y = 3x + 1$

19. $y = -x - 1$

20. $y = -3x - 2$

21. $y = \frac{1}{2}x + 2$

22. $y = -\frac{4}{5}x - 5$

23. A car is traveling at 45 mi/h. Write an equation that models the total distance *d* traveled after *h* hours. What is the graph of the equation?

Name ______________________ Class ____________ Date ____________

5-3 Standardized Test Prep

Slope-Intercept Form

Multiple Choice

For Exercises 1–5, choose the correct letter.

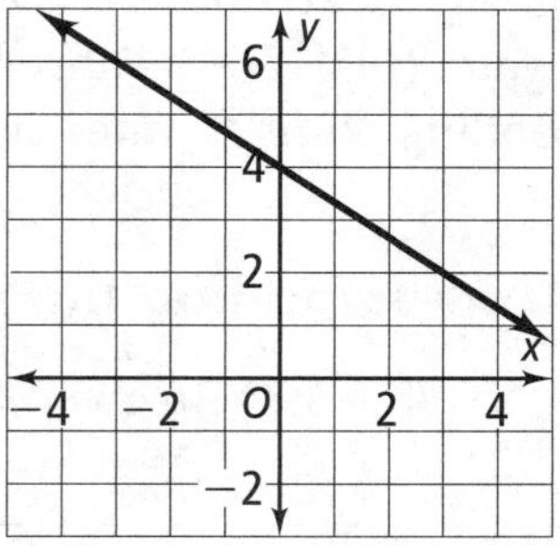

1. What is an equation of the line shown in the graph at the right?

A. $y = -\frac{3}{2}x + 4$ **C.** $y = -\frac{2}{3}x + 4$

B. $y = \frac{2}{3}x + 4$ **D.** $y = -\frac{2}{3}x + 6$

2. What is an equation of the line that has slope −4 and passes through the point (−2, −5)?

F. $y = -4x - 8$ **G.** $y = -4x - 13$ **H.** $y = -4x - 5$ **I.** $y = -4x + 3$

3. What is an equation of the line that passes through the points (−4, 3) and (−1, 6)?

A. $y = -x - 7$ **B.** $y = -x - 1$ **C.** $y = 7x + 1$ **D.** $y = x + 7$

4. The data shown in the table is linear. Which equation models the data?

x	y
2	13
6	15
10	17

F. $y = \frac{1}{2}x + 12$ **H.** $y = 2x + 9$

G. $y = \frac{1}{2}x + 6$ **I.** $y = 2x - 3$

5. Karissa earns $200 per week plus $25 per item she sells. Which equation models the relationship between her pay p per week and the number of items n she sells?

A. $p = 200n + 25$ **C.** $n = 25p + 200$

B. $p = 25n + 200$ **D.** $n = 200p + 25$

Short Response

6. What is an equation of the line that passes through (−8, 2) and has slope $-\frac{3}{4}$? What is the graph of the equation?

Name ______________________ Class ____________ Date ____________

5-4 Think About a Plan
Point-Slope Form

Boiling Point The relationship between altitude and the boiling point of water is linear. When the altitude is 8000 ft, water boils at 197.6°F. When the altitude is 4500 ft, water boils at 203.9°F. Write an equation giving the boiling point *b* of water (in degrees Fahrenheit) in terms of the altitude *a* (in feet). What is the boiling point of water at 2500 ft?

Understanding the Problem

1. What are you given?

____

2. In general, how can this information be used to answer the question?

____

Planning the Solution

3. What is the slope formula?

____

4. Substitute given values into the slope formula and simplify. Show your work.

____

5. Which point can be used to write the point-slope form of the equation?

____

6. What strategy can you use to solve this problem?

____

7. How can you determine the boiling point of water at 2500 ft?

____

Getting an Answer

8. Write an equation giving the boiling point *b* of water (in degrees Fahrenheit) in terms of the altitude *a*.

____

9. What is the boiling point of water at 2500 ft? Show your work.

____

____

Name ______________________ Class ____________ Date ____________

5-4 Practice
Form K

Point-Slope Form

Write an equation in point-slope form of the line that passes through the given point and has the given slope.

1. $(1, 3)$; $m = 5$

2. $(-2, -1)$; $m = -3$

3. $(4, -7)$; $m = -\frac{1}{4}$

Graph each equation.

4. $y + 1 = 3(x - 2)$

5. $y - 4 = -1(x + 2)$

6. $y - 3 = -2(x + 4)$

Graph the line that passes through the given point and has the given slope *m*.

7. $(-1, -3)$; $m = 2$

8. $(-3, -2)$; $m = -4$

9. $(-2, 6)$; $m = -\frac{1}{2}$

10. Open-Ended Write an equation in each of the following forms that has a slope of $-\frac{2}{3}$.

a. point-slope form

b. slope-intercept form

11. Writing Describe what you know about the graph of a line represented by the equation $y + 4 = -5(x - 1)$.

Name ______________________ Class ____________ Date ____________

5-4 Practice (continued)

Form K

Point-Slope Form

Model the data in each table with a linear equation in slope-intercept form. What do the slope and *y*-intercept represent?

12.

Hours Worked	Money Earned ($)
4	49
6	73.50
11	134.75
15	183.75

13.

Time Running (min)	Distance (mi)
20	2
40	4
60	6
100	10

Write an equation in point-slope form of each line.

14.

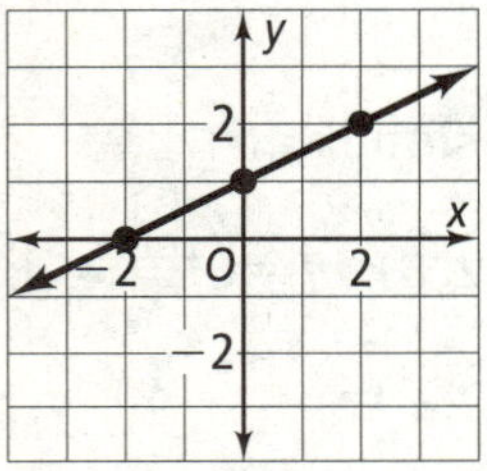

15.

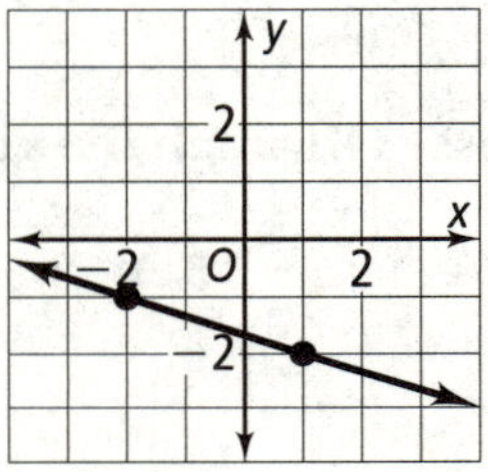

Write an equation in point-slope form of the line that passes through the given points. Then write the equation in slope-intercept form.

16. (5, 1), (0, 2)

17. (−2, −3), (4, 3)

18. (−3, −2), (2, 3)

19. (2, 5), (8, −7)

20. Writing Describe how you would use the point-slope form to write the equation of a line that passes through the points (2, 3) and (−1, 6) in slope-intercept form.

21. A restaurant's goal is to serve 600 customers in 8 hours and 900 customers in 12 hours. Write an equation in point-slope form that represents the number of customers served per hour. What is the graph of the equation?

Name ______________________ Class ____________ Date ____________

5-4 Standardized Test Prep

Point-Slope Form

Multiple Choice

For Exercises 1–5, choose the correct letter.

1. Which equation is equivalent to $y - 6 = -12(x + 4)$?

A. $y = -6x - 48$ **C.** $y = -12x - 42$

B. $y = 6x - 48$ **D.** $y = -12x - 54$

2. Which point is located on the line represented by the equation $y + 4 = -5(x - 3)$?

F. $(-4, -5)$ **G.** $(-5, -4)$ **H.** $(3, -4)$ **I.** $(-3, 4)$

3. Which equation represents the line that passes through the points $(6, -3)$ and $(-4, -9)$?

A. $y + 4 = -\frac{3}{5}(x + 9)$ **C.** $y - 3 = \frac{3}{5}(x + 6)$

B. $y + 4 = \frac{5}{3}(x + 9)$ **D.** $y + 3 = \frac{3}{5}(x - 6)$

4. Which equation represents the line shown in the graph?

F. $y = -3x - 2$

G. $y = 3x + 2$

H. $y + 4 = -3(x - 2)$

I. $y + 8 = -3(x - 2)$

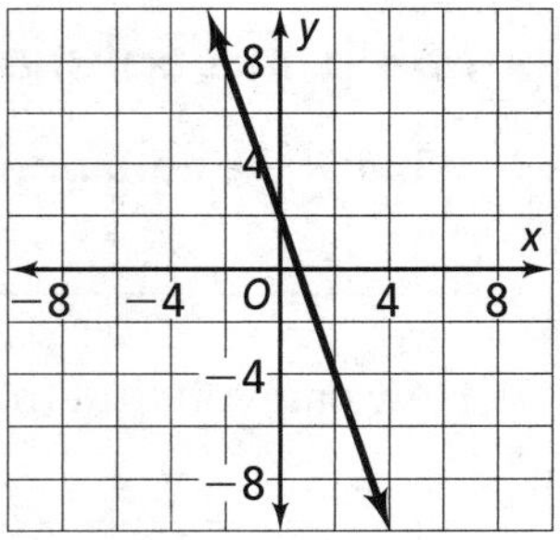

5. The population of a city increases by 4000 people each year. In 2025, the population is projected to be 450,000 people. What is an equation that gives the city's population p (in thousands of people) x years after 2010?

A. $p = 4x + 450$ **C.** $p - 15 = 4(x - 450)$

B. $p - 450 = 4(x - 5)$ **D.** $p = 4x + 15$

Short Response

6. The table shows the cost of a large cheese pizza with additional toppings on it.

Toppings	Cost ($)
2	10.50
3	11.75
5	14.25

a. What is an equation in point-slope form that represents the relationship between the number of toppings and the cost of the pizza?

b. What is the graph of the equation?

Name ______________________ Class ____________ Date ____________

5-5 Think About a Plan

Standard Form

Sports A football team scores 63 points. All of the points come from field goals worth 3 points and touchdowns (with successful extra-point attempts) worth 7 points. Write and graph a linear equation that represents this situation. List every possible combination of field goals and touchdowns the team could have scored.

Understanding the Problem

1. What are you given?

____

2. How can touchdowns and field goals be represented? How can these be written as terms to represent the point value of each?

____

Planning the Solution

3. What is the equation in standard form that models the situation?

____

4. How can you find the *y*-intercept?

____

5. How can you find the *x*-intercept?

____

6. How can you use the intercepts to graph the line?

____

Getting an Answer

7. Graph the relation on a coordinate grid.

8. Use the graph to determine and list all of the combinations.

____

Name ______________________ Class ____________ Date ____________

5-5 Practice
Standard Form

Form K

Find the *x*- and *y*-intercepts of the graph of each equation.

1. $x + y = -3$

2. $2x - 4y = -8$

3. $x + 5y = -10$

4. $-3x + 2y = 12$

Draw a line with the given intercepts.

5. *x*-intercept: 2
y-intercept: −3

6. *x*-intercept: −4
y-intercept: −2

Graph each equation using *x*- and *y*-intercepts.

7. $3x + y = -2$

8. $-2x + y = 1$

9. $x - y = 4$

10. $-6x + y = -4$

11. $2x - 3y = -6$

12. $6x + 8y = 24$

For each equation, tell whether its graph is a *horizontal* or a *vertical* line.

13. $x = -1$

14. $y = 5$

Graph each equation.

15. $x = -5$

16. $y = 6$

Name ______________________ Class ____________ Date ____________

5-5 Practice (continued) Form K

Standard Form

17. Writing Explain how $y - 2 = 2(x + 6)$ can be rewritten into standard form. Then show your work in transforming the equation to standard form.

Write each equation in standard form using integers.

18. $y = x + 6$

19. $y + 5 = -(x + 3)$

20. $y - 1 = -\frac{1}{2}(x - 4)$

21. $y = -\frac{2}{3}x + 6$

22. You work two jobs. At the first job, you earn \$10 per hour. At the second job, you earn \$12 per hour. You earned \$440 last week. Write and graph an equation that represents this situation. What are three combinations of hours you could have worked at each job?

23. Mike was the kicker for the football team. He scored 56 points during the season kicking field goals (3 points) and extra points (1 point). Write and graph an equation that represents this situation. What are three combinations of field goals x and extra points y he could have made?

For each graph, find the x- and y-intercepts. Then write an equation in standard form using integers.

24.

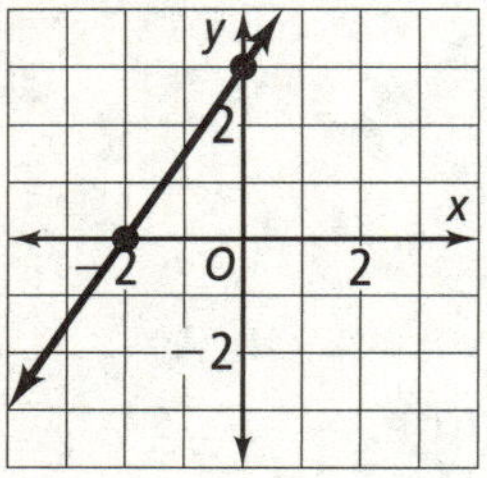

25.

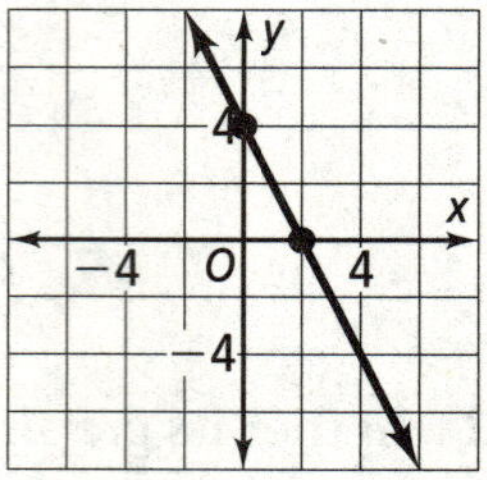

Find the x- and y-intercepts of the line that passes through the given points.

26. (2, −2), (6, −4)

27. (−1, −3), (4, 2)

Name ______________________ Class ____________ Date ____________

5-5 Standardized Test Prep

Standard Form

Multiple Choice

For Exercises 1–4, choose the correct letter.

1. What is $y = -\frac{5}{3}x - 6$ written in standard form using integers?

A. $\frac{5}{3}x + y = -6$ **B.** $5x + 3y = -6$ **C.** $5x + 3y = -18$ **D.** $-5x + 3y = 6$

2. Which of the following is an equation of a vertical line?

F. $4x + 5y = 0$ **G.** $-4 = 16x$ **H.** $3y = -9$ **I.** $4x + 5y = -1$

3. What are the x- and y-intercepts of the graph of $-7x + 4y = -14$

A. x-intercept: -7
y-intercept: 4

B. x-intercept: 7
y-intercept: -4

C. x-intercept: -2
y-intercept: 3.5

D. x-intercept: 2
y-intercept: -3.5

4. Cheryl is planning to spend \$75 on a Christmas gift for her father. He needs new socks and ties. A store has socks s and ties t on sale for \$4 and \$11, respectively. Which equation models this situation?

F. $4s + 11t = 75$

G. $11s + 4t = 75$

H. $s = 15t + 75$

I. $t = 4s - 11$

Extended Response

5. The grocery store is selling eggs for \$2 per dozen and bacon for \$5 per pound. You plan to spend \$50 in food for the benefit breakfast. Write and graph an equation that represents this situation. What are three combinations of dozens of eggs and pounds of bacon you can purchase?

Name ______________________ Class ____________ Date ____________

5-6 Think About a Plan

Parallel and Perpendicular Lines

Agriculture Two farmers use combines to harvest corn from their fields. One farmer has 600 acres of corn, and the other has 1000 acres of corn. Each farmer's combine can harvest 100 acres per day. Write two equations for the number of acres y of corn not harvested after x days. Are the graphs of the equations *parallel, perpendicular,* or *neither*? How do you know?

Understanding the Problem

1. What is the difference between the two farms? What is the same?

____

2. How can you determine if the graphs of two equations are parallel, perpendicular, or neither?

____

Planning the Solution

3. What is an algebraic expression that represents the amount of corn each farmer can harvest per day?

____

4. Write an equation representing the number of acres y of corn not harvested after x days on the farm with 600 acres.

____

5. Write an equation representing the number of acres y of corn not harvested after x days on the farm with 1000 acres.

____

Getting an Answer

6. Write the equations in Steps 4 and 5 in slope-intercept form.

____

7. What are the slopes of the equations?

____

8. Are the graphs of the equations parallel, perpendicular, or neither? Explain.

____

Name ______________________ Class ____________ Date ____________

5-6 Practice

Form K

Parallel and Perpendicular Lines

Write an equation in slope-intercept form of the line that passes through the given point and is parallel to the graph of the given equation.

1. $(-1, 3); y = 2x - 8$

2. $(2, 6); y = -3x + 5$

3. $(-3, 12); y = -\frac{1}{3}x + 7$

4. $(8, -10); y = \frac{3}{4}x + 1$

Determine whether the graphs of the given equations are *parallel, perpendicular,* or neither. Explain.

5. $y = -5x + 9$
   $5x + y = -21$

6. $x = \frac{1}{10}$
   $y = \frac{1}{10}$

7. $y = -4x + 14$
   $-x + 4y = 14$

8. $y = \frac{6}{7}x + 4$
   $y = -\frac{6}{7}x - 5$

Determine whether each statement is *always, sometimes,* or *never* true. Explain.

9. Two lines with different slopes are parallel.

10. Two lines with the same y-intercept are perpendicular.

11. Two lines whose slopes are opposites of each other are perpendicular.

5-6 Practice (continued) Form K

Parallel and Perpendicular Lines

Write an equation of the line that passes through the given point and is perpendicular to the graph of the given equation.

12. (6, −2); $y = -3x + 4$

13. (2, 7); $y = \frac{1}{2}x - 11$

14. (−5, −6); $x + y = 6$

15. (4, −5); $2x + 2y = 6$

16. Open-Ended Write the equations of three lines whose graphs are parallel to $y = 2x + 11$.

17. Open-Ended Write the equations of two lines whose graphs are perpendicular to $y = -\frac{1}{3}x - 9$.

18. What is the slope of a line that is parallel to $y = 2$?

19. What is the slope of a line that is perpendicular to $y = 2$?

20. What is the slope of a line that is parallel to $x = -4$?

21. What is the slope of a line that is perpendicular to $x = -4$?

22. On a map, Center St. passes through coordinates (5, −3) and (3, 7). Merrie Rd. intersects Center St. and passes through coordinates (2, 6) and (−3, 5). Are these streets perpendicular? Explain.

Name ______________________ Class ____________ Date ____________

5-6 Standardized Test Prep

Parallel and Perpendicular Lines

Multiple Choice

For Exercises 1–5, choose the correct letter.

1. Which equation has a graph parallel to the graph of $9x + 3y = -22$?

A. $y = 3x - 22$ **B.** $y = -3x + 8$ **C.** $y = \frac{1}{3}x + 12$ **D.** $y = -\frac{1}{3}x - 2$

2. Which equation has a graph perpendicular to the graph of $7x = 14y - 8$?

F. $y = -2x - 7$ **G.** $y = -\frac{1}{2}x + 4$ **H.** $y = \frac{1}{2}x - 1$ **I.** $y = 2x + 9$

3. Which equation is the equation of a line that passes through $(-10, 3)$ and is perpendicular to $y = 5x - 7$?

A. $y = 5x + 53$ **B.** $y = -\frac{1}{5}x - 7$ **C.** $y = -\frac{1}{5}x + 1$ **D.** $y = \frac{1}{5}x + 5$

4. Which of the following coordinates for P will make $\overleftrightarrow{MN}$ parallel to $\overleftrightarrow{OP}$ in the diagram at the right?

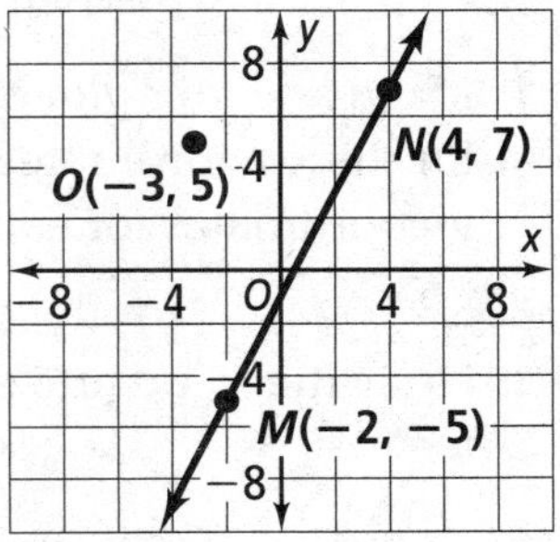

F. $(-2, -5)$ **G.** $(-3, 6)$ **H.** $(3, 2)$ **I.** $(3, 5)$

5. Segment XY represents the path of an airplane that passes through the coordinates $(2, 1)$ and $(4, 5)$. What is the slope of a line that represents the path of another airplane that is traveling parallel to the first airplane?

A. -2 **B.** $-\frac{1}{2}$ **C.** $\frac{1}{2}$ **D.** 2

Short Response

6. A city designer is drawing the road map for a new housing development. Palm St. runs through the coordinates $(11, 5)$ and $(-1, 1)$ on the map. Pepperdine St. is going to run perpendicular to Palm St. The coordinates of Pepperdine St. are $(4, 7)$ and $(7, y)$. What is the value of y? What is the equation for the line representing Pepperdine St. in slope-intercept form?

Name ________________________________ Class _____________ Date _____________

5-7 Think About a Plan

Scatter Plots and Trend Lines

U.S. Population Use the data below.

Estimated Population of the United States (thousands)

Year	2000	2001	2002	2003	2004	2005	2006
Male	138,482	140,079	141,592	142,937	144,467	145,973	147,512
Female	143,734	145,147	146,533	147,858	149,170	150,533	151,886

Source: U.S. Census Bureau

a. Make a scatter plot of the data pairs (male population, female population).

b. Draw a trend line and write its equation.

c. Use your equation to predict the U.S. female population if the U.S. male population increases to 150,000,000.

d. Reasoning Consider a scatter plot of the data pairs (year, male population). Would it be reasonable to use this scatter plot to predict the U.S. male population in 2035? Explain your reasoning.

1. Make a scatter plot of the data pairs using the male population for the x-coordinates and the female population for the y-coordinates for each year.

2. Draw the trend line onto the scatter plot.

3. How do you determine the equation of a trend line? What is the equation of this trend line? Show your work.

____

4. Substitute 150,000,000 for x to predict the female population. ____________

5. Make a scatter plot of the data pairs (year, male population).

6. Would it be reasonable to use this scatter plot to predict the U.S. male population in 2035? Explain your reasoning.

____

____

Name ______________________ Class ____________ Date ____________

5-7 Practice

Form K

Scatter Plots and Trend Lines

For each table, make a scatter plot of the data. Describe the type of correlation the scatter plot shows.

1.

Tips Earned by Waiter

Hours Worked	2	3	6	8	9
Tips ($)	36	62	120	148	165

2.

Foots Size and Height

Foot Size (in.)	10	13	8	6	11
Height (in.)	70	77	66	61	72

3. Use the table below and a graphing calculator.

Ohio Resident Population

Year	1960	1970	1980	1990	2000	2005	2010
Population (thousands)	9706	10,652	10,798	10,847	11,353	11,478	11,576

Source: U.S. Census Bureau

a. Make a scatter plot of the data pairs (years since 1960, population).

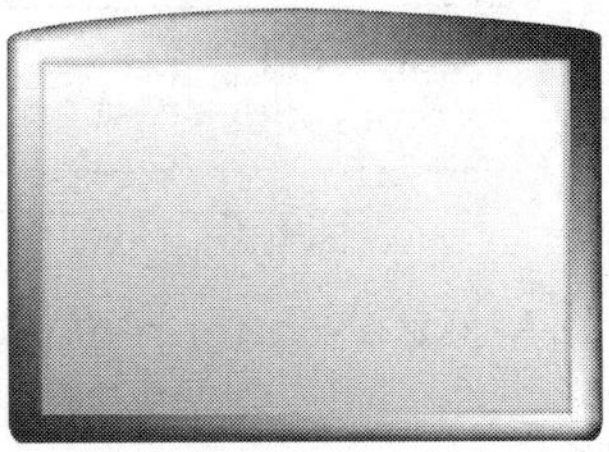

b. Draw a line of best fit for the data.

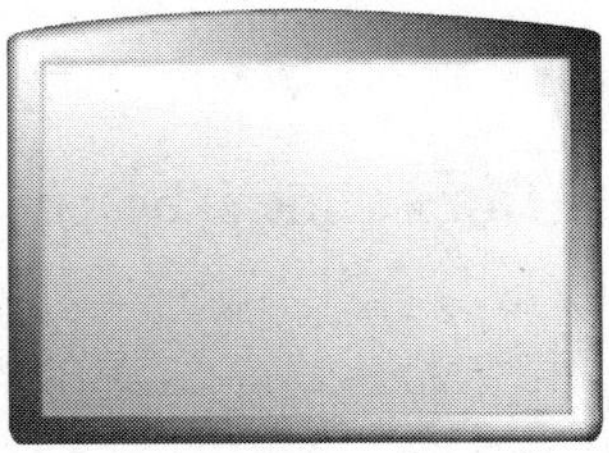

c. Write an equation for the line of best fit.

d. According to the data, what will the estimated resident population in Ohio be in 2030?

Name ______________________ Class ____________ Date ____________

5-7 Practice (continued)

Form K

Scatter Plots and Trend Lines

In each situation, tell whether a correlation is likely. If it is, tell whether the correlation reflects a causal relationship. Explain your reasoning.

4. the number of cabinets Omar assembles and the amount of time it takes him to assemble one

5. the number of darts thrown at the dart board and Jackie's average score in the game of darts

6. the dates of the summer beach vacation and the weather

7. **Open-Ended** Describe a real world situation that would show a strong positive correlation. Explain your reasoning.

8. **Writing** Describe how extrapolation could be useful in a business application.

9. **Use the table below and a graphing calculator.**

Sales of Hybrid Cars in the U.S.

Year	2001	2002	2003	2004	2005	2006	2007
Cars Sold (thousands)	20	38	54	84	206	252	288

Source: hybridcars.com

a. Make a scatter plot of the data pairs (years since 2001, cars sold).

b. Draw a line of best fit for the data.

c. Write an equation for the line of best fit.

d. According to the data, about how many hybrid cars will be sold in 2020?

Name ______________________ Class ____________ Date ____________

5-7 Standardized Test Prep

Scatter Plots and Trend Lines

Multiple Choice

For Exercises 1–5, choose the correct letter.

1. For the following situation, determine if there is a correlation. If there is a correlation, is it a causal relationship?
the number of hours practicing at the batting cages and your batting average
A. negative correlation and a causal relationship
B. positive correlation but not a causal relationship
C. positive correlation and a causal relationship
D. no correlation

2. When evaluating data on a scatter plot, what can be used to make predictions about the future?
F. interpolation
G. extrapolation
H. correlation coefficient
I. causation

3. Mr. Bolton has worked for the same company for 17 years. What relationship would you expect between the number of years he has been with the company and his annual salary?
A. positive correlation
B. negative correlation
C. no correlation
D. none of the above

4. A city had a population of 150,000 people in 1990. The population growth of the city is represented by the equation $p = 5t + 150$ where p is the population in thousands and t is the time in years since 1990. In what year will the population have doubled?
F. 1993 **G.** 2000 **H.** 2020 **I.** 2030

5. What type of correlation is represented by the data in the scatter plot?
A. positive correlation
B. negative correlation
C. no correlation
D. none of the above

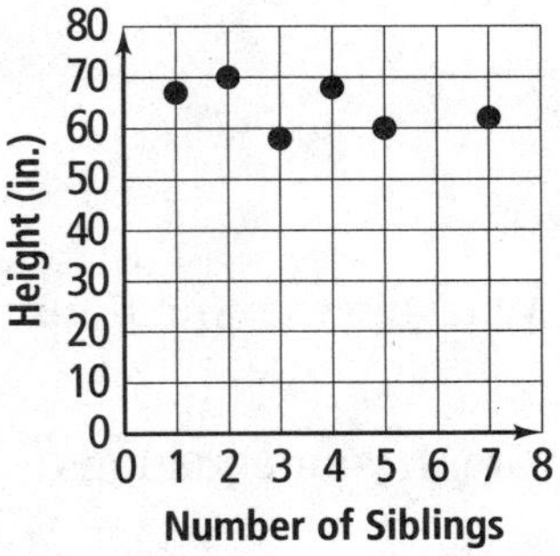

Short Response

6. Use the scatter plot to answer the following questions.
a. What is an equation of the trend line for the data?

b. What would the earnings be for 40 hours worked?

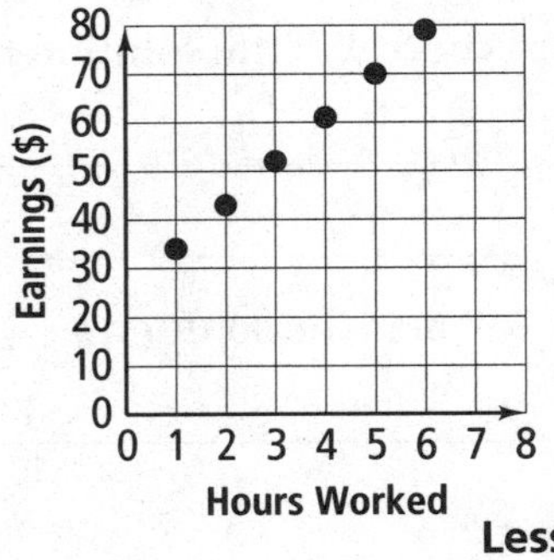

Name ______________________ Class ______________ Date ______________

6-1 Think About a Plan

Solving Systems by Graphing

Cell Phone Plans A cell phone provider offers plan 1 that costs $40 per month plus $.20 per text message sent or received. A comparable plan 2 costs $60 per month but offers unlimited text messaging.

a. How many text messages would you have to send or receive in order for the plans to cost the same each month?

b. If you send and receive an average of 50 text messages each month, which plan would you choose? Why?

Know

1. What equations can you write to model the situation?

☐	times	☐	plus	☐	=	y (total)

Cell phone plan #2 cost per month ______________

Cell phone plan #1 cost per month ______________

2. How will graphing the equations help you find the answers?

____

Need

3. How will you find the best plan?

____

Plan

4. What are the equations that represent the two plans? __________ and __________

5. Graph your equations.

6. Where will the solution be on the graph?

____

____

7. What is the solution?

____

Name ______________________ Class ____________ Date ____________

6-1 Practice

Form K

Solving Systems by Graphing

Solve each system by graphing. Check your solution.

1. $x - y = 4$
   $x + 2y = -8$

2. $2x + y = 1$
   $x - y = 2$

3. $3x + y = 6$
   $2x + 3y = 13$

4. $2x + 5y - 6 = 0$
   $-2x + y - 2 = 0$

5. $x - y = 4$
   $x + 2y = -8$

6. $x + 3y = 6$
   $4x - 5y = 7$

7. **Reasoning** If the graphs of two linear equations in a system do not intersect each other, what does that tell you about the solution of the system? Explain.

8. **Writing** Describe how to determine the solution of a system of two linear equations by graphing.

9. **Reasoning** Can you determine whether a system of two linear equations has one solution, an infinite number of solutions, or no solution by simply examining the equations without graphing the lines? Explain.

10. **Reasoning** Without graphing, decide whether the following system of linear equations has *one solution, infinitely many solutions*, or *no solution*. Explain.

    $8x = 2y - 16$

    $y = 4x$

Name ______________________ Class ____________ Date ____________

6-1 Practice (continued) *Form K*

Solving Systems by Graphing

11. Right now Seth's age is $\frac{4}{5}$ the age of his brother Eric. Twenty-one years ago, Eric was twice as old as Seth. What are their ages now?

12. The sum of two numbers is 62, and their difference is 8. What are the numbers?

13. One of the measures of the angles of a triangle is 25°. If the sum of the measures of the other two angles is 155° and the difference between their measures is 5°, what are the measures of the unknown angles?

Solve each system by graphing. Tell whether the system has *one solution*, *infinitely many solutions*, or *no solution*.

14. $x + 2y = 3$
$4x + y = 19$

15. $2x + y = 2$
$\frac{1}{2}y = -x + 1$

16. $5x + y = -5$
$10x + 2y - 10 = 0$

17. $-2x - y = -4$
$x + 3y = -3$

18. $2x - y = -5$
$3x + 2y = 3$

19. $4x + 6y - 10 = 0$
$2x + 3y = 5$

20. Writing If two equations represent the same line, what can you conclude about the solution of the equations? Why? Explain.

Name ______________________ Class ____________ Date ____________

6-1 Standardized Test Prep

Solving Systems by Graphing

Multiple Choice

For Exercises 1–4, choose the correct letter.

1. Which best describes a system of equations that has no solution?

A. consistent, independent
C. consistent, dependent
B. inconsistent, dependent
D. inconsistent

2. How many solutions does this system have? $2x + y = 3$, $6x = 9 - 3y$

F. 1 **G.** none **H.** infinite **I.** 2

3. What is the approximate solution of the linear system represented by the graph at the right?

A. $(4, -3)$ **B.** $(6, -1)$ **C.** $(-1, 4)$ **D.** $(4, -1)$

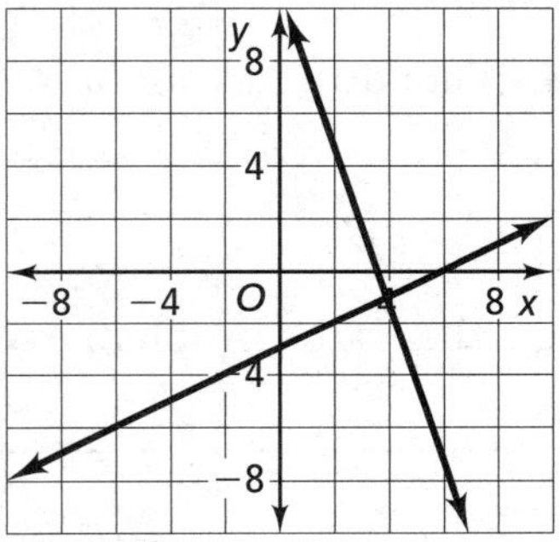

4. Which cannot describe a system of linear equations?

F. no solution
H. infinite solutions
G. exactly two solutions
I. exactly one solution

Extended Response

5. A farmer feeds his cows 200 pounds of feed each day and has 700 pounds of feed in his barn. Another farmer feeds his cows 350 pounds of feed each day and has 1000 pounds of feed in his barn.

a. In how many days will the two farmers have the same amount of feed left?

____

b. Does your answer make sense? Explain.

____

____

c. How would your answer change if both farmers got an additional 1000 pounds of feed?

____

Name ______________________ Class __________ Date __________

6-2 Think About a Plan

Solving Systems Using Substitution

Art An artist is going to sell two sizes of prints at an art fair. The artist will charge $20 for a small print and $45 for a large print. The artist would like to sell twice as many small prints as large prints. The booth the artist is renting for the day costs $510. How many of each size print must the artist sell in order to break even at the fair?

Understanding the Problem

1. How much will the artist spend to rent a booth? ______________________

2. What do you know about selling prices of the prints? ______________________

3. What do you know about the number of prints the artist would like to sell? ______________________

4. What is the problem asking you to determine? ______________________

____

Planning the Solution

5. What variables are needed? ______________________

6. What equation can be used to determine the number of prints that the artist would like to sell based on size? __________

7. What equation can be used to determine how many prints the artist has to sell to break even? ______________________

Getting an Answer

8. What is the solution to the system of equations?

Name ______________________ Class ____________ Date ____________

6-2 Practice

Form K

Solving Systems Using Substitution

Solve each system using substitution. Check your solution.

1. $x = y$
$x - 3y = 4$

2. $y = -2x + 5$
$3y = -x - 5$

3. $4y = 5x - 1$
$3x - 2y = 1$

4. $4x - y = -11$
$y = -\frac{1}{2}x + 2$

5. $2x + 3y = 12$
$x - 2y = -4.5$

6. $y = \frac{-x}{4} + 4$
$x + 2y = 6$

7. Writing Explain how a solution found using substitution can be checked.

8. Writing With the substitution method, explain how you find the value of the second variable once you have determined the value of one of the variables.

9. Reasoning For the system of equations $\begin{array}{l} x - 2y = -5 \\ 2x - 3y = -3 \end{array}$, which variable will you solve for first? Once you have solved for the first variable, which equation will you use to substitute into? Explain. Solve the system of equations.

10. If the difference of two numbers is 43 and the sum of the numbers is 13, what are the numbers?

11. David earns \$1.50 per hour more than Peter. Together, they earn \$940 if they both work 40 hours in a week. How much money per hour do David and Peter earn?

6-2 Practice (continued) Form K

Solving Systems Using Substitution

12. The fifth-grade teachers took their classes on a field trip to a museum. The first group had 25 students and two teachers and cost \$97.50. The second group had 32 students and three teachers and cost \$127. What is the cost per student and per teacher?

13. Diana purchased 6 pounds of strawberries and 4 pounds of apples for \$18.90. Then she realized that this was not enough and purchased 3 more pounds of each fruit for \$10.74. What was the cost per pound for each type of fruit?

14. If the width of the rectangle is three times the length and the perimeter of the rectangle is 72 ft, what are the length and width of the rectangle?

15. There are 785 students in the senior class. If there are 77 more females in the class than males, how many male and female seniors are there in the class?

Solve each system by substitution. Tell whether the system has *one solution, infinitely many solutions*, or *no solution*.

16. $6x - 3y = 15$
$y = 2x - 5$

17. $4x + y = -2$
$-3x - y = 0$

18. $5x + 2y = 6$
$3y = 2x + 9$

19. $2x - 6y = 12$
$3y = x + 6$

20. $4x + y = 0$
$2x - y = -12$

21. $4x + 2y = 7$
$y = -2x + 3.5$

22. $y = 5x - 1$
$5x + y = 1$

23. $y = 3x - 6$
$-3x + y = 6$

Name ______________________ Class ____________ Date ____________

6-2 Standardized Test Prep

Solving Systems Using Substitution

Gridded Response

Solve each exercise and enter your answer on the grid provided.

1. For the following system of equations, what is the x-value of the solution?

$-x + 2y = 6$

$6y = x + 18$

2. The sum of the measures of angle X and angle Y is 90. If the measure of angle X is 30 less than twice the measure of angle Y, what is the measure of angle X?

3. One number is 4 less than 3 times a second number. If 3 more than two times the first number is decreased by 2 times the second number, the result is 11. Use the substitution method. What is the first number?

4. An investor bought 3 shares of stock A and 2 shares of stock B for a total of $41. Stock A costs $2.00 more per share than stock B. What is the cost of a share of stock A in dollars?

5. Solve the following system of equations using substitution. What is the value of y?

$2x + 3y = 105$

$x + 2y = 65$

1. 2. 3. 4. 5.

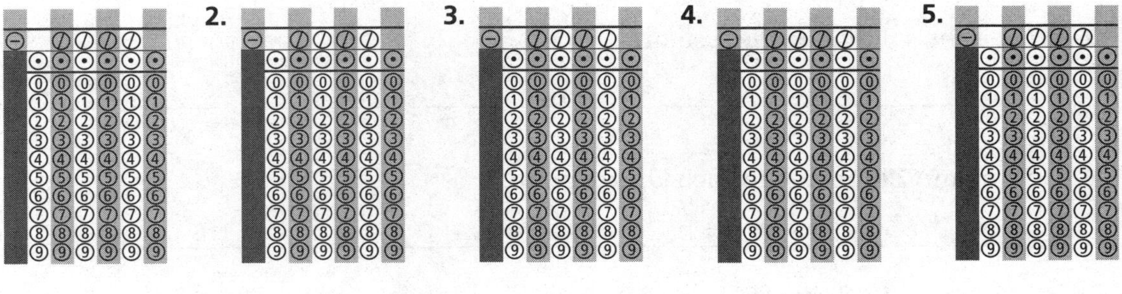

Name ______________________ Class ____________ Date ____________

6-3 Think About a Plan

Solving Systems Using Elimination

Nutrition Half a pepperoni pizza plus three fourths of a ham-and-pineapple pizza contains 765 Calories. One fourth of a pepperoni pizza plus a whole ham-and-pineapple pizza contains 745 Calories. How many Calories are in a whole pepperoni pizza? How many Calories are in a whole ham-and-pineapple pizza?

Know

1. What equation will represent the 765 Calories combination of pizza? ____________

2. What equation will represent the 745 Calories combination of pizza? ____________

Need

3. What possible methods can you use to solve the system of equations?

____

Plan

4. How can you solve the system of equations by elimination?

____

____

5. How can you eliminate one of the variables to solve the system of equations?

____

6. Solve the system of equations.

7. What is the solution of the system?

____

8. How many Calories are in each kind of pizza?

____

____

Name ______________________ Class ____________ Date ____________

6-3 Practice

Form K

Solving Systems Using Elimination

Solve each system using elimination.

1. $x + y = 7$
$x - y = 3$

2. $2x + y = -5$
$3x - y = -10$

3. $x + 3y = 4$
$-x + 2y = -4$

4. $2x + 3y = -12$
$-2x + y = 4$

5. $x - 3y = 27$
$3x - 3y = 39$

6. $4x + 2y = 2$
$3x + y = 4$

7. Writing Solve the system $\begin{matrix} 3x + y = 5 \\ -2x - y = -5 \end{matrix}$ using elimination. Explain how you can check the solution both algebraically and graphically.

8. Open-Ended Write a system of equations that can be solved using elimination without multiplication.

9. There are 72 members of the show choir. There are 6 more boys than girls in the choir.

a. Write the model of a system for the above situation.

b. Do you need to multiply any of the equations by a constant before solving by elimination? Explain.

10. Writing Explain the process you use to determine which variable is the best variable to eliminate in a system of two equations in two variables.

6-3 Practice (continued) Form K

Solving Systems Using Elimination

11. The sum of two numbers is 19, and their difference is 55. What are the two numbers?

12. For the fundraiser, Will sold 225 candy bars. He earns $1 for each almond candy bar he sells and $0.75 for each caramel candy bar he sells. If he earned a total of $187.50, how many of each type of candy bar did he sell for the fundraiser?

13. There were 155 people at the basketball game. Tickets for the game are $2.50 for students and $4 for adults. If the total money received for admission was $492.50, how many students and adults attended the game?

14. Jocelyn has $0.75 in her pocket made up of 27 nickels and dimes. How many of each type of coin does she have?

Solve each system using elimination. Tell whether the system has *one solution, infinitely many solutions,* or *no solution.*

15. $x - 2y = -1$
$2x + y = 4$

16. $x + 3y = 4$
$2x - 6y = 8$

17. $y = -\frac{1}{2}x - 3$
$x + 2y = -6$

18. $6x - 3y = -18$
$-2x + 4y = 18$

19. $2x - 8y = -16$
$y = \frac{1}{4}x - 2$

20. $3x - y = -1$
$y = 3x - 5$

21. $2x - y = 3$
$5x + 2y = 30$

22. $12x - 8y = 18$
$6x = 4y + 9$

6-3 Standardized Test Prep

Solving Systems Using Elimination

Multiple Choice

For Exercises 1–5, choose the correct letter.

1. What is the solution for the following system of equations? $5x + 7y = 3$, $2x + 3y = 1$

A. $(-2, 1)$ B. $(1, -2)$ C. $(2, -1)$ D. $(-1, 2)$

2. The perimeter of a rectangle is 24 in. and its length l is 3 times the width w. What is the length and width (l, w) of the rectangle?

F. $(3, 9)$ G. $(14.4, 4.8)$ H. $(12, 4)$ I. $(9, 3)$

3. What do both dependent and inconsistent systems have in common?

A. no solution
B. same y-intercept
C. same slope
D. same slope and y-intercept

4. Two linear equations have the same y-intercept and different slopes. How would you classify the system?

F. consistent, independent
G. consistent, dependent
H. dependent, inconsistent
I. independent, inconsistent

5. What is the solution of the following system of equations?

$5x + 7y = 3$
$2x = -3y + 1$

A. $(11, 17)$ B. $(2, -1)$ C. $(11.5, 8)$ D. $(-2, 1)$

Short Response

6. A hotel is offering the two weekend specials described below.

Plan 1: 3 nights and 4 meals for \$233

Plan 2: 3 nights and 3 meals for \$226.50.

For accounting purposes, the hotel will record income for the stay and the meals separately. So the cost per night for each special must be the same, and the cost per meal for each special must be the same.

a. What is a system of equations for the situation?
b. Solve the system. What is the cost per night and the cost per meal?

Name ______________________ Class ____________ Date ____________

6-4 Think About a Plan

Applications of Linear Systems

Chemistry In a chemistry lab, you have two vinegars. One is 5% acetic acid, and one is 6.5% acetic acid. You want to make 200 mL of a vinegar with 6% acetic acid. How many milliliters of each vinegar do you need to mix together?

Know

1. What types of vinegar do you have available?

2. What amount of mixed vinegar do you need?

3. What percentage of acetic acid do you want in the mixed vinegar?

Need

4. What do you need to find to solve the problem?

Plan

5. How will you define the two variables for this problem?

6. What is an equation for the total amount of vinegar you want to make?

7. What is an equation for the acetic acid content?

8. What method will you use to solve?

9. What is the solution of the system of equations?

10. How much of each type of vinegar should you mix together?

6-4 Practice

Form K

Applications of Linear Systems

Solve each word problem.

1. The concession stand is selling hot dogs and hamburgers during a game. At halftime, they sold a total of 78 hot dogs and hamburgers and brought in \$105.50. How any of each item did they sell if hamburgers sold for \$1.50 and hot dogs sold for \$1.25?

2. The sum of two numbers is 67. The smaller number is 3 less than the larger number. What are the two numbers?

3. There are two different jobs Jordan is considering. The first job will pay her \$4200 per month plus an annual bonus of \$4500. The second job pays \$3100 per month plus \$600 per month toward her rent and an annual bonus of \$500. Which job should she take?

4. The perimeter of a rectangle is 66 cm and its width is half its length. What are the length and the width of the rectangle?

5. A chemist is mixing one solution that is 32% sodium and another solution that is 12% sodium. How many liters of each type should the chemist use to produce 50 liters of the solution that is 20% sodium?

6-4 Practice (continued) Form K

Applications of Linear Systems

6. A community sponsored a charity square dance where admission was \$3 for adults and \$1.50 for children. If 168 people attended the dance and the money raised was \$432, how many adults and how many children attended the dance?

   a. What are the two systems of equations that you could write to solve this problem?

   b. What method would you use to solve the system? Why?

Solve each system. Explain why you chose the method you used.

7. $3y = 4x + 1$
   $8x - 2y = 10$

8. $-2y = -4x - 2$
   $3x + 2y = 9$

9. $3x - 3y = -3$
   $-2x - 3y = 17$

10. $x - 2y = 9$
    $x + 3y = -1$

11. **Open-Ended** Write a system of equations for which you would use substitution to solve.

12. A student invested \$5000 in two different savings accounts. The first account pays an annual interest rate of 3%. The second account pays an annual interest rate of 4%. At the end of one year, she had earned \$185 in interest. How much money did she invest in each account?

Name ______________________ Class ____________ Date ____________

6-4 Standardized Test Prep

Applications of Linear Systems

Multiple Choice

For Exercises 1–5, choose the correct letter.

1. You solved a linear system with two equations and two variables and got the equation $-6 = -6$. How many solutions does the system of equations have?

A. no solution **C.** exactly 1 solution
B. infinitely many solutions **D.** 2 solutions

2. The sum of two numbers is 12. The difference of the same two numbers is -4. What is the larger of the two numbers?

F. 4 **H.** 7 **G.** 5 **I.** 8

3. You solved a linear system and got the equation $-6 = 0$. How many solutions does the system of equations have?

A. no solution **C.** exactly 1 solution
B. infinitely many solutions **D.** 2 solutions

4. What is the solution of the system of equations? $\begin{aligned} -y + 3x &= 6 \\ y &= -6x + 12 \end{aligned}$

F. $(-2, 0)$ **H.** $(2, 0)$ **G.** $(0, -2)$ **I.** $(0, 2)$

5. A kayaker paddles upstream for 1.5 hours, then turns his kayak around and returns to his tent in 1 hour. He travels 3 miles each way. What is the rate of the river's current?

A. 0.5 mi/h **B.** 2 mi/h **C.** 1 mi/h **D.** 1.5 mi/h

Short Response

6. Rectangle *EFGH* has a perimeter of 24 inches, and triangle *BCD* has a perimeter of 18 inches.

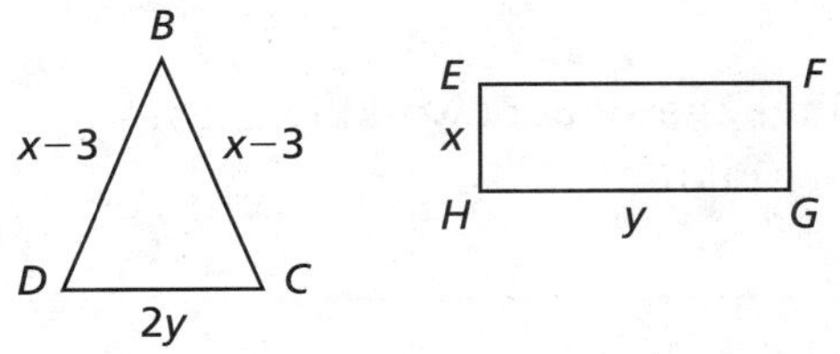

a. What is a system of equations for the perimeters of the figures?

b. Without solving, what method you would use to solve the system? Explain.

Name ______________________ Class ____________ Date ____________

6-5 Think About a Plan

Linear Inequalities

Employment A student with two summer jobs earns $10 per hour at a café and $8 per hour at a market. The student would like to earn at least $800 per month.

a. Write and graph an inequality to represent the situation.

b. The student works at the market for 60 h per month and can work at most 90 h per month. Can the student earn at least $800 each month? Explain how you can use your graph to determine this.

Understanding the Problem

1. What do you know about the student's hourly rates?

____

2. What do you know about how much the student would like to earn each month?

____

3. What do you know about the number of hours the student can work each month?

____

Planning the Solution

4. What inequality represents the number of hours that the student can work each month? ____________

5. What inequality represents the amount that the student can earn each month?

____

Getting an Answer

6. How can you use these two inequalities to find out if the student working 60 hours a month at the market can make $800 per month?

____

____

7. How can you determine the number of hours that the student should work each month? What are the number of hours the student should work at the market and at the cafe to make at least $800 per month?

____

____

Name ______________________ Class ____________ Date ____________

6-5 Practice

Form K

Linear Inequalities

Graph each linear inequality.

1. $x \geq -7$

2. $y < -5$

3. $-x + y \geq 2$

4. $-4x + 5y < -3$

5. $x - y \geq 8$

6. $2x + 3y > 9$

7. $y \geq x$

8. $3x > y$

9. $x - 2y > -4$

10. $5x + 5y > -10$

11. $4x - \frac{1}{2}y < 3$

12. $x \leq -3y$

6-5 Practice (continued) — Form K

Linear Inequalities

13. Writing How can you check to see that you have shaded the correct half of the coordinate plane after graphing a linear inequality? Explain.

Determine whether the ordered pair is a solution of the linear inequality.

14. $4x + 3y > -2; (-3, -1)$

15. $x + y > -3; (-2, 2)$

16. $y - 4x \leq 0; (1, 4)$

17. $2x - 4y > 5; (5, -1)$

18. $y \leq 2x - 3; (-1, -4)$

19. $y < -3x + 1; (3, 5)$

Write a linear inequality that represents each graph.

20.

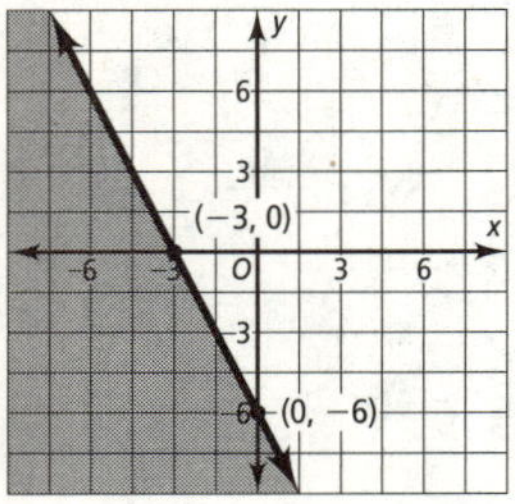

21.

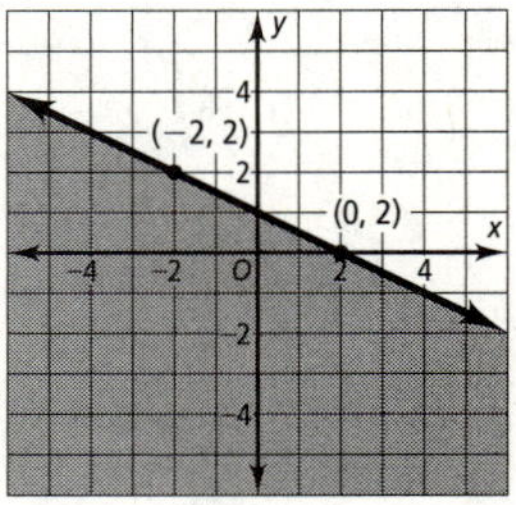

22. A friend has \$75 to buy some new shirts and pants. Each shirt *s* costs \$11. Each pair of pants *p* costs \$19.

a. Write and graph an inequality that shows how many shirts and pants your friend can buy.

b. Which side of the boundary line should you shade?

c. What inequality symbol did you use? Explain.

23. Admission to the movie theater costs \$7.50 for adults and \$3.50 for students. The theater must bring in at least \$200 per movie. Write an inequality for the number of tickets the theater needs to sell to make a profit. If the theater sells 15 adult tickets, how many student tickets do they need to sell to make a profit?

24. Each child at the birthday party was given \$5 to spend at the arcade on games and rides. Each game costs \$0.25 and each ride costs \$0.50. Write an inequality for the number of games and rides a child can enjoy for \$5. What is the maximum number of games or rides each child can enjoy?

Name ______________________ Class ____________ Date ____________

6-5 Standardized Test Prep

Linear Inequalities

Multiple Choice

For Exercises 1–5, choose the correct letter.

1. What point on the axes satisfies the inequality $y < x$?

A. $(0, 1)$ **B.** $(-1, 0)$ **C.** $(1, 0)$ **D.** $(0, 0)$

2. For the graph of the inequality $x - 2y \geq 4$, what is a value of x for a point that is on the boundary line and the axes?

F. 4 **G.** -2 **H.** 2 **I.** -4

3. If $x \geq 0$ and $y \geq 0$, then which quadrant holds the solutions?

A. IV **B.** III **C.** I **D.** II

4. Which is the y-value of a boundary point that is an intersecting point not on the axes for this region: $x \geq 0, y \geq 0, x \leq 4$ and $y \leq 3$?

F. 4 **G.** 0 **H.** 1 **I.** 3

5. How do you decide where to shade an inequality whose boundary does not go through the origin?

A. For $<$, shade above the boundary.
B. If $(0, 0)$ is a solution, shade where $(0, 0)$ is.
C. For $<$, shade below the boundary.
D. If $(0, 0)$ is a solution, shade where $(0, 0)$ is not.

Short Response

6. A school fundraiser sells holiday cards and wrapping paper. They are trying to raise at least \$400. They make a profit of \$1.50 on each box of holiday cards and \$1.00 on each pack of wrapping paper.

a. What is an inequality for the profit the school wants to make for the fundraiser?

b. If the fundraiser sells 100 boxes of cards and 160 packs of wrapping paper, will they reach their goal? Show your work.

Name ______________________ Class ____________ Date ____________

6-6 Think About a Plan

Systems of Linear Inequalities

Gift Certificates You received a $100 gift certificate to a clothing store. The store sells T-shirts for $15 and dress shirts for $22. You want to spend no more than the amount of the gift certificate. You want to leave at most $10 of the gift certificate unspent. You need at least one dress shirt. What are all of the possible combinations of T-shirts and dress shirts you could buy?

Understanding the Problem

1. What do you know about the cost of each type of shirt that you want to buy?

____

2. What do you know about how much you can spend? What do you know about how much you want to leave unspent?

____

3. What do you know about the number of dress shirts that you want to buy?

____

Planning the Solution

4. What inequality represents the amount of shirts you can buy? ____________

5. What inequality represents the amount of the gift certificate which could be unspent? ____________

6. What inequality represents the number of dress shirts you want to buy? ____________

Getting an Answer

7. How can you use these inequalities to find out the number of T-shirts and dress shirts you can buy? ______________________________

8. Graph the system of linear inequalities. Point out the region that shows the answer.

9. What combinations of T-shirts and dress shirts are possible? ______________________________

10. Are there any other possible combinations? Explain.

____

Name ____________________ Class ____________ Date ____________

6-6 Practice

Form K

Systems of Linear Inequalities

Solve each system of inequalities by graphing.

1. $y \leq 2x - 1$
   $y \geq -x + 3$

2. $3x - 2y \leq 4$
   $x + 3y \leq 6$

3. $x + y \geq -3$
   $2x + 2y \leq -2$

4. $-y \leq 3x + 4$
   $-3x + 3y \leq -9$

5. **Writing** Describe when you use a solid line or a broken line when graphing inequalities. What does each type of line mean?

6. **Open-Ended** Create a system of inequalities that has no solution. Demonstrate by drawing a graph.

7. The owner of an ice cream stand needs to order waffle cones and sugar cones. There is room to store 10 boxes of cones. Each box of sugar cones costs $100, and each box of waffle cones costs $150. He has $1250 budgeted for the purchase of cones.
   a. What variables will you use?
   b. How will you decide which inequality signs to use and where to shade?
   c. What system of inequalities represents the information?

Name ______________________ Class ______________ Date ______________

6-6 Practice (continued) Form K

Systems of Linear Inequalities

Determine whether the ordered pair is a solution of the given system.

8. $(2, -1)$; $3 - 3y \leq 3y$
$3y > 2x + 1$

9. $(-3, -3)$; $5x + 4y > -4$
$2x + 3y > 2$

10. A friend makes \$15 per hour at his first job and \$11 per hour at his second job. His goal is to make at least \$600 per week. He does not want to work any more than 55 hours in a week. Write a system of inequalities for the given situation and graph the inequalities.

11. For the school fundraiser, a class is selling stationary and greeting cards. The goal for the class is to sell at least 100 items. The school receives \$2.50 for each stationary set that is sold and \$3 for each set of greeting cards that is sold. The goal is to raise at least \$300. Write a system of inequalities for the given situation and graph the inequalities.

12. A woman is purchasing fruit for some pies she is making for a party. She wants to purchase at least 10 pounds of strawberries and blueberries. Strawberries are sold for \$2 per pound, and blueberries are sold for \$3 per pound. She does not want to spend more than \$25 total for the fruit. Write a system of inequalities for the given situation and graph the inequalities.

Solve each system of inequalities by graphing.

13. $3x + 4y < -14$
$x - 3y \geq 17$

14. $x - 5y - 6 \geq 0$
$2x + 4y + 1 \leq -1$

Name _______________ Class _______________ Date _______________

6-6 Standardized Test Prep

Systems of Linear Inequalities

Multiple Choice

For Exercises 1–4, choose the correct letter.

1. You and a friend both would like a salad and a small drink. Between the two of you, you have \$8.00. A salad costs \$2.49 and a small drink is \$.99. Can either of you have a second salad or drink?

A. yes, 1 salad **B.** yes, 1 of each **C.** yes, 1 drink **D.** no, you cannot

2. Which of the following systems of inequalities represents the graph?

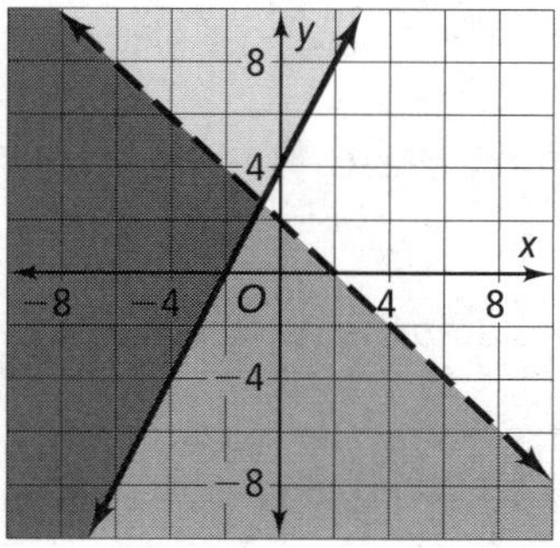

F. $y > 2x + 4$, $y \leq -x + 2$ **G.** $2x - y \geq 4$, $y < -x + 2$

H. $y \geq 2x + 4$, $-x + y < 2$ **I.** $-2x + y \geq 4$, $x + y < 2$

3. For the graph above, what is the approximate *y*-value of the point of intersection?

A. −1 **B.** 4 **C.** 3 **D.** 2

4. A student spends no more than 2 hours on his math and English homework. If math takes about twice as long as English, what is the maximum time that the student can spend on English?

F. $\frac{1}{3}$ hour **G.** $\frac{1}{2}$ hour **H.** 1 hour **I.** $\frac{2}{3}$ hour

Short Response

5. A young woman wants to make at least \$200 a week and can work no more than 30 hours a week. She works at the library for \$8 an hour and babysits for \$6 an hour.

a. What system of inequalities shows the possible combination of hours and jobs she can work?

b. Why did you exclude points to the left of the *y*-axis and below the *x*-axis?

Name ______________________ Class ____________ Date ____________

7-1 Think About a Plan

Zero and Negative Exponents

Manufacturing A company is making metal rods with a target diameter of 1.5 mm. A rod is acceptable when its diameter is within 10^{-3} mm of the target diameter. Write an inequality for the acceptable range of diameters.

Understanding the Problem

1. What is the target diameter for the metal rods? ______________________

2. How do you know if a rod is acceptable? ______________________

3. What is the problem asking you to determine? ______________________

____

Planning the Solution

4. What does the word "within" tell you about the acceptable range of diameters? ______________________

____

5. What does this tell you about the type of inequality that you should use?

____

Getting an Answer

6. Write 10^{-3} as a fraction and as a decimal.

7. Find the acceptable range for the diameters of the rods.

8. Write your answer as a single inequality. ______________________

Name ____________________ Class ____________ Date ____________

7-1 Practice

Form K

Zero and Negative Exponents

Simplify each expression.

1. 37^0

2. 3^{-4}

3. $\frac{5}{5^{-2}}$

4. $\frac{3}{6^{-1}}$

5. $-(5)^{-2}$

6. 112^{-1}

7. -11^0

8. $-(7n)^{-2}$

9. $-(15p)^0$

10. $\left(\frac{3}{5}\right)^{-2}$

11. $4x^{-3}y^0$

12. $\frac{8m^{-2}}{4n^{-1}}$

13. $\frac{-6a^{-2}(bc)^2}{d^{-4}}$

14. $\left(\frac{5s}{6t}\right)^{-2}$

15. $4^{-2}h^{-4}j^3$

16. $-(6yz)^{-2}x^0$

17. $\frac{10fg^{-5}h^0}{h^{-2}}$

18. $\frac{6t^{-1}}{11(uv)^{-3}w^4}$

7-1 Practice (continued)

Form K

Zero and Negative Exponents

Evaluate each expression for $x = -2$, $y = 4$, and $z = 2$.

19. $4x^{-1}$

20. z^{-3}

21. $2xy^{-2}z^{2}$

22. $6x^{3}z^{0}$

23. $-x^{-2}$

24. $(-y)^{-3}$

Write each number as a power of 10 using negative exponents.

25. $\frac{1}{10{,}000}$

26. $\frac{1}{100{,}000}$

Write each expression as a decimal.

27. 10^{-6}

28. 6×10^{-3}

29. The population of a suburb is 4000 people. The population of the suburb is expected to double each decade. The expression $4000 \cdot 2^{d}$ models the population of the suburb after each decade d. Evaluate the expression for $d = -2$. Describe what the value of the expression represents in this situation.

30. Writing Describe how a power with a zero exponent and a power with a negative exponent can be simplified.

Name ________________________ Class ____________ Date ____________

7-1 Standardized Test Prep

Zero and Negative Exponents

Multiple Choice

For Exercises 1–6, choose the correct letter.

1. What is the simplified form of $3a^4b^{-2}c^3$?

   A. $\frac{81a^4c^3}{b^2}$　　B. $\frac{81a^4}{b^2c^3}$　　C. $\frac{3a^4}{b^2c^3}$　　D. $\frac{3a^4c^3}{b^2}$

2. What is $-a^{-2}$ if $a = -5$?

   F. -25　　G. 25　　H. $-\frac{1}{25}$　　I. $\frac{1}{25}$

3. Which of the following simplifies to a negative number?

   A. -4^{-4}　　B. $(-4)^{-4}$　　C. 4^{-4}　　D. $\frac{1}{4^{-4}}$

4. What is the simplified form of $-(14x)^0 y^{-7} z$?

   F. $-\frac{14z}{y^7}$　　G. $\frac{14z}{y^7}$　　H. $\frac{z}{y^7}$　　I. $-\frac{z}{y^7}$

5. What is $(-m)^{-3}n$ if $m = 2$ and $n = -24$?

   A. 3　　B. -3　　C. 4　　D. -4

6. What is the simplified form of $\left(-\frac{5a}{3}\right)^{-3}$?

   F. $\frac{27}{125a^3}$　　G. $-\frac{27}{125a^3}$　　H. $\frac{125a^3}{27}$　　I. $-\frac{125a^3}{27}$

Short Response

7. The number of bacteria in a culture quadruples every hour. There were 65,536 bacteria in the culture at 8:00 A.M. The expression $65{,}536 \cdot 4^h$ models the number of bacteria in the culture h hours after 8:00 A.M.

   a. What is the value of the expression for $h = -4$?

   b. What does the value of the expression in part a represent?

Name ______________________ Class ____________ Date ____________

7-2 Think About a Plan

Scientific Notation

Physics The radius of a water molecule is about 1.4 angstroms. One angstrom is 0.00000001 cm. What is the diameter of a water molecule in centimeters? Use scientific notation.

1. What geometric facts and arithmetic operation(s) you are going to need to use to solve the problem? What is the relationship between diameter and radius? How do you convert between the given units?

____

____

____

____

2. How many angstroms are there in the diameter of a water molecule? ____________

How will you turn angstroms into centimeters? ____________________

____

3. Rewrite 0.00000001 in scientific notation. Recall that a number written in scientific notation is in the form $a \times 10^n$.

$a =$ ____________ $n =$ ____________ 0.00000001 = ____________

4. Multiply the number of angstroms in the diameter of a water molecule by the length of an angstrom in centimeters to find the number of centimeters in the diameter of a water molecule.

____

Name ______________________ Class ____________ Date ____________

7-2 Practice

Form K

Scientific Notation

Is the number written in scientific notation? If not, explain.

1. 50.1×10^3

2. 3.1×10^{11}

3. 4.6×10^{-5}

4. $0.7 \times 10^{3.4}$

Write each number in scientific notation.

5. 5,400,000

(hint: a is 5.4, and $5.4 \times 1{,}000{,}000 = 5{,}400{,}000$. In scientific notation you have $\boxed{a} \times 10^{\square}$.)

6. 8200

7. 60,500,000

8. 0.00063 (hint: $a = 6.3$)

9. 3.5 million

Write each number in standard notation.

10. 2.5×10^5

11. 4.12×10^7

12. 3.2×10^{-4}

13. 3.5×10^0

Name ______________________ Class ____________ Date ____________

7-2 Practice (continued)

Form K

Scientific Notation

Simplify. Write each answer using scientific notation.

14. $2(6.4 \times 10^4)$

(hint: Multiply 2 and 6.4. You have 12.8×10^4 but 12.8 cannot be *a*, since it is greater than 10. 12.8×10^4 becomes $(1.28 \times 10) \times 10^4$.)

15. $4(8.5 \times 10^6)$

16. $87(6.4 \times 10^5)$

17. $3(6 \times 10^{-7})$

18. $0.03(4.5 \times 10^6)$

19. Open-Ended Scientific notation is often used for working with very small or very large numbers. Write one situation where using scientific notation might be appropriate.

20. Reasoning Write a number larger than 1 million in scientific notation. How does this number change when you multiply the number by 100?

21. Country A has a population of 8.7×10^9. You hear that country B has twice as many people as country A . How many people live in country B?

Write a number in scientific notation that is between the two given numbers.

22. $3.4 \times 10^5, 8.6 \times 10^5$

23. $2.5 \times 10^{-4}, 6.3 \times 10^{-4}$

24. $6.5 \times 10^5, 4.3 \times 10^6$

25. $4.1 \times 10^{-2}, 5.7 \times 10^{-3}$

Name ______________________________ Class ______________ Date ______________

7-2 Standardized Test Prep

Scientific Notation

Multiple Choice

For Exercises 1–6, choose the correct letter.

1. Which of the following expressions is written in scientific notation?

A. 73.4×10^5 **B.** 0.09×10^7 **C.** 80×10^3 **D.** 4.22×10^{-5}

2. Which of the following is 0.0000000708 written in scientific notation?

F. 7.08×10^{-8} **G.** 7.8×10^{-8} **H.** 708×10^{-10} **I.** 70.8×10^{-9}

3. Which expression represents the largest number?

A. 40.1×10^{-6} **B.** 4.1×10^{-7} **C.** 0.411×10^{-6} **D.** 0.04001×10^{-5}

4. Which expression is equal to $\frac{1}{8000}$ written in scientific notation?

F. 8.0×10^3 **G.** 1.25×10^{-4} **H.** 125×10^{-5} **I.** 1.25×10^4

5. Which of the following statements is *not* true regarding an expression written in scientific notation in the form $a \times 10^n$?

A. The value of a must be greater than or equal to 1 and smaller than 10.
B. The value of n must be an integer.
C. Doubling n results in a doubling of the value of the expression.
D. Doubling a results in a doubling of the value of the expression.

6. Which number is equal to $7(3.5 \times 10^4)$ written in scientific notation?

F. 24.5×70^4 **G.** 2.45×10^5 **H.** 24.5×10^4 **I.** 1.05×10^5

Short Response

7. A state government has 5.7×10^7 dollars invested in a pension fund for retired employees. It expects this investment to double in value every 8 years. What is the value of the investment after 8 years, 16 years and 24 years? Write your response in scientific notation.

Name ______________________ Class __________ Date __________

7-3 Think About a Plan

Multiplying Powers With the Same Base

Chemistry In chemistry, a *mole* is a unit of measure equal to 6.02×10^{23} atoms of a substance. The mass of a single neon atom is about 3.35×10^{-23}g. What is the mass of 2 moles of neon atoms? Write your answer in scientific notation.

Understanding the Problem

1. What is the mass of a single atom of neon?

____

2. How many atoms are in 1 mole?

____

Planning the Solution

3. Without solving, explain how you can determine the mass of 1 mole of neon atoms. How about 2 moles of neon atoms?

____

____

4. What exponent rules and guidelines will help you with your calculations?

____

____

Getting an Answer

5. Demonstrate how the numbers can be arranged to simplify the multiplication.

____

____

6. Complete your calculations.

____

____

7. Is your answer in scientific notation? Explain.

____

____

Name ______________________ Class ____________ Date ____________

7-3 Practice

Form K

Multiplying Powers with the Same Base

Rewrite each expression using each base only once.

1. $10^7 \cdot 10^2$
2. $6^3 \cdot 6^1 \cdot 6^8$
3. $7^8 \cdot 7^{-1} \cdot 7^{-5}$
4. $4^{-6} \cdot 4^3 \cdot 4^4$
5. $12^2 \cdot 12^{-9} \cdot 12^{12}$
6. $3^4 \cdot 3^5 \cdot 3^{-6}$

Simplify each expression.

7. t^3t^9
8. $-3y^8 \cdot 5y^{-5}$
9. $(7a^{-1})(-3a^5)$
10. $-3j^6 \cdot 12j$
11. $(m)(m^4)(m^2)$
12. $(8h^3)(-5h^{-4})$
13. $x^3y^{-1} \cdot xy \cdot x^{-2}y^2$
14. $(-3f^2g^{-3})(2fg)(7f^3g^{-2})$

Simplify each expression. Write each answer in scientific notation.

15. $(2 \times 10^6)(4 \times 10^9)$
16. $(-3 \times 10^8)(3 \times 10^{-5})$
17. $(-7 \times 10^{11})(-8 \times 10^{-4})$
18. $(6 \times 10^{-7})(-6 \times 10^{-4})$

Find the area of each figure.

19.

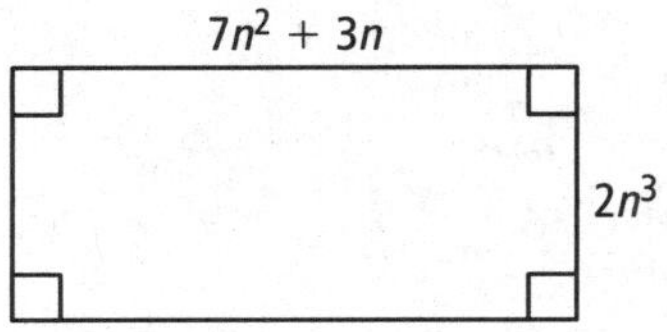

20.

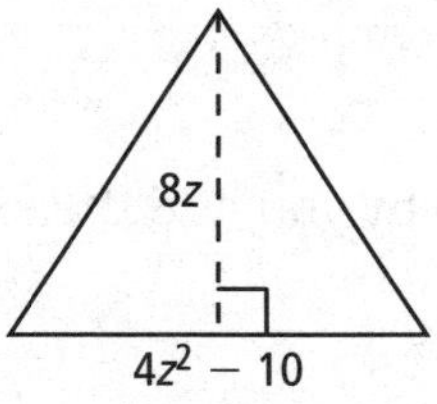

Name ______________________ Class ____________ Date ____________

7-3 Practice (continued) — Form K

Multiplying Powers with the Same Base

Write each answer in scientific notation.

21. In the 2004 presidential election, John Kerry received approximately 5.9×10^7 votes. President Bush received approximately 1.05 times the number of votes as Senator Kerry. Approximately, how many votes did President Bush receive?

22. Lake Ontario is the smallest of the Great Lakes with a surface area of 7.34×10^3 mi^2. The surface area of all 5 Great Lakes is 12.8 times the surface area of Lake Ontario. What is the surface area of all 5 Great Lakes?

Complete each equation.

23. $3^{-5} \cdot 3^{\square} = 3^{10}$

24. $8^3 \cdot 8^{-5} = 8^{\square}$

25. $w^{-3} \cdot w^{-8} = w^{\square}$

26. $a^{-5} \cdot a^{\square} \cdot a^{-4} = a^3$

Simplify each expression. Write each answer in scientific notation.

27. $(9 \times 10^{-14})(-6 \times 10^{-12})$

28. $(5 \times 10^4)(0.6 \times 10^{-10})$

29. $(0.2 \times 10^{22})(0.9 \times 10^{-30})$

30. $(0.25 \times 10^7)(12 \times 10^{-15})$

31. The area of a trapezoid can be found using the formula $A = \frac{1}{2}(b_1 + b_2)h$, where h is the height of the trapezoid and b_1 and b_2 are the bases of the trapezoid. What is the area of a trapezoid with height $14xy^2$ cm, a base $3x^2$ cm, and another base $7x^2$ cm?

32. Reasoning Show why you add the exponents when multiplying $4^3 \cdot 4^4$.

Name ______________________ Class __________ Date __________

7-3 Standardized Test Prep

Multiplying Powers With the Same Base

Multiple Choice

For Exercises 1–5, choose the correct letter.

1. What is the simplified form of $(-3x^3y^2)(5xy^{-1})$?

A. $\frac{-15x^3}{y^2}$ **B.** $-15x^3y^2$ **C.** $-15x^4y$ **D.** $15x^4y$

2. What is the simplified form of $-9m^{-2}n^5 \cdot 2m^{-3}n^{-6}$?

F. $-18m^5n$ **G.** $\frac{-18}{m^5n}$ **H.** $\frac{-18m^6}{n^{30}}$ **I.** $-18m^6n^{30}$

3. A rectangular pasture has a fence around the perimeter. The length of the fence is $16x^7$ and the width is $48x^4$. What is the area of the pasture?

A. $3x^3$ **B.** $128x^{11}$ **C.** $768x^{11}$ **D.** $768x^{28}$

4. What is the simplified form of $(3.25 \times 10^3)(7.8 \times 10^6)$ written in scientific notation?

F. 2.535×10^{10} **G.** 2.535×10^{18} **H.** 2.535×10^{19} **I.** 25.35×10^9

5. The size of a certain cell is 2.5×10^{-9} m. Another cell is 1.5×10^3 times larger. How large is the larger cell in scientific notation?

A. 4×10^{-27} m **B.** 4×10^{-12} m **C.** 3.75×10^6 m **D.** 3.75×10^{-6} m

Extended Response

6. The distance between two astronomical bodies is 6.75×10^6 miles. The distance from the first body to a third body is 3.56×10^4 times the distance between the first two bodies.

a. Write an expression that represents the distance between the first and third bodies.

b. Simplify the distance in part a.

c. Write an expression that represents the distance light would travel from the first body to the third body and back to the first.

d. Simplify the distance the light travels in part c.

Name ______________________ Class ____________ Date ____________

7-4 Think About a Plan

More Multiplication Properties of Exponents

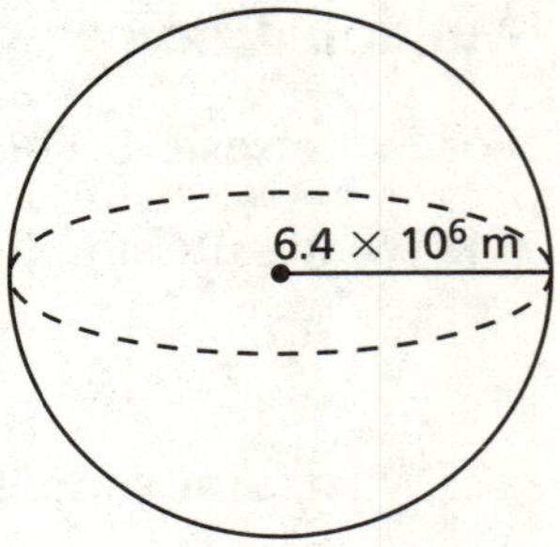

a. **Geography** Earth has a radius of about 6.4×10^6 m. What is the approximate surface area of Earth? Use the formula for the surface area of a sphere, $S = 4\pi r^2$. Write your answer in scientific notation.

b. Oceans cover about 70% of the surface of the Earth. About how many square meters of Earth's surface are covered by ocean water?

c. The oceans have an average depth of 3790 m. Estimate the volume of water in Earth's oceans.

1. What can you substitute into the formula?

____

2. What numbers need to be squared?

____

3. Calculate the surface area using 3.14 for π. Show your work. Write your answer in scientific notation.

____

____

4. For part b, set up a percent proportion with the appropriate units.

____

5. Solve your proportion. Show your work. Leave your answer in scientific notation.

____

____

6. Since you calculated the surface area of the ocean, how can you use your calculation to determine the volume of the water?

____

____

7. Determine the volume. Show your work. Write your answer in scientific notation.

____

____

7-4 Practice

Form K

More Multiplication Properties of Exponents

Simplify each expression.

1. $(v^4)^2$
2. $(a^5)^7$
3. $(n^4)^{-6}$
4. $h(h^{-3})^{-10}$
5. $(x^3)^4y^3$
6. $(3q)^5$
7. $(a^4)^6(b^5)^{-2}$
8. $(m^2)^8(n^0)^4$
9. $(2t^3)^{-4}$
10. $(5k^9)^{-3}$
11. $(3s^4)^3s^2$
12. $(bc^3)^5$
13. $(mnp)^0$
14. $(f^2g^3)(fg^4)^{-1}$
15. $a(a^{-3}b^{-4})^{-2}b^{-3}$
16. $(5x^{-2})^2(y^7z^{-5})^{-4}$
17. $c^{10}(c^4d^{-3})^4d^3$
18. $7t^{11}u^3(-4t^{-9})^2u^{-5}$

Simplify. Write each answer in scientific notation.

19. $(4 \times 10^3)^2$
20. $(7 \times 10^8)^4$
21. $(1.4 \times 10^{-8})^3$
22. $(5 \times 10^{-7})^3$
23. $(2.5 \times 10^{10})^2$
24. $(4.8 \times 10^4)^{-2}$
25. The radius of a cylinder is 2.9×10^5 in. The height of the cylinder is 3.8×10^4 in. What is the volume of the cylinder? (Hint: $V = \pi r^2h$)
26. The side length of a square is 9.5×10^2 cm. What is the area of the square?

Name ______________________ Class ____________ Date ____________

7-4 Practice (continued) *Form K*

More Multiplication Properties of Exponents

Complete each equation.

27. $(n^3)^5 = n^{\square}$

28. $(a^7)^{\square} = a^{-21}$

29. $(j^{\square})^{-8} = j^{72}$

30. $(t^{-2})^{\square} = t^{-8}$

31. $(5g^4)^{\square} = \frac{1}{125g^{12}}$

32. $(m^2n^{-4})^{\square} = \frac{m^4}{n^8}$

33. Reasoning Demonstrate why you multiply the exponents when simplifying $(3^4)^3$.

Simplify each expression.

34. $(4.895)^{-11}(4.895)^{11}$

35. $-7xy^{-3}z^3(0)^{-10}$

36. $4^2(8d)^3$

37. $(10^8)^{-5}(3.6 \times 10^{-8})^3$

38. The volume of a sphere can be determined by the formula $V = \frac{4}{3}\pi r^3$, where r is the radius. Find the volume of the sphere shown at the right in terms of x. Use 3.14 for π.

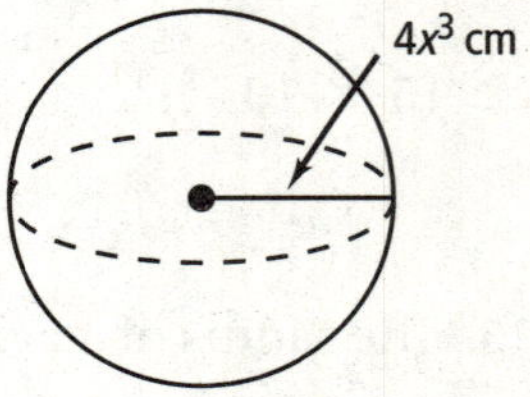

39. The volume of a circular cone can be determined by the formula $V = \frac{1}{3}\pi r^2 h$, where r is the radius of the base and h is the height of the cone. Find the volume of the cone shown at the right in terms of b. Use 3.14 for π.

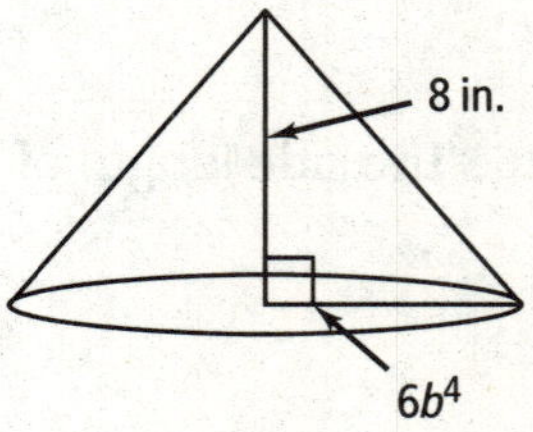

Name ______________________ Class ____________ Date ____________

7-4 Standardized Test Prep

More Multiplication Properties of Exponents

Gridded Response

Solve each exercise and enter your answer on the grid provided.

1. What is the simplified form of $(2 \times 10^2)^2$ in standard notation?

2. What is the simplified form of $(0.00038 \times 10^3)^2$ in standard notation?

3. The side of a square measures $2x^2y^3$. What is the area of the square if $x = -2$ and $y = 2$?

4. The side of a square measures $3mn^2$. What is the area of the square if $m = 4$ and $n = -2$?

5. The radius of a circle is 0.00012×10^5 ft. What is the area of the circle? Use the formula $A = \pi r^2$.

1.
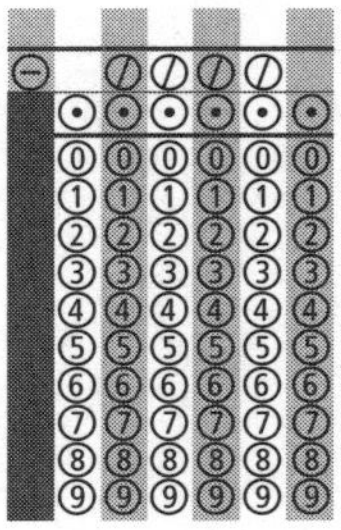

2.
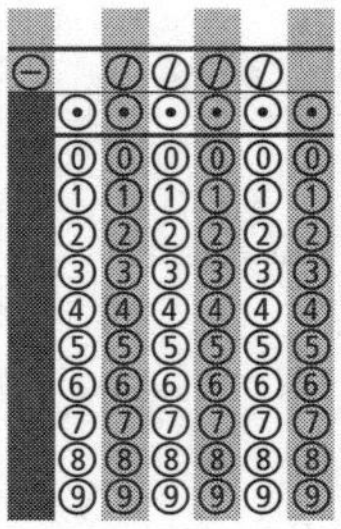

3.
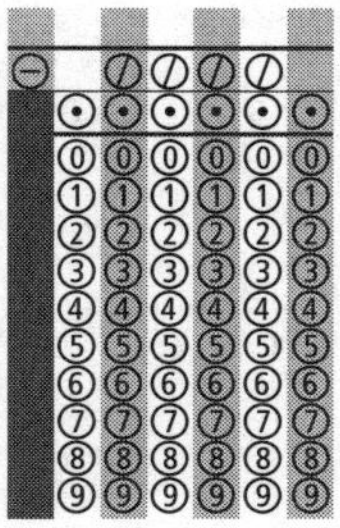

4.
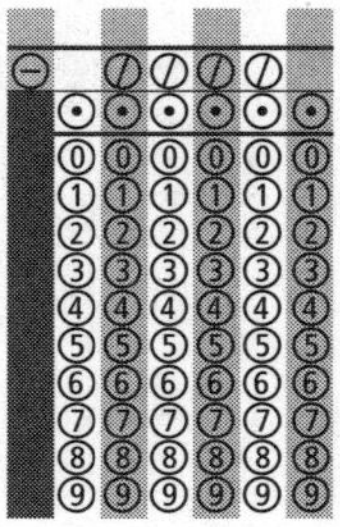

5.
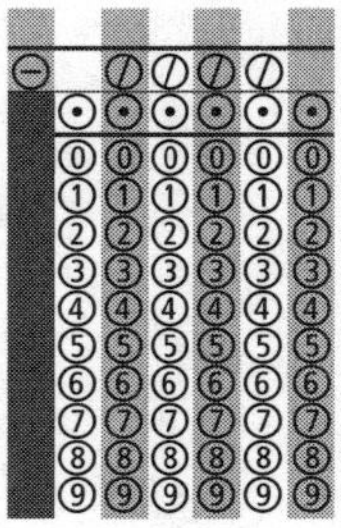

Name ______________________ Class ____________ Date ____________

7-5 Think About a Plan

Division Properties of Exponents

Physics The wavelength of a radio wave is defined as speed divided by frequency. An FM radio station has a frequency of 9×10^7 waves per second. The speed of the waves is about 3×10^8 meters per second. What is the wavelength of the station?

1. Wavelength is speed divided by frequency. Which of the given values needs to be divided by the other?

   ______________________ divided by ______________________

2. What is the quotient of the first part of the numbers?

3. What is the quotient of the powers of 10?

4. What is the quotient, written in scientific notation, of the speed divided by the frequency?

5. How many meters is the wavelength of the station?

7-5 Practice

Form K

Division Properties of Exponents

Simplify each expression.

1. $\frac{3^5}{3^2} = \frac{3 \times 3 \times 3 \times 3 \times 3}{3 \times 3} = 3^{\square}$

2. $\frac{6^7}{6^3}$

3. $\frac{y^7}{y^4}$

4. $\frac{m^4}{m}$

5. $\frac{x^6y^9}{x^2y^5}$

6. $\frac{21m^3}{3m^2}$

7. $\left[\frac{2}{7}\right]^4 = \frac{2}{7} \times \frac{2}{7} \times \frac{2}{7} \times \frac{2}{7} = \frac{2^4}{7^4} = \square$

8. $\left[\frac{3}{2}\right]^3$

9. $\left[\frac{5x}{3y}\right]^2$

10. $\left[\frac{3x^4}{2y^3}\right]^3$

11. $\left[\frac{2m^3}{5p}\right]^0$

12. $\left[\frac{xy^3}{x^3y}\right]^2$

7-5 Practice (continued) — Form K

Division Properties of Exponents

13. Writing Explain how you divide powers with like bases. Discuss why the bases have to be the same. How are these rules similar to the rules for multiplying powers with like bases?

Explain why each expression is *not* in simplest form.

14. 2^4y^3

15. $(3x)^2$

16. x^3y^0

17. $\frac{y^5}{y}$

Simplify each quotient. Write each answer in scientific notation.

18. $\frac{6 \times 10^7}{3 \times 10^5}$

19. $\frac{2.4 \times 10^3}{8.2 \times 10^2}$

20. Error Analysis A student simplifies the expression $\left[\frac{6^4}{3^2}\right]^3$ as follows: $\left[\frac{6^4}{3^2}\right]^3 = [(6 \div 3)^{4-2}]^3 = (2^2)^3 = 64$. What mistake did the student make in simplifying the expression? What is the correct simplification of the expression?

21. The area of a rectangle is $20x^6y^4$. The length of the rectangle is x^2y^3 What is the width of the rectangle?

22. Open-Ended First simplify the expression $\left[\frac{2m^5}{10m}\right]^2$ by raising each factor in the brackets to the second power then simplify the result. Next simplify by some other method. Explain your method. Are the results the same? Which method do you prefer?

7-5 Standardized Test Prep

Division Properties of Exponents

Multiple Choice

For Exercises 1–6, choose the correct letter.

1. Which of the following is equivalent to $\frac{x^5y^2}{xy^2}$ when $x \neq 0$ and $y \neq 0$?

   A. x^6y^5 B. x^5y C. x^4y D. x^4

2. Which expression is *not* equal to 125?

   F. $5\left(\frac{5^3}{\frac{2}{5}}\right)^2$ G. $\left(\frac{5^3}{5^4}\right)^{-3}$ H. $\frac{5^{-2}}{5^{-5}}$ I. $5\left(\frac{5^5}{5^3}\right)$

3. A fraction reduces to 36. If its numerator is $(6x)^5$, what is its denominator?

   A. 6^3x B. 6^3x^5 C. $6x^5$ D. 6^7x^5

4. Which is the correct simplification of $\frac{5.4 \times 10^{12}}{1.2 \times 10^3}$ written in scientific notation?

   F. 4.5×10^7 G. 4.5×10^9 H. 45×10^6 I. 6.48×10^7

5. Which of the following statements is *not* true regarding operations with exponents?

   A. To divide powers with the same base, subtract the exponents.
   B. To subtract powers with the same base, divide the exponents.
   C. To multiply powers with the same base, add the exponents.
   D. To raise a power to a power, multiply the exponents.

6. Which of the following expressions is written in simplest form?

   F. 3^5x^2 G. $(5y)^3$ H. a^0b I. x^2y^3z

Short Response

7. A rectangle has an area of $12x^3y^4$ cm^2. It has a width of $3xy$ cm. What ratio would you set up to determine the length? What is the length of the rectangle?

Name ______________________ Class ____________ Date ____________

7-6 Think About a Plan

Exponential Functions

Computers A computer valued at $1500 loses 20% of its value each year.

a. Write a function rule that models the value of the computer.

b. Find the value of the computer after 3 yr.

c. In how many years will the value of the computer be less than $500?

1. Make a table for which one column represents the number of years since the computer was purchased and the other represents the value of the computer at the end of each year.

Years Since Purchase	Value of Computer
0	$1500
1	
2	
3	
4	

2. Use the table to determine whether the function is exponential. Is there a common ratio? If so, what is it? What does the common ratio have to do with the situation represented in the problem? Where does it show up in an exponential function?

3. Remember the general form of an exponential function: $f(x) = a \cdot b^x$. Given your table and situation, determine values for a and b. Write the appropriate exponential function.

4. Use the exponential function to answer part b.

5. Set your exponential function equal to $500 and solve or extend your table to determine the answer to part c.

Name ______________________ Class ____________ Date ____________

7-6 Practice

Form K

Exponential Functions

Determine whether each table represents an exponential function. Explain why or why not. Remember an exponential function exists when you have a constant ratio between the *y* values and a constant difference between the *x* values.

1.

x	1	2	3	4	5	6
y	2	4	8	12	24	48

2.

x	1	2	3	4	5	6
y	1	4	9	16	25	36

Determine whether each equation represents an exponential function. Remember, an exponential function takes the form $y = a \cdot b^x$ where $a \neq 0$ and $b > 0$, $b \neq 1$.

3. $y = 3 \cdot 2^x$

4. $y = 4 \cdot x^5$

5. $y = 5x - 8$

6. $y = 5 \cdot 1.07^x$

Evaluate each function for the given value.

7. $y = 4^x$ for $x = 3$

8. $f(x) = 2 \cdot 3^x$ for $x = 5$

9. $h(t) = 60 \cdot 1.07^t$ for $t = 8$

10. $y = 5 \cdot 7^x$ for $x = 0$

Name ______________________ Class ____________ Date ____________

7-6 Practice (continued)

Form K

Exponential Functions

11. An investment of \$2000 in a bank account doubles every 5 years. The function that models the growth of this investment is $f(x) = 2000 \cdot 2^x$, where x is the number of doubling periods. How much will the investment be worth after two doubling periods, or 10 years?

12. The city library will be increasing the number of books it has to loan at a rate of 5% per year. The library currently has 40,000 books. The number of books they will have in any given year is modeled by the function $h(t) = 40{,}000 \cdot 1.05^t$, where t is the number of years. How many books will the library have 8 years from now?

Graph each exponential function.

13. $y = 2^x$

14. $y = 3 \cdot 2^x$

15. $y = 5^x$

16. $y = 3 \cdot 5^x$

17. Writing Discuss the similarities and differences between the four graphs that you sketched in Exercises 13–16.

Solve each equation.

18. $2^x = 16$

19. $10 \cdot 3^x = 90$

20. $5^x - 4 = 21$

21. $4^x + 6 = 70$

Name ______________________ Class ____________ Date ____________

7-6 Standardized Test Prep

Exponential Functions

Multiple Choice

For Exercises 1–6, choose the correct letter.

1. Which of the following equations represents an exponential function?

   A. $y = 3x^2$ B. $y = 3(2^x)$ C. $y = 2x^3$ D. $y = 5x + 4$

2. What is the solution to $4 \cdot 3^x = 36$?

   F. 2 G. 3 H. 4 I. 6

3. Which function has the greatest value for $x = 3$?

   A. $f(x) = 2 \cdot 4^x$ B. $f(x) = 4 \cdot 2^x$ C. $f(x) = 4 \cdot x^2$ D. $f(x) = 2 \cdot x^4$

4. When graphed, which function will not have an x-intercept?

   F. $y = 2x + 3$ G. $y = 2x^3$ H. $y = 3x^2$ I. $y = 3 \cdot 2^x$

5. Which of the following statements is *not* true regarding the function $y = 2^x$?

   A. The function is an exponential function.
   B. The function has a domain of all real numbers.
   C. As the value of x gets very large, the value of y gets close to zero.
   D. As the value of x increases by one, the value of y doubles.

6. Which of the following ordered pairs is on the graph of $y = 3 \cdot 4^x$?

   F. (0, 0) G. (1, 81) H. (2, 24) I. (2, 48)

Short Response

7. You invest $1000 at 7% interest compounded annually. What is the exponential equation that models this situation? According to your equation, how much will the investment be worth 3 years later?

Name ______________________ Class ____________ Date ____________

7-7 Think About a Plan

Exponential Growth and Decay

Business You open a bank account to save for college and deposit $400 in the account. Each year, the balance in your account will increase 5%.

a. Write a function that models your annual balance.

b. What will be the *total* amount in your account after 7 yr?

1. Make a table that has one column representing the number of years the account has been open, a second column representing the balance in the given year, and a third column representing the *total* balance.

Years Account Open	Balance this Year	Total Balance
0		
1		
2		
3		

2. The first row of the table represents year 0. Year 0 is the start up year, the year with a balance of $400. If you want to know how much you have after three years, you will read your balance from the fourth line of the table, which starts with the number 3. In order to answer the question in part b, what line of the table should you use? What number would start that line? Why?

____

____

____

3. Recall that the general form of an exponential function is $f(x) = a \cdot b^x$. Given the situation described, what is a? What is b? Write the function that models your annual balance. Check to make sure the function you created provides the same values you put into your table for years 1, 2 and 3.

a = ____________ b = ____________ $f(x)$ = ____________

4. Use the exponential function and extend the table to answer part b.

Years Account Open	Balance this Year	Total Balance
0		
1		
2		
3		
4		
5		
6		
7		

Name ______________________ Class ____________ Date ____________

7-7 Practice

Form K

Exponential Growth and Decay

Identify the initial amount *a* and the growth factor *b* in each exponential function. (Hint: In the exponential equation $y = a \cdot b^x$, *a* is the initial amount and *b* is the growth factor when $b > 1$.)

1. $f(x) = 2 \cdot 3^x$

2. $y = 5 \cdot 1.06^x$

3. $g(t) = 6^t$

4. $h(x) = -3 \cdot 2^x$

Use the given function to find the balance in each account after the given period.

5. \$3000 principal earning 4% compounded annually, after 6 years
$f(x) = 3000 \cdot (1.04)^6$

6. \$2000 principal earning 6.8% compounded annually, after 3 years
$f(x) = 2000 \cdot (1.068)^3$

Find the balance in each account after the given period.

7. \$5000 principal earning 4% compounded annually, after 10 years

8. \$3500 principal earning 3.6% compounded annually, after 2 years

Identify the initial amount *a* and the decay factor *b* in each exponential function. (Hint: In the exponential equation $y = a \cdot b^x$, *a* is the initial amount and *b* is the *decay* factor when $b < 1$.)

9. $y = 4 \cdot 0.2^x$

10. $f(x) = 3 \cdot 0.9^x$

Tell whether the equation represents *exponential growth, exponential decay,* or *neither.*

11. $y = 2 \cdot 3^x$

12. $f(x) = 6 \cdot 0.5^x$

13. $f(x) = 5 \cdot x^2$

14. $y = 0.3^x$

7-7 Practice (continued) Form K

Exponential Growth and Decay

15. The town manager reports that incoming revenues for a given year were \$2 million. The budget director predicts that revenues will increase by 4% per year. How much revenue will the town have available 10 years from the date of the town manager's report if the equation that models the growth is $f(x) = 2{,}000{,}000 \cdot (1.04)^x$?

16. A fisheries manager determines that there are approximately 3000 bass in a lake.

a. The population is growing at a rate of 2% per year. The function that models that growth is $y = 3000 \cdot 1.02^x$. How many bass will live in the lake after 4 years?

b. How many bass will live in the lake after 7 years?

c. About how long will it be before there are 4000 bass in the lake?

17. A business purchases a computer system for \$2000. The tax code allows them to take off a portion of that purchase for each year the computer system is used. If the value of the system is *depreciated* at a rate of 15% per year, the function that models the current value of the system is $f(x) = 2000 \cdot 0.85^t$. How much is the computer worth after 4 years?

Tell whether each represents an *exponential growth function*, an *exponential decay function*, or *neither*.

18.

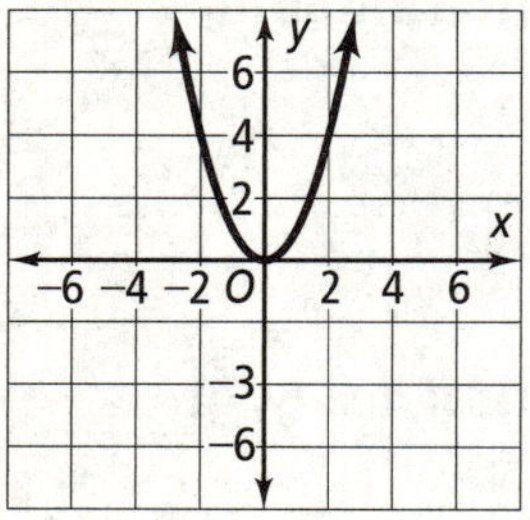

19.

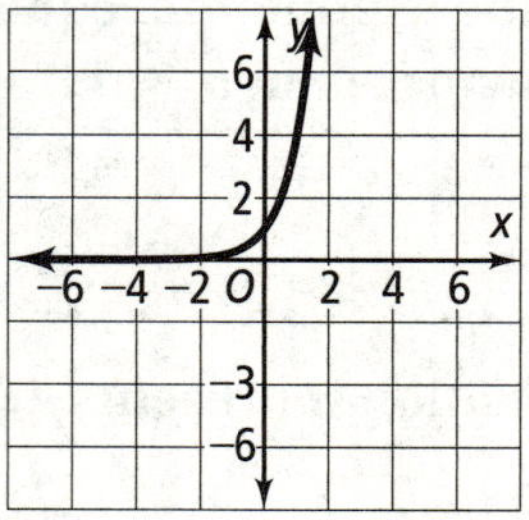

20.

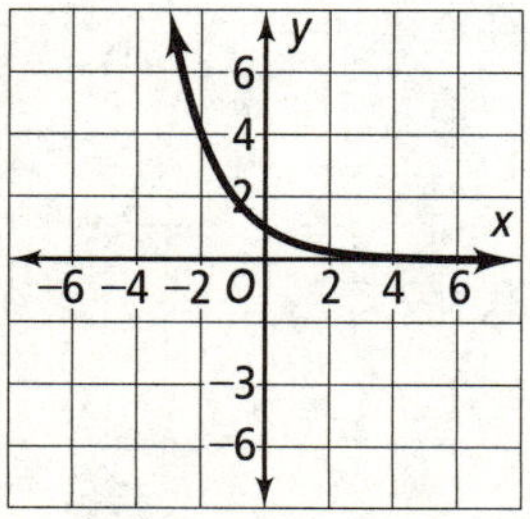

21.

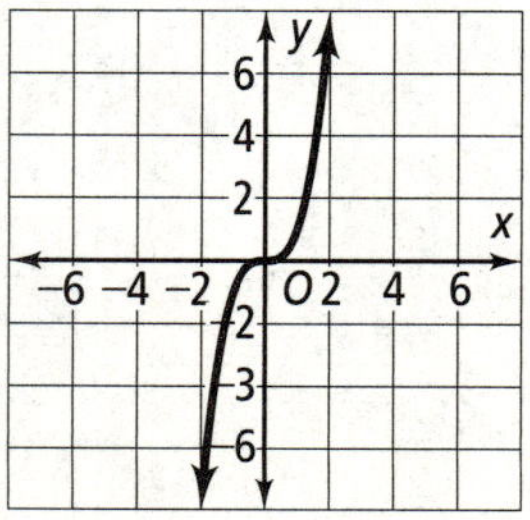

Name ______________________ Class ____________ Date ____________

7-7 Standardized Test Prep

Exponential Growth and Decay

Multiple Choice

For Exercises 1–5, choose the correct letter.

1. Which of the following functions models exponential decay?
   A. $f(x) = 12 \cdot 3^x$ **B.** $y = 2 \cdot 0.8^x$ **C.** $y = -3x^2$ **D.** $f(x) = 1.8^x$

2. Suppose you deposit $500 into an account earning 7.8% interest compounded annually. How long will it take for the account to be worth $1000?
   F. between 6 and 7 years
   G. between 7 and 8 years
   H. between 8 and 9 years
   I. between 9 and 10 years

3. What is always true regarding functions that model exponential growth?
   A. Their graphs are always symmetric about the *y*-axis.
   B. The range depends on the growth factor.
   C. The value of *y* is always greater than the value of *x*.
   D. The value of *y* decreases as *x* gets more negative.

4. What is $3 \cdot 2^x$ if $x = 3$?
   F. 18 **G.** 24 **H.** 125 **I.** 216

5. Where will the graphs of $y = 4^x$, $y = 1.2^x$ and $y = 0.6^x$ intersect?
   A. (0, 0) **B.** (1, 0) **C.** (0, 1) **D.** (1, 1)

Short Response

6. Suppose you deposit $2000 into an account earning 5% interest compounded quarterly. To the nearest dollar, what is the balance after 4 years?

Name ______________________ Class ____________ Date ____________

8-1 Think About a Plan

Adding and Subtracting Polynomials

Geometry The perimeter of a trapezoid is $39a - 7$. Three sides have the following lengths: $9a$, $5a + 1$, and $17a - 6$. What is the length of the fourth side?

Understanding the Problem

1. What is the perimeter of the trapezoid? ______________________

2. What are the lengths of the sides you are given? __________, __________, __________

3. How many sides does a trapezoid have? ______________________

4. How do you find the perimeter of a trapezoid? ______________________

5. What is the problem asking you to determine? ______________________

____

Planning the Solution

6. Draw a diagram of the trapezoid and label the information you know.

7. Write an equation that can be used to determine the length of the fourth side.

____

Getting an Answer

8. Solve your equation to find the length of the fourth side of the trapezoid.

8-1 Practice

Form K

Adding and Subtracting Polynomials

Find the degree of each monomial.

1. $3s^3t^3$
2. $3n$
3. $5xy$
4. 7
5. $\frac{1}{4}k^5$
6. d

Simplify.

7. $3mn^4 + 6mn^4$
8. $12g^2 - 7g^2$
9. $-11c^4d + 12c^4d$
10. $42z^3 - 15z^3$

Write each polynomial in standard form. Then name each polynomial based on its degree and number of terms.

11. $7a + 4 - a^2$
12. $5b^2 + 2n$
13. $-11d^4$
14. $2x^3 - 9 + 2x + 8 - 4x$

15. A pizza shop owner is monitoring the amount of cheese he uses each week. The polynomials below model the pounds of cheese ordered in the past, where p represents pounds.

    Mozzarella: $3p^3 - 6p^2 + 14p + 125$

    Cheddar: $12.5p^2 + 18p + 75$

    Write a polynomial that models the total number of pounds of cheese that were ordered.

8-1 Practice (continued)

Form K

Adding and Subtracting Polynomials

Simplify.

16. $\begin{array}{r} 3r + 5 \\ + \ 7r + 3 \\ \hline \end{array}$

17. $(t^4 - 4t^2 + 9) + (-t^3 + 3t)$

18. $\begin{array}{r} 7b^2 + 6 \\ + \ 4b^2 + 5 \\ \hline \end{array}$

19. $\begin{array}{r} 4z + 7 \\ - \ (6z + 1) \\ \hline \end{array}$

20. $(-6k^3 + 3k) - (-5k^3 + 3k^2 - 8k)$

21. $\begin{array}{r} 3p^4 + 1 \\ - \ (9p^4 + 5) \\ \hline \end{array}$

22. A city wants to compare the number of people who own their own home and who rent their home. The polynomials below show expressions for each.

Own: $4p^2 + 360p + 22{,}178$

Rent: $6p^2 + 125p + 5286$

In each polynomial, $p = 0$ corresponds to the first year in a 10-year period. Write a polynomial for how many more own their home than rent their home.

23. The wallpaper border that runs all the way around a room is $5f^2 + 19f + 11$ long. Three sides of the room have the following lengths of border: $6f$, $5f - 7$, $2f^2 + 2$. What is the length of the fourth side of the room?

24. Open-Ended Write two different polynomials with a difference of $-3x^2 + 5x - 7$.

Name ____________________ Class ____________ Date ____________

8-1 Standardized Test Prep

Adding and Subtracting Polynomials

Multiple Choice

For Exercises 1–6, choose the correct letter.

1. What is the degree of the monomial $3x^2y^3$?

A. 2 **B.** 3 **C.** 5 **D.** 6

2. What is the simplified form of $8b^3c^2 + 4b^3c^2$?

F. $12bc$ **G.** $12b^3c^2$ **H.** $12b^6c^4$ **I.** $12b^9c^4$

3. How is $6d - 8 + 4d^2$ written in standard form?

A. $4d^2 + 6d - 8$ **B.** $4d^2 + 6d + 8$ **C.** $4d^2 - 6d - 8$ **D.** $4d^2 - 6d + 8$

4. What is the simplified form of $(4j^2 + 6) + (2j^2 - 3)$?

F. $6j^2 - 3$ **G.** $6j^2 + 3$ **H.** $6j^2 + 9$ **I.** $4j^4 + 3$

5. What is the difference of the following polynomials?

$$\begin{array}{r} 6x^3 - 2x^2 + 4 \\ \underline{-\ (2x^3 + 4x^2 - 5)} \end{array}$$

A. $4x^3 - 2x^2 - 1$ **B.** $8x^3 + 6x^2 - 1$ **C.** $4x^3 - 2x^2 + 1$ **D.** $4x^3 - 6x^2 + 9$

6. What is the simplified form of $(3x^2 - 4x + 6x) + (5x^3 + 2x^2 - 3x)$ in standard form?

F. $5x^3 + 10x^2 - x$ **G.** $8x^3 - 2x^2 + 3x$ **H.** $5x^3 + 10x^2 - 5x$ **I.** $5x^3 + 5x^2 - x$

Short Response

7. Suppose you have been given this polynomial.

$$5b + 4b^2 - 3b^4 + 3$$

a. How can you write this polynomial in standard form?

____

b. What is the degree of this polynomial? Explain. ____________________

____

Name ______________________ Class ____________ Date ____________

8-2 Think About a Plan

Multiplying and Factoring

a. Factor $n^2 + n$.

b. Writing Suppose n is an integer. Is $n^2 + n$ *always, sometimes,* or *never* an even integer? Justify your answer.

1. Factor out n from the expression.

$$n(\square + \square)$$

2. What are the two factors? __________, __________

3. What is an integer? ______________________________

____

4. Are n and $n + 1$ consecutive integers? Explain. ______________________________

____

5. What do you know about the product of odd and even integers?

EVEN × EVEN = ______________

ODD × ODD = ______________

EVEN × ODD = ______________

ODD × EVEN = ______________

6. Out of two consecutive integers, how many are odd? ______________

7. Is the product of consecutive integers *odd* or *even*? Explain. ______________________________

____

8. $n^2 + n$ is $\square$ an even integer because ______________________________

______________________________.

Name ______________________ Class ____________ Date ____________

8-2 Practice

Form K

Multiplying and Factoring

Simplify each product.

1. $3w(w + 2)$

2. $(z + 5)2z$

3. $3m^2(4 + m)$

4. $2p(p^2 - 6p + 1)$

5. $-y(5y^3 - 3y^2 + 2y)$

6. $3a(-3a^2 + 2a - 7)$

7. $6x^3(3x^2 - x + 10)$

8. $-4h(-h^3 - 8h^2 + 2h)$

9. $4n(n^2 + 5n + 6)$

Find the GCF of the terms of each polynomial.

10. $16q + 32$

11. $4t^3 - 24t$

12. $32y - 24$

13. $x^3 + 3x^2 + 5x$

14. $5d^3 + 20d - 35$

15. $2m^3 + 10m^2 + 12m$

16. $7g^4 + 21g^3 - 14g^2$

17. $15z^3 + 3z^2 - 27z$

18. $33w^7 + 55w^5 - 22w^3$

Factor each polynomial.

19. $9t - 3$

20. $12j^3 + 28$

21. $72x^2 - 63x$

22. $12k^3 - 9k^2 + 6$

23. $30n^3 + 18n^2 + 54n$

24. $32z^4 - 80z^3 + 112z^2$

25. $12n^4 + 16n^3 + 20n^2$

26. $24y^6 + 36y^4 + 42y^2$

27. $7q^5 + 21q^3 - 49q$

Name ______________________ Class ____________ Date ____________

8-2 Practice (continued) — Form K

Multiplying and Factoring

28. You are painting a rectangular wall with length $5x^2$ ft and width $12x$ ft. There is a rectangular door that measures x ft by $2x$ ft that will not be painted. What is the area of the wall that is to be painted? Write your answer in factored form.

Simplify. Write in standard form.

29. $-3m(2m^2 - 5m + 10)$

30. $-5t^2(-6t^3 + 12t)$

31. $10x(-4x^2 + x - 3)$

32. $-2v(3v^3 - 6v^2 + 2v)$

33. $5y(y + 2) - y(y - 3)$

34. $-2b^2(-4b^2 + 3b)$

Factor each polynomial.

35. $13cd^3 + 39c^2d^2$

36. $5x^3y^4 - 25xy^2$

37. $42m^5n + 28m^4$

38. $36fg^2 + 54f^2g^4$

39. $8s^8t^4 + 20s^4t^3$

40. $12a^2b^5 + 156a^2b^3$

41. Open-Ended Write a quadratic monomial and a cubic trinomial. Then find their product and write it in standard form.

42. A rectangle has a length of $6x^3y^2 - 1$ and a width of $3xy + 2$. The formula for the perimeter of a rectangle is $P = 2l + 2w$, where l is the length and w is the width. What is the perimeter of the rectangle? Simplify your answer.

Name ______________________ Class ____________ Date ____________

8-2 Standardized Test Prep

Multiplying and Factoring

Multiple Choice

For Exercises 1–5, choose the correct letter.

1. How can this product be simplified?

$$5x^2(2x - 3)$$

A. $5x^2 + 2x - 3$ B. $10x^3 - 15x^2$ C. $-5x^2$ D. $7x^3 - 15x^2$

2. What is the GCF of the terms of $8c^3 + 12c^2 + 10c$?

F. 2 G. 4 H. $2c$ I. $4c$

3. How can the polynomial $6d^4 + 9d^3 - 12d^2$ be factored?

A. $3d^2(2d^2 + 3d - 4)$

B. $3d^2(3d^2 + 6d - 9)$

C. $3d(d^3 + 3d^2 - 4)$

D. $6d^2(d^2 + 3d^3 - 6)$

4. There is a circular garden in the middle of a square yard. The radius of the circle is $4x$. The side length of the yard is $20x$. What is the area of the part of the yard that is not covered by the circle?

F. $4x(5)$ G. $8x^2(5 - \pi)$ H. $16x(25 + \pi)$ I. $16x^2(25 - \pi)$

5. What is the simplified form of $-3z^2(z + 2) - 4(z^2 + 1)$?

A. $-7z^2 + 1$

B. $-3z^3 - 4z^2 - 6z - 4$

C. $-3z^3 - 2z^2 - 4$

D. $-3z^3 - 10z^2 - 4$

Short Response

6. A rectangular blacktop with a length of $5x$ and a width of $3x$ has been erected inside a rectangular field that has a length of $12x$ and a width of $7x$.

a. What is the area of the part of the field that is not blacktop?

b. There is a circular fountain in the rectangular field that has a radius of $3x$. What is the area of the part of the field that does not include the blacktop or the fountain? Factor your answer.

Name ______________________ Class ____________ Date ____________

8-3 Think About a Plan

Multiplying Binomials

Geometry The dimensions of a rectangular prism are n, $n + 7$, and $n + 8$. Use the formula $V = lwh$ to write a polynomial in standard form for the volume of the prism.

Know

1. What are the dimensions of the rectangular prism? __________, __________, __________

2. What is the formula for the volume of a rectangular prism? ______________________

3. In the volume formula, what do l, w, and h represent? __________, __________, __________

4. Explain how to write a polynomial in standard form. ______________________

____

Need

5. To solve the problem you need to find ______________________

____.

Plan

6. Draw a diagram of the rectangular prism and label the information you know.

7. Write an expression for the volume of the rectangular prism.

____

8. Write the volume of the rectangular prism as a polynomial in standard form.

Name ______________________ Class __________ Date __________

8-3 Practice
Form K

Multiplying Binomials

Simplify each product using the Distributive Property.

1. $(b - 2)(b + 1)$

2. $(x + 6)(x + 5)$

3. $(3n + 1)(n - 8)$

4. $(2t - 7)(t - 5)$

5. $(y + 3)(y + 7)$

6. $(b - 6)(b + 3)$

Simplify each product using a table.

7. $(x + 1)(x - 11)$

8. $(h - 2)(3h + 5)$

9. $(8w - 3)(4w - 7)$

10. $(3c + 13)(13c + 3)$

11. $(3a + 2)(a - 2)$

12. $(t + 7)(2t - 4)$

13. $(3q^2 + 6)(2q - 5)$

14. $(x + 6)(x - 7)$

15. $(p - 10)(2p + 5)$

16. $(j - 12)(j - 11)$

17. $(3z - 4)(7z - 5)$

18. $(2m + 11)(6m - 1)$

19. $(7h + 6)(7h - 6)$

20. $(-3z + 7)(4z - 8)$

21. $(-3t + 5)(-3t - 2)$

8-3 Practice (continued)

Form K

Multiplying Binomials

22. The radius of a circle is $(7x + 3)$ cm. Write an expression to represent the area of the circle in simplified form.

23. A rectangle has a length of $(x + 2)$ in. and a width of $(2x + 3)$ in. Find an expression that represents the area of the rectangle. Write the expression in simplified form.

Simplify each product using the FOIL method.

24. $(x + 4)(x + 6)$

25. $(a - 5)(2a - 6)$

26. $(6d^2 + 4)(8d - 3)$

27. $(t - 4)(t - 9)$

28. $(n + 8)(2n - 7)$

29. $(f - 7)(f + 3)$

Simplify each product.

30. $(c + 4)(c^2 - 3c + 5)$

31. $(p^2 - 2p + 5)(p - 7)$

32. $(4x^2 + 2x + 3)(3x - 8)$

33. $(5t^2 + 3t - 11)(6t - 1)$

34. A community center is expanding the size of its rectangular meeting hall. The hall is currently 300 ft long and 150 ft wide. The center plans to expand both the length and the width of the meeting hall by $3x$ ft. What polynomial in standard form represents the area of the expanded meeting hall?

35. Open-Ended Write a cubic monomial and a fourth-degree trinomial. Then find their product and write it in standard form.

Name ______________________ Class ____________ Date ____________

8-3 Standardized Test Prep

Multiplying Binomials

Multiple Choice

For Exercises 1–5, choose the correct letter.

1. What is the simplified form of $(x - 2)(2x + 3)$? Use the Distributive Property.

   A. $2x^2 - x - 6$ B. $2x^2 - 6$ C. $2x^2 - 7x - 6$ D. $2x^2 + x - 6$

2. What is the simplified form of $(3x + 2)(4x - 3)$? Use a table.

   F. $12x^2 + 18x + 6$ G. $12x^2 + x - 6$ H. $12x^2 + 18x - 6$ I. $12x^2 - x - 6$

3. What is the simplified form of $(4p - 2)(p - 4)$?

   A. $4p^2 + 6p - 16$ B. $4p^2 - 18p + 8$ C. $4p^2 - 14p - 6$ D. $4p^2 - 6p + 16$

4. The radius of a cylinder is $3x - 2$ cm. The height of the cylinder is $x + 3$ cm. What is the surface area of the cylinder?

   F. $2\pi(3x^2 + 10x - 8)$
   G. $2\pi(12x^2 + 7x - 2)$
   H. $2\pi(12x^2 - 2x + 13)$
   I. $2\pi(12x^2 - 5x - 2)$

5. What is the simplified form of $(2x^2 + 4x - 3)(3x + 1)$?

   A. $6x^3 + 10x^2 - 5x + 3$
   B. $6x^3 + 14x^2 + 5x - 3$
   C. $6x^3 + 14x^2 - 5x - 3$
   D. $6x^3 - 10x^2 - 5x - 3$

Short Response

6. A soup can that is a cylinder has a radius of $2x - 1$ and a height of $3x$. What is the surface area of the soup can? Show your work.

Name ____________________ Class __________ Date __________

8-4 Think About a Plan

Multiplying Special Cases

Construction A square deck has a side length of $x + 5$. You are expanding the deck so that each side is four times as long as the side length of the original deck. What is the area of the new deck? Write your answer in standard form.

Understanding the Problem

1. What is the shape of the deck? ____________________

2. How long is each side of the deck? ____________________

3. The new deck has sides that are __________ times longer than the original sides.

4. What is the problem asking you to find? ____________________
____

Planning the Solution

5. Write an expression for the new side length of the deck.

6. Write an expression for the area of the new deck.

Getting an Answer

7. What is the standard form of the expression for the area of the new deck?

Name ______________________ Class ____________ Date ____________

8-4 Practice

Form K

Multiplying Special Cases

Simplify each expression.

1. $(y + 1)^2$

2. $(n + 11)^2$

3. $(t + 7)^2$

4. $(3m + 6)^2$

5. $(4x + 1)^2$

6. $(3n + 2)^2$

7. $(t - 3)^2$

8. $(7v - 3)^2$

9. $(6p - 5)^2$

The figures below are squares. Find an expression for the area of each shaded region. Write your answers in standard form.

10.

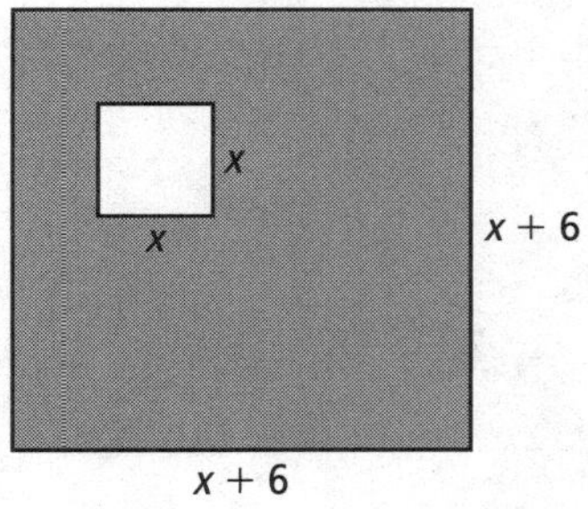

11.

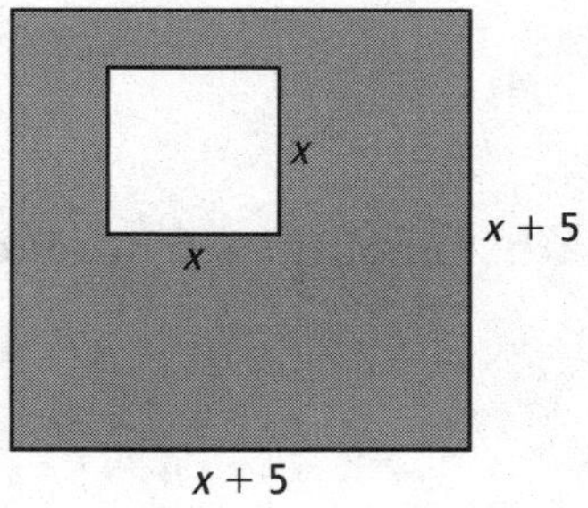

12. A flat, square roof needs a square patch in the corner to seal a leak. The side length of the roof is $(x + 12)$ ft and the side length of the patch is x ft. What is the area of the good part of the roof?

13. A white, square quilt has a purple square in the center. The side length of the purple square is $(x - 5)$ inches and the width of the quilt is 60 inches. What is the area of the white part of the quilt?

Name ______________________ Class ____________ Date ____________

8-4 Practice (continued) — Form K

Multiplying Special Cases

Mental Math Simplify each product.

14. 52^2

15. 18^2

16. 119^2

17. 495^2

18. 72^2

19. 151^2

Simplify each product.

20. $(x + 1)(x - 1)$

21. $(m + 5)(m - 5)$

22. $(a - 4)(a + 4)$

23. $(s - 13)(s + 13)$

24. $(2z - 3)(2z + 3)$

25. $(4d + 6)(4d - 6)$

Mental Math Simplify each product.

26. $99 \cdot 101$

27. $48 \cdot 52$

28. $178 \cdot 182$

Simplify each product.

29. $(s + 3t)^2$

30. $(2x + y)^2$

31. $(4a - b)^2$

32. $(m^2 + 3n)(m^2 - 3n)$

33. $(9f^2 + 4g)(9f^2 - 4g)$

34. $(6m^4 - n^3)(6m^4 + n^3)$

35. The formula $V = \pi r^2 h$ gives the volume of a cylinder with radius r and height h. Find the volume of a cylinder with radius $(x + 4)$ cm and height 5 cm. Write your answer in standard form.

Name ____________________ Class __________ Date __________

8-4 Standardized Test Prep

Multiplying Special Cases

Gridded Response

Solve each exercise and enter your answer on the grid provided.

1. What is coefficient of the x-term in the simplified form of $(2x + 4)^2$?

2. What is 27^2? Use mental math.

3. What is constant in the simplified form of $(x - 6)^2$?

4. What is the product of 38 and 42? Use mental math.

`5. How much greater is the product of 73 and 67 than the product of 74 and 66?

1.
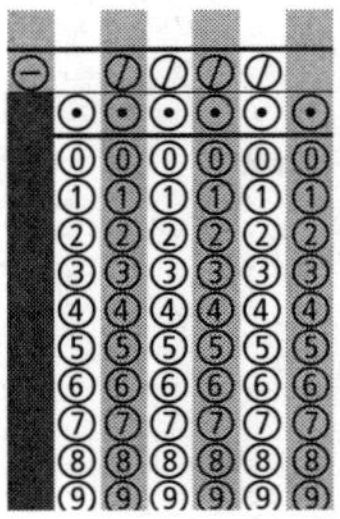

2.
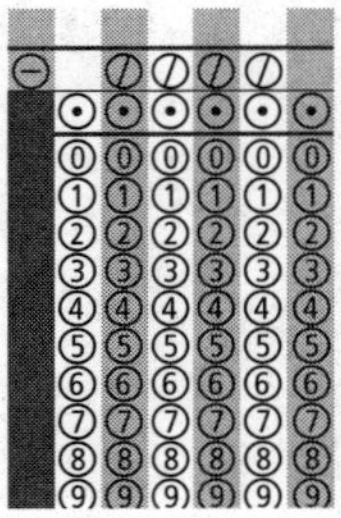

3.
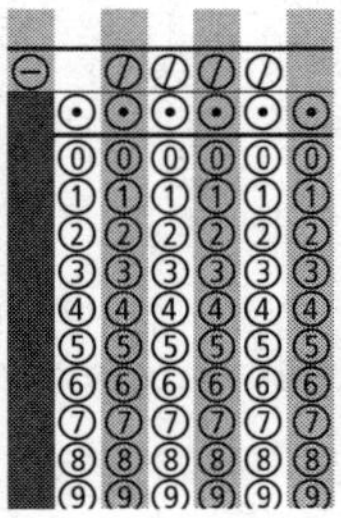

4.
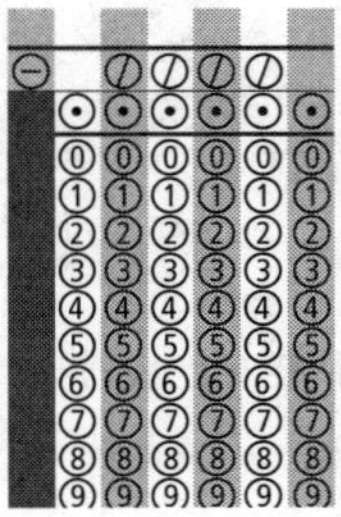

5.
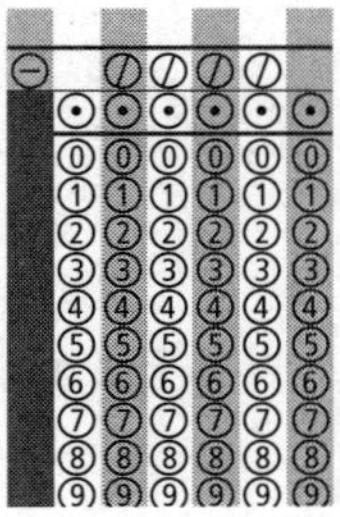

Name ______________________ Class ____________ Date ____________

8-5 Think About a Plan

Factoring $x^2 + bx + c$

Recreation A rectangular skateboard park has an area of $x^2 + 15x + 54$. What are possible dimensions of the park? Use factoring.

Know

1. The area of the skateboard park is ______________.

2. The dimensions of a rectangle are its __________ and __________.

3. The __________ of the area polynomial are possible dimensions of the skateboard park.

Need

4 To solve the problem I need to find ______________________________

____

Plan

5. Complete the table. List the pairs of factors of ☐.

   Identify the pair that has a sum of ☐.

Factors of 54	Sum of Factors

6. Write the factored polynomial.

7. What are possible dimensions of the skateboard park?

8. Justify your answer.

____

____

____

Name ______________________ Class ____________ Date ____________

8-5 Practice

Form K

Factoring $x^2 + bx + c$

Complete.

1. $n^2 + 9n + 18 = (n + 3)(n + \square)$

2. $t^2 + 9t + 14 = (t + 2)(t + \square)$

3. $d^2 + 11d + 30 = (d + 5)(d + \square)$

4. $v^2 + 2v + 1 = (v + 1)(v + \square)$

5. $m^2 - 8m + 15 = (m - 5)(m - \square)$

6. $a^2 - 13a + 22 = (a - 2)(a - \square)$

7. $z^2 - 17z + 72 = (z - 8)(z - \square)$

8. $w^2 - 7w + 12 = (w - 3)(w - \square)$

Factor each expression. Check your answer.

9. $g^2 + 6g + 8$

10. $y^2 + 10y + 24$

11. $r^2 + 12r + 35$

12. $k^2 + 9k + 8$

13. $x^2 - 16x + 60$

14. $h^2 - 19h + 78$

Complete.

15. $g^2 + 5g - 24 = (g - 3)(g + \square)$

16. $b^2 - 6b - 7 = (b - 7)(b + \square)$

17. $y^2 + 4y - 45 = (y + 9)(y - \square)$

18. $k^2 + 4k - 12 = (k + 6)(k - \square)$

19. $p^2 - 7p - 60 = (p + 5)(p - \square)$

20. $n^2 - 6n - 40 = (n - 10)(n + \square)$

Name ______________________ Class ____________ Date ____________

8-5 Practice (continued)

Form K

Factoring $x^2 + bx + c$

Factor each expression. Check your answer.

21. $x^2 - 4x - 5$

22. $t^2 + t - 20$

23. $z^2 - z - 72$

24. $m^2 - 6m - 27$

25. $a^2 + 4a - 21$

26. $v^2 - 4v - 12$

27. $c^2 - 7c - 44$

28. $r^2 + 6r - 16$

29. $f^2 + f - 6$

30. $j^2 - 6j - 55$

31. $y^2 + 3y - 54$

32. $n^2 - 10n - 11$

33. The area of a rectangular window is given by the trinomial $x^2 - 14x + 48$. The window's length is $(x - 8)$. What is the window's width?

34. The area of a rectangular area rug is given by the trinomial $f^2 - 4f - 77$. The length of the rug is $(f + 7)$. What is the width of the rug?

35. Reasoning Write possible expressions for the length and the width of a rectangle with area $x^2 + 13x + 42$.

36. A rectangular tabletop has an area of $t^2 + 2t - 99$. What are possible dimensions of the tabletop? Use factoring.

Name ______________________ Class ____________ Date ____________

8-5 Standardized Test Prep

Factoring $x^2 + bx + c$

Multiple Choice

For Exercises 1–7, choose the correct letter.

1. Which number makes this equation true?

$$v^2 + 10v + 16 = (v + 8)(v + \square)$$

A. 2 **B.** 4 **C.** 6 **D.** 8

2. What is the factored form of $x^2 + 6x + 8$?

F. $(x + 5)(x + 3)$ **G.** $(x + 4)(x + 2)$ **H.** $(x + 7)(x + 1)$ **I.** $(x + 3)(x + 3)$

3. What is the factored form of $x^2 - 7x + 12$?

A. $(x - 5)(x - 3)$ **B.** $(x - 6)(x - 1)$ **C.** $(x - 2)(x - 5)$ **D.** $(x - 4)(x - 3)$

4. Which number makes this eqtuation true?

$$q^2 + 3q - 18 = (q + 6)(q - \square)$$

F. 1 **G.** 2 **H.** 3 **I.** 12

5. What is the factored form of $x^2 + 3x - 10$?

A. $(x + 5)(x - 2)$ **C.** $(x - 2)(x - 5)$

B. $(x - 5)(x + 2)$ **D.** $(x + 5)(x + 2)$

6. The area of a garden is given by the trinomial $g^2 - 2g - 24$. The garden's length is $g + 4$. What is the garden's width?

F. $g - 2$ **G.** $g - 6$ **H.** $g - 8$ **I.** $g + 2$

7. What is the factored form of $x^2 + 3xy - 28y^2$?

A. $(x + 14y)(x - 2y)$ **B.** $(x + 2y)(x - 14y)$ **C.** $(x + 4y)(x - 7y)$ **D.** $(x - 4y)(x + 7y)$

Short Response

8. The area of a rectangular backyard is given by the trinomial $b^2 + 5b - 24$. What are possible dimensions of the backyard? Show why your answer is correct.

Name ______________________ Class ____________ Date ____________

8-6 Think About a Plan

Factoring $ax^2 + bx + c$

Carpentry The top of a rectangular table has an area of $18x^2 + 69x + 60$. The width of the table is $3x + 4$. What is the length of the table?

Know

1. The area of the table top is ______________.

2. The width of the table top is ______________.

3. Some quadratic trinomials can be written as the product of two ______________.

4. One of the factors of the polynomial $18x^2 + 69x + 60$ is ______________.

Need

5. To solve the problem I need to find ____

____.

Plan

6. Find the missing factor.

What can you multiply by $3x$ to get $18x^2$? $3x \cdot \square = 18x^2$

What can you multiply by 4 to get 60? $4 \cdot \square = 60$

7. What is the factored form of $18x^2 + 69x + 60$? ______________

8. What is the length of the table? Check your answer.

____

____

____

Name ______________________ Class ____________ Date ____________

8-6 Practice

Form K

Factoring $ax^2 + bx + c$

Factor each expression.

1. $3n^2 - 8n - 3$
2. $5a^2 - 22a + 8$
3. $2s^2 + 13s + 6$
4. $6t^2 + 21t - 12$
5. $9b^2 - 65b + 14$
6. $5z^2 + 11z + 6$
7. $7r^2 - 9r - 10$
8. $2m^2 + m - 21$
9. $3g^2 + 20g + 32$
10. The area of a rectangular driveway is $2x^2 + 15x + 25$. The width of the driveway is $x + 5$. What is the length of the driveway?
11. The area of a rectangular floor is $8x^2 + 6x - 20$. The width of the floor is $2x + 4$. What is the length of the floor?
12. The area of a rectangular desktop is $6x^2 + 3x - 3$. The width of the desktop is $2x + 1$. What is the length of the desktop?

Factor each expression completely.

13. $24n^2 + 2n - 12$
14. $72q^2 - 12q - 40$
15. $30j^2 - 27j - 21$
16. $60h^2 + 280h + 45$
17. $40a^2 + 126a + 44$
18. $45f^2 + 24f - 189$

8-6 Practice (continued)

Form K

Factoring $ax^2 + bx + c$

Open-Ended Find two different values that complete each expression so that the trinomial can be factored into the product of two binomials. Factor your trinomials.

19. $4n^2 + \square n - 3$

20. $12r^2 + \square + 6$

21. $24a^2 + \square a - 15$

22. $18b^2 + \square b + 8$

23. A parallelogram has an area of $8x^2 - 2x - 45$. The height of the parallelogram is $4x + 9$.

a. Write the formula for the area of a parallelogram.

b. What is the length of the base of the parallelogram?

c. **Writing** Explain how you solved the problem.

24. A rectangular athletic field has an area of $40x^2 + 190x - 50$. The width of the athletic field is $8x - 2$. What is the length of the athletic field?

Factor each expression.

25. $96d^2 - 76d - 77$

26. $48h^2 - 86h + 35$

27. $24m^2 + 18m - 15$

28. $36c^2 + 27c - 55$

Name ______________________ Class ____________ Date ____________

8-6 Standardized Test Prep

Factoring $ax^2 + bx + c$

Multiple Choice

For Exercises 1–5, choose the correct letter.

1. What is the factored form of $4x^2 + 12x + 5$?
   A. $(2x + 4)(2x + 3)$ B. $(4x + 5)(x + 1)$ C. $(2x + 1)(2x + 5)$ D. $(4x + 1)(x + 5)$

2. What is the factored form of $2x^2 + x - 3$?
   F. $(2x + 3)(x - 1)$ G. $(2x + 1)(x - 3)$ H. $(2x - 3)(x + 1)$ I. $(2x - 1)(x + 3)$

3. The area of a rectangular swimming pool is $10x^2 - 19x - 15$. The length of the pool is $5x + 3$. What is the width of the pool?
   A. $2x - 18$ B. $2x - 5$ C. $5x - 5$ D. $5x - 22$

4. What is the factored form of $16x^2 - 16x - 12$?
   F. $4(2x - 2)(2x + 2)$
   G. $4(4x - 6)(x + 2)$
   H. $4(2x - 2)(2x + 3)$
   I. $4(2x - 3)(2x + 1)$

5. What is the factored form of $3x^2 + 21x - 24$?
   A. $3(x + 8)(x - 1)$
   B. $3(x + 6)(x + 1)$
   C. $3(x + 5)(x - 3)$
   D. $3(x + 7)(x - 3)$

Short Response

6. The perimeter around a dog's running space is $20x^2 + 28x + 8$. The length of the dog's running space is $10x + 4$. What is the width of the dog's running space? Show why your answer is correct.

Name ______________________ Class ____________ Date ____________

8-7 Think About a Plan

Factoring Special Cases

Interior Design A square rug has an area of $49x^2 - 56x + 16$. A second square rug has an area of $16x^2 + 24x + 9$. What is an expression that represents the difference of the areas of the rugs? Show two different ways to find the solution.

1. What are two methods you could use to solve this problem? ______________________

2. How would you find the difference without factoring? ______________________

3. What polynomial do you get when you use this method? ______________________

4. Can you factor that polynomial? ______________________

5. How could you use factoring to solve the problem? ______________________

6. What do the shape of the rug and the polynomials tell you about how to factor the polynomials for the area of the rugs? ______________________

   ____

7. Factor each trinomial.

   $49x^2 - 56x + 16 = (\square - \square)(\square - \square) = (\square\square\square)^2$

   $16x^2 + 24x + 9 = (\square + \square)(\square + \square) = (\square\square\square)^2$

8. Use your results from Exercise 7 to write an expression for the difference in the areas.

   ____

9. Factor the expression from Exercise 8 using the difference of two squares. Simplify the expressions within each set of parentheses.

   ____

10. Do the two methods give you the same result?

Name ______________________ Class ____________ Date ____________

8-7 Practice

Form K

Factoring Special Cases

Factor each expression.

1. $c^2 + 2c + 1$
2. $d^2 - 10d + 25$
3. $p^2 - 24p + 144$
4. $w^2 + 14w + 49$
5. $s^2 + 16s + 64$
6. $9g^2 + 24g + 16$
7. $25m^2 - 60m + 36$
8. $4q^2 - 32q + 64$
9. $49y^2 - 84y + 36$
10. $121n^2 - 66n + 9$
11. $81x^2 - 18x + 1$
12. $100t^2 - 100t + 25$

The given expression represents the area. Find the side length of the square.

13.

$36w^2 + 12w + 1$

14.

$81w^2 - 72w + 16$

15.

$9w^2 - 48w + 64$

16.

$121w^2 - 66w + 9$

17. **Writing** How can you tell that $x^2 - 19x + 90$ is not a perfect square trinomial?

Name ______________________ Class ____________ Date ____________

8-7 Practice (continued) — Form K

Factoring Special Cases

Factor each expression.

18. $b^2 - 121$

19. $d^2 - 81$

20. $f^2 - 625$

21. $108x^2 - 3$

22. $50n^2 - 8$

23. $405z^2 - 245$

24. $216h^2 - 150$

25. $28y^2 - 28$

26. $50t^2 + 40t + 8$

27. $12n^2 - 36n + 27$

28. $180a^2 - 300a + 125$

29. $250k^2 - 200k + 40$

30. Writing Explain how to recognize a difference of two squares.

31. a. Open-Ended Write an expression that shows the factored form of a perfect-square trinomial.

b. Explain how you know your expression is a perfect-square trinomial when expanded.

Mental Math For Exercises 32–34, find a pair of factors for each number by using the difference of two squares.

32. 84

33. 55

34. 80

35. Writing The area of a square painting is $225x^4 + 240x^2 + 64$. Explain how you would find a possible length of one side of the painting.

Name ______________________ Class ____________ Date ____________

8-7 Standardized Test Prep

Factoring Special Cases

Multiple Choice

For Exercises 1–6, choose the correct letter.

1. What is the factored form of $q^2 - 12q + 36$?

   A. $(q + 6)(q - 6)$ B. $(q - 6)(q - 6)$ C. $(q - 9)(q + 4)$ D. $(q + 4)(q + 9)$

2. What is the factored form of $9x^2 + 12x + 4$?

   F. $(3x + 2)^2$ G. $(3x + 3)^2$ H. $(3x - 2)^2$ I. $(3x - 3)^2$

3. What is the factored form of $x^2 - 196$?

   A. $(x - 14)^2$ B. $(x + 14)^2$ C. $(x - 28)(4x + 7)$ D. $(x - 14)(x + 14)$

4. What is the factored form of $9x^2 - 64$?

   F. $(3x - 8)^2$ G. $(3x + 8)^2$ H. $(3x - 8)(3x + 8)$ I. $(9x - 8)(x + 8)$

5. What is the factored form of $12m^2 - 75$?

   A. $3(2m - 5)^2$ B. $3(2m + 5)(2m - 5)$ C. $3(2m + 5)^2$ D. $(6m - 25)(2m + 3)$

6. What is the factored form of $49x^2 - 56x + 16$?

   F. $(7x - 4)^2$ G. $(7x + 4)(7x - 4)$ H. $(7x + 4)^2$ I. $(7x - 8)^2$

Extended Response

7. A four-sided building has an area of $36x^2 + 48x + 16$. Explain how to find a possible length and width of the building. What is a possible shape of the building?

Name ______________________ Class ____________ Date ____________

8-8 Think About a Plan

Factoring by Grouping

Art The pedestal of a sculpture is a rectangular prism with a volume of $63x^3 - 28x$. What expressions can represent the dimensions of the pedestal? Use factoring.

KNOW

1. The pedestal of the sculpture is shaped like a ______________________.

2. The volume of the pedestal is ____________.

3. The formula you can use to find the dimensions of the pedestal is __________.

NEED

4. To solve the problem you need to find ______________________

____

PLAN

5. Factor out the GCF from the volume of the pedestal. ______________________

6. What type of expression is of the remaining expression? ______________________

7. Factor the expression completely. ______________________

8. What expressions represent possible dimensions of the pedestal?

____

8-8 Practice

Form K

Factoring by Grouping

Find the GCF of the first two terms and the GCF of the last two terms for each polynomial.

1. $6n^3 + 3n^2 + 10n + 5$

2. $12z^3 + 36z^2 + 4z + 12$

3. $9k^3 + 45k^2 + 2k + 10$

4. $11a^3 + 33a^2 + 8a + 24$

5. $2f^3 + 5f^2 - 4f - 10$

6. $16d^3 - 24d^2 - 6d + 9$

Factor each expression.

7. $6x^3 - 4x^2 + 15x - 10$

8. $5q^3 - 40q^2 - 4q + 32$

9. $28m^3 + 7m^2 - 8m - 2$

10. $3p^3 + 5p^2 + 9p + 15$

11. $18y^3 - 6y^2 - 63y + 21$

12. $3t^3 - 18t^2 + 5t - 30$

13. $250c^3 - 250c^2 + 100c - 100$

14. $18g^3 - 33g^2 + 30g - 55$

15. $88n^3 + 77n^2 - 72n - 63$

16. $50h^3 - 40h^2 + 60h - 48$

17. $24b^3 - 96b^2 - 14b + 56$

18. $54r^3 + 9r^2 - 6r - 1$

8-8 Practice (continued) — Form K

Factoring by Grouping

Factor completely.

19. $7s^3 + 14s^2 + 14s + 4$

20. $32h^4 + 72h^3 + 36h^2 + 81h$

21. $42z^4 - 48z^3 - 7z^2 + 8z$

22. $60p^3 + 48p^2 + 25p + 20$

23. $26n^4 - 14n^3 + 91n^2 - 49n$

24. $40t^3 + 28t^2 - 30t - 21$

25. $45k^4 - 9k^3 + 10k^2 - 2k$

26. $18b^5 - 3b^4 + 30b^3 - 5b^2$

Find linear expressions for the possible dimensions of each rectangular prism.

27.

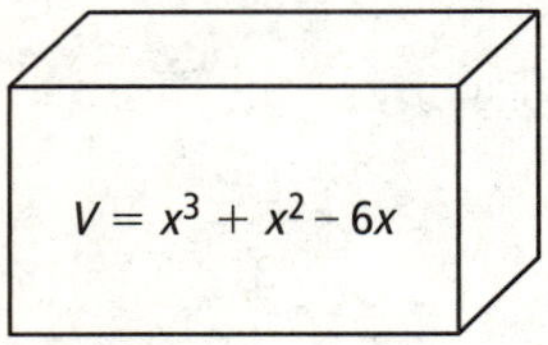

28.

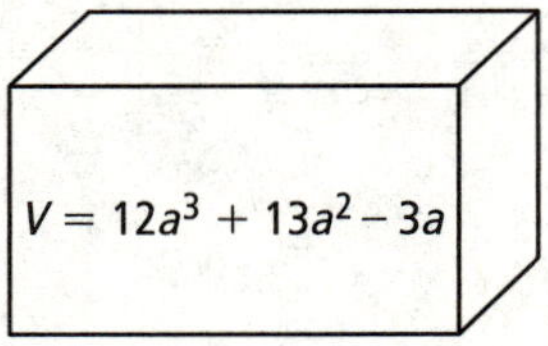

29. A storage bin in the shape of a rectangular prism has a volume of $10x^3 + 15x^2 + 2x$. What linear expressions can represent possible dimensions of the tub?

30. Writing Describe the first step to look for in factoring a cubic expression containing four terms.

31. Open-Ended Write a 4-term expression that you can factor by grouping. Factor your polynomial.

Name ______________________ Class ____________ Date ____________

8-8 Standardized Test Prep

Factoring by Grouping

Multiple Choice

For Exercises 1–5, choose the correct letter.

1. What is the GCF of the first two terms of the polynomial $4y^3 + 8y^2 + 5y + 10$?

A. $4y$ **B.** $4y^2$ **C.** $4y^3$ **D.** 4

2. What is the factored form of $4x^3 + 3x^2 + 8x + 6$?

F. $(2x^2 + 3)(2x + 3)$

G. $(2x^2 + 2)(2x + 3)$

H. $(x^2 + 2)(2x + 3)$

I. $(x^2 + 2)(4x + 3)$

3. What is the factored form of $9x^4 - 6x^3 + 18x^2 - 12x$?

A. $3x(x^2 - 2x)(x - 4)$

B. $3x(x^2 - 2)(3x + 2)$

C. $3x(x^2 + 2)(3x - 2)$

D. $3x(3x^2 - 2x)(6x - 4)$

4. What is the factored form of $20p^3 + 40p^2 + 15p + 30$?

F. $5(2p^2 + 3)(p + 2)$

G. $5(2p^2 + 6)(p + 4)$

H. $5(4p^2 + 3)(p + 2)$

I. $5(4p^2 + 8p)(3p + 6)$

5. A box in the shape of a rectangular prism has a volume of $9x^3 + 24x^2 + 12x$. Which is not one of the possible dimensions? (Its dimensions are all linear expressions with integer coefficients.)

A. $2x + 3$ **B.** $3x + 2$ **C.** $3x$ **D.** $x + 2$

Short Response

6. The polynomial $3\pi x^3 + 24\pi x^2 + 48\pi x$ represents the volume of a cylinder. The formula for the volume of a cylinder with radius r and height h is $V = \pi r^2 h$.

a. Factor $3\pi x^3 + 24\pi x^2 + 48\pi x$.

b. Write a linear expression for a possible radius of the cylinder. Explain.

Name ______________________ Class ____________ Date ____________

9-1 Think About a Plan

Quadratic Graphs and Their Properties

Physics In a physics class demonstration, a ball is dropped from the roof of a building, 72 feet above the ground. The height h (in feet) of the ball above the ground is given by the function $h = -16t^2 + 72$, where t is the time in seconds.

a. Graph the function.

b. How far has the ball fallen from time $t = 0$ to $t = 1$?

c. **Reasoning** Does the ball fall the same distance from time $t = 1$ to time $t = 2$ as it does from $t = 0$ to $t = 1$? Explain?

1. Complete the following table of values.

t	$h = -16t^2 + 72$	(t, h)
0		
1		
2		
3		

2. Use the completed table to graph the function $h = -16t^2 + 72$.

3. What was the height of the ball at $t = 0$? ____________

What was the height of the ball at $t = 1$? ____________

How far has the ball fallen from time $t = 0$ to $t = 1$? ____________

4. What is the height of the ball at $t = 2$? ____________

How far has the ball fallen from time $t = 1$ to $t = 2$? ____________

5. Does the ball fall the same distance from time $t = 1$ to $t = 2$ as it does from $t = 0$ to $t = 1$? Explain.

____

____

____

____

Name ______________________ Class ____________ Date ____________

9-1 Practice

Form K

Quadratic Graphs and Their Properties

Identify the vertex of each graph. Tell whether it is a maximum or a minimum.

1. 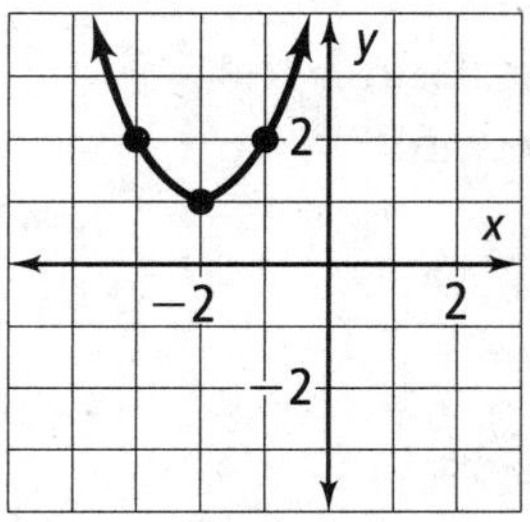

2. 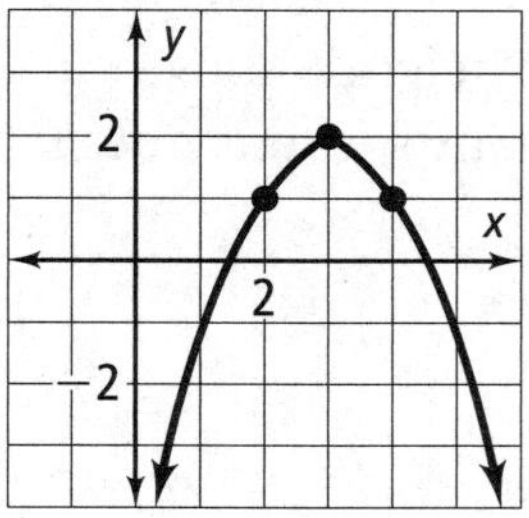

Graph each function.

3. $f(x) = 5x^2$

4. $f(x) = -3x^2$

5. $f(x) = -\frac{2}{3}x^2$

6. $f(x) = -\frac{3}{5}x^2$

Order each group of quadratic functions from widest to narrowest graph.

7. $y = -2x^2, y = -4x^2, y = -3x^2$

8. $y = \frac{1}{3}x^2, y = 3x^2, y = \frac{1}{6}x^2$

Graph each function.

9. $f(x) = x^2 + 3$

10. $f(x) = x^2 - 5$

11. $f(x) = -\frac{1}{3}x^2 - 1$

12. Jared is casting his fishing line with a lead sinker attached over the edges of a pier. The pier is 15 feet above the water. The function $h = -16t^2 + 15$ gives the sinker's height h above the water (in feet) after t seconds. Graph the function. How many seconds does it take for the sinker to hit the water?

13. A roofer is going to drop his hammer to the ground from the roof after making sure the area is clear. The roof is 25 feet high. The function $h = -16t^2 + 25$ gives the hammer's height h above the ground (in feet) after t seconds. Graph the function. How many seconds does it take for the hammer to hit the ground?

Identify the domain and range of each function.

14. $y = 4x^2 - 3$

15. $y = -\frac{1}{4}x^2 - 2$

16. $y = \frac{2}{3}x^2 + 1$

17. $f(x) = -2x^2 + 6$

18. Writing Discuss how the graph of $y = x^2 - 7$ differs from the graph of $y = x^2$.

19. Writing Explain how you can determine if the parabola has been shifted up or down by examining the equation.

20. Open-Ended Write the equation of a quadratic function for which the graph opens in the same direction as the graph of $y = x^2$, is wider than the graph of $y = x^2$, and is shifted up compared to the graph of $y = x^2$.

Name ______________________ Class ____________ Date ____________

9-1 Standardized Test Prep

Quadratic Graphs and Their Properties

Multiple Choice

For Exercises 1–4, choose the correct letter.

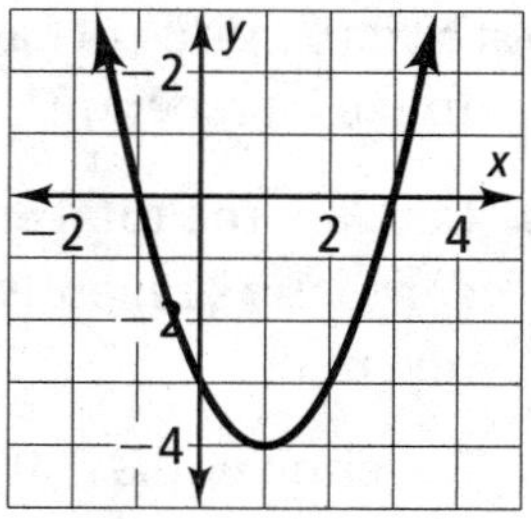

1. What is the vertex of the parabola shown at the right?

   A. $(-1, 0)$ C. $(1, -4)$

   B. $(0, -3)$ D. $(3, 0)$

2. Which of the following has a graph that is wider than the graph of $y = 3x^2 + 2$?

   F. $y = 3x^2 + 3$ H. $y = -4x^2 - 1$

   G. $y = 0.5x^2 + 1$ I. $y = 4x^2 + 1$

3. Which graph represents the function $y = -2x^2 - 5$?

   A.
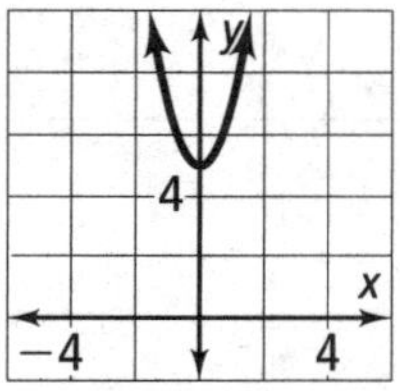

   B.
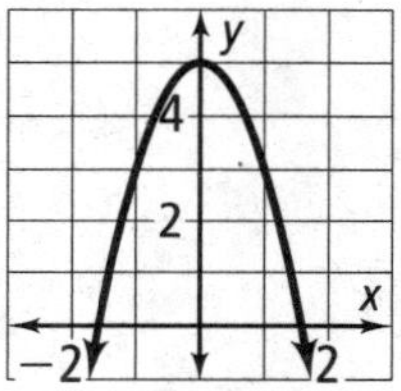

   C.
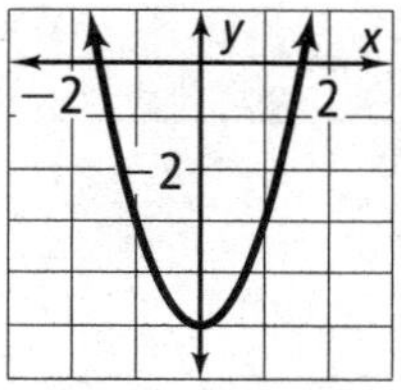

   D.
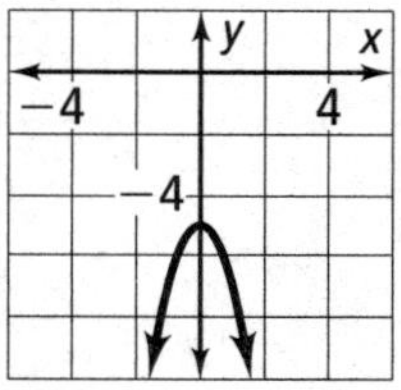

4. What is the order, from narrowest to widest graph, of the quadratic functions $f(x) = -10x^2, f(x) = 2x^2$, and $f(x) = 0.5x^2$?

   F. $f(x) = -10x^2, f(x) = 2x^2$, and $f(x) = 0.5x^2$

   G. $f(x) = 2x^2, f(x) = -10x^2$, and $f(x) = 0.5x^2$

   H. $f(x) = 0.5x^2, f(x) = 2x^2$, and $f(x) = -10x^2$

   I. $f(x) = 0.5x^2, f(x) = -10x^2$, and $f(x) = 2x^2$

Short Response

5. A ball fell off a cliff into the river from a height of 25 feet. The function $h = -30t^2 + 25$ gives the ball's height h above the water after t seconds. Graph the function. How much time does it take for the ball to hit the water?

Name ______________________ Class __________ Date __________

9-2 Think About a Plan

Quadratic Functions

Business A cell phone company sells about 500 phones each week when it charges $75 per phone. It sells about 20 more phones per week for each $1 decrease in price. The company's revenue is the product of the number of phones sold and the price of each phone. What price should the company charge to maximize its revenue?

1. Let $d =$ the total amount of dollar decrease to the price. Let $r =$ the company's revenue. Write a quadratic function that reflects the company's revenue.

Revenue equals 500 phones plus *d* times 20 phones times $75 less *d*.

$r = (\boxed{} + (d \times \boxed{})) \times (\boxed{} - d)$

$r =$ ______________________

$r =$ ______________________

$r =$ ______________________

2. Find the vertex of the quadratic function above. How will finding the vertex help you determine at what price the company should charge to maximize its revenue?

____

____

3. What price should the company charge?

Name ____________________ Class ____________ Date ____________

9-2 Practice

Form K

Quadratic Functions

Find the equation of the axis of symmetry and the coordinates of the vertex of the graph of each function.

1. $y = 3x^2 + 1$

2. $y = x^2 - 6x + 2$

3. $y = x^2 - 8x + 12$

4. $y = -2x^2 - 5$

5. $y = 3x^2 + 6x - 8$

6. $y = -6x^2 + 12x - 3$

Graph each function. Label the axis of symmetry and the vertex.

7. $f(x) = x^2 + 6x - 2$

8. $f(x) = -3x^2 + 9x - 8$

9. $f(x) = 4x^2 - 8x + 1$

10. $f(x) = 5x^2 + 10x - 4$

11. A baseball player hit a ball with an upward velocity of 46 ft/s. Its height h in feet after t seconds is given by the function $h = -16t^2 + 46t + 6$. What is the maximum height the ball reaches? How long will it take the baseball to reach the maximum height? How long does it take for the ball to hit the ground?

12. A golf ball is chipped into the air from a small hill with an upward velocity of 50 ft/s. Its height h in feet after t seconds is given by the function $h = -16t^2 + 50t + 10$. What is the maximum height the ball reaches? How long will it take the ball to reach the maximum height? How long does it take for the ball to hit the ground?

9-2 Practice (continued)

Form K

Quadratic Functions

Graph each function. Label the axis of symmetry and the vertex.

13. $f(x) = \frac{3}{4}x^2 + 12x - 2$

14. $f(x) = \frac{1}{3}x^2 + 4x + 2$

15. $f(x) = \frac{2}{5}x^2 - 8x + 1$

16. $f(x) = -\frac{1}{2}x^2 + 8x - 6$

For Exercises 17 and 18, give an example of a quadratic function with the given characteristic(s). Justify your answer by graphing the function.

17. Its graph opens down and has its vertex at (0, 4).

18. Its graph opens upward and has its vertex at (0, −2).

Name ______________________ Class ____________ Date ____________

9-2 Standardized Test Prep

Quadratic Functions

Multiple Choice

For Exercises 1–5, choose the correct letter.

1. Which equation represents the axis of symmetry of the function $y = -2x^2 + 4x - 6$?

A. $y = 1$ **B.** $x = 1$ **C.** $x = 3$ **D.** $x = -3$

2. What are the coordinates of the vertex of the graph of the function $y = -x^2 + 6x - 11$?

F. $(3, -2)$ **G.** $(3, 16)$ **H.** $(-3, -29)$ **I.** $(-3, -20)$

3. What are the coordinates of the vertex of the graph of the function $y = 3x^2 - 12x + 3$?

A. $(-2, 29)$ **B.** $(2, -15)$ **C.** $(2, -9)$ **D.** $(3, -6)$

4. Which graph represents the function $y = 3x^2 + 12x - 6$?

F.
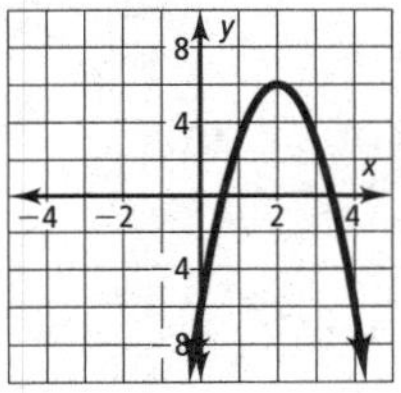

G.
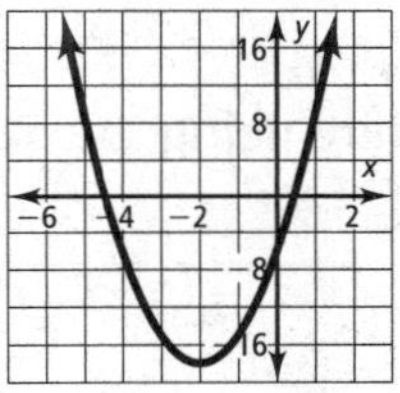

H.
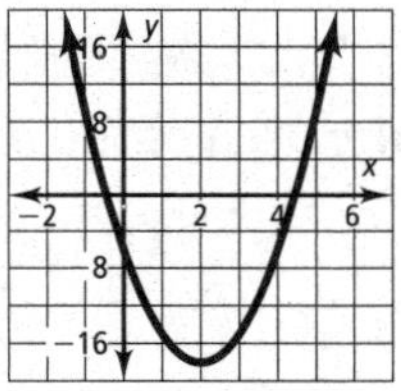

I.
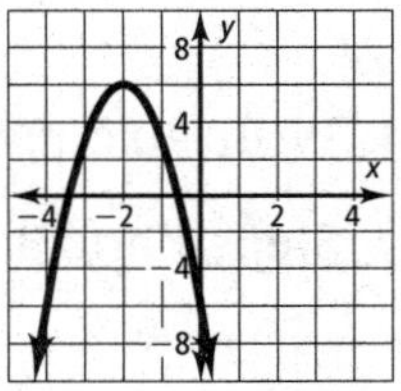

5. Which equation matches the graph shown at the right?

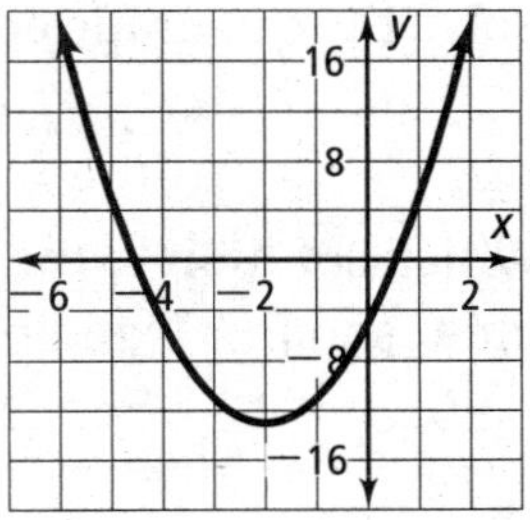

A. $y = 8x^2 + 2x - 5$

B. $y = 8x^2 + 2x + 5$

C. $y = 2x^2 + 8x + 5$

D. $y = 2x^2 + 8x - 5$

Short Response

6. A golf ball is driven in the air toward the hole from an elevated tee with an upward velocity of 160 ft/s. Its height h in feet after t seconds is given by the function $h = -16t^2 + 160t + 18$. How long will it take for the golf ball to reach its maximum height? What is the ball's maximum height?

Name ________________________ Class ____________ Date ____________

9-3 Think About a Plan

Solving Quadratic Equations

Quilting You are making a square quilt with the design shown at the right. Find the side length of the inner square that would make the area of the inner square equal to 50% of the total area of the quilt. Round to the nearest tenth of a foot.

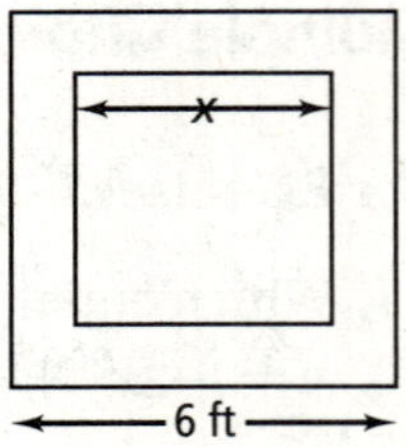

1. What is an expression for the area of the inner square? ____________________

2. What is the area of the entire quilt? ____________________

3. What is 50% of the area of the entire quilt? ____________________

4. Write an equation for the area of the inner square using the expressions from Steps 1 and 3. ____________________

5. Solve the quadratic equation.

6. Which solution to the quadratic equation best describes the side length of the inner square? Explain.

____

____

____

Name ______________________ Class ____________ Date ____________

9-3 Practice

Form K

Solving Quadratic Equations

Solve each equation by graphing the related function. If the equation has no real-number solution, write *no solution.*

1. $x^2 + 9 = 0$

2. $x^2 - 36 = 0$

3. $4x^2 = 0$

4. $\frac{1}{9}x^2 - 1 = 0$

5. $x^2 - 21 = -21$

6. $2x^2 - 32 = 0$

Solve each equation by finding square roots. If the equation has no real-number solution, write *no solution.*

7. $z^2 = 49$

8. $f^2 = 256$

9. $h^2 - 25 = -125$

10. $16n^2 - 36 = 0$

11. $6c^2 = 24$

12. $5p^2 + 45 = 0$

13. $64 - a^2 = 0$

14. $49t^2 - 81 = 0$

Model each problem with a quadratic equation. Then solve. If necessary, round to the nearest tenth.

15. Find the length of a side of a square with an area of 225 m^2.

16. Find the radius of a circle with an area of 121 yd^2.

Name ______________________________ Class ____________ Date ____________

9-3 Practice (continued) — Form K

Solving Quadratic Equations

17. The square yard you are mowing has an area of 9600 ft^2. What is the side length of the yard? Round your answer to the nearest tenth of a foot if necessary.

18. What is the radius of the largest circular quilt that can be made with an area less than or equal to 70 ft^2? Round your answer to the nearest tenth of a foot if necessary.

Mental Math **Tell how many solutions each equation has.**

19. $m^2 + 46 = 46$

20. $w^2 - 72 = 0$

Solve each equation by finding square roots. If the equation has no real-number solution, write *no solution*. If a solution is irrational, round to the nearest tenth.

21. $25n^2 + 44 = 144$

22. $-\frac{3}{4}y^2 + 5 = -22$

23. $\frac{1}{2}a^2 - 8 = 0$

24. $2.68b^2 + 4.75 = -2.25$

Find the value of *x* for the square and triangle. If necessary, round to the nearest tenth.

25.

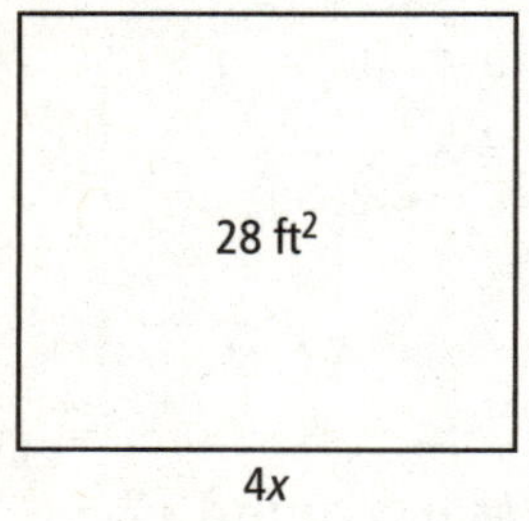

26.

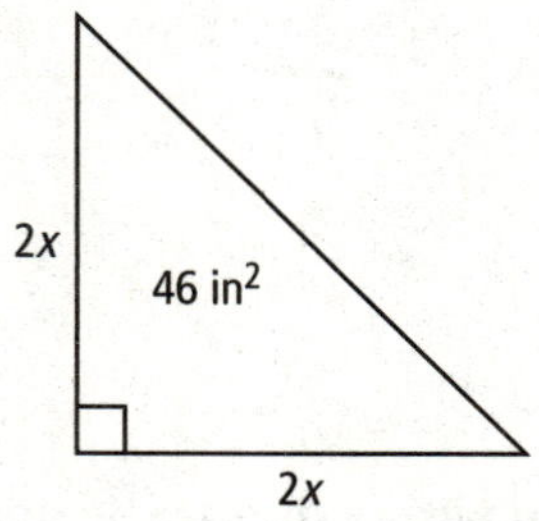

Name ______________________ Class __________ Date __________

9-3 Standardized Test Prep

Solving Quadratic Equations

Multiple Choice

For Exercises 1–7, choose the correct letter.

1. What is the solution of $n^2 - 49 = 0$?

   A. -7 B. 7 C. ± 7 D. no solution

2. What is the solution of $x^2 + 64 = 0$?

   F. -5 G. 8 H. ± 8 I. no solution

3. What is the solution of $a^2 + 17 = 42$?

   A. -5 B. 5 C. ± 5 D. no solution

4. What is the side length of a square with an area of $144x^2$?

   F. 12 G. $12x$ H. $\pm 12x$ I. no solution

5. What is the value of b in the triangle shown at the right?

   A. -4 in.
   B. 4 in.
   C. ± 4 in.
   D. no solution

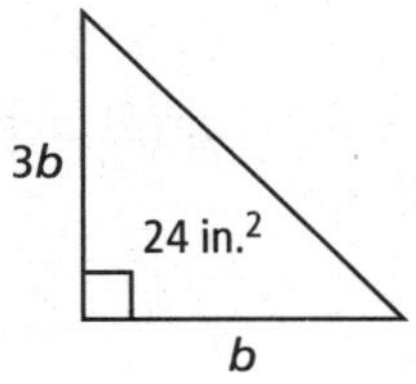

6. What is the radius of a sphere whose surface area is 100 square centimeters? Use the formula for determining the surface area of a sphere, $S = 4\pi r^2$, and 3.14 for π. Round your answer to the nearest hundredth.

   F. 2.82 cm G. 5 cm H. 5.64 cm I. 125,600 cm

7. What is the value of z so that -9 and 9 are both solutions of $x^2 + z = 103$?

   A. -22 B. 3 C. 22 D. 184

Extended Response

8. A ball is dropped from the top of a building that is 250 feet tall. The height h of the ball in feet after t seconds is modeled by the function $h = -16t^2 + 250$. Round to the nearest tenth if necessary.
   a. How long will it take for the ball to reach the ground? Show your work.
   b. How long will it take for the ball to reach a height of 75 feet? Show your work.

Name ______________________ Class ____________ Date ____________

9-4 Think About a Plan

Factoring to Solve Quadratic Equations

Sports You throw a softball into the air with an initial upward velocity of 38 ft/s and an initial height of 5 ft.

a. Use the vertical motion model to write an equation that gives the ball's height h (in feet) at time t (in seconds).

b. The ball's height is 0 ft when it is on the ground. Solve the equation you wrote in part (a) for $h = 0$ to find when the ball lands.

What do you know?

1. Write a vertical motion model that best describes the equation for the ball's height h at time t. What are the values of v and c?

   $h = -16t^2 + v \cdot t + c$

   $h = -16t^2 + \square \cdot t + \square$

2. How would graphing the quadratic equation help you understand the problem?

   ____

   ____

   ____

How do you solve the problem?

3. The ball's height is 0 ft when it is on the ground. Solve the equation you wrote in part (a) for $h = 0$ to find when the ball lands.

Name ______________________ Class ____________ Date ____________

9-4 Practice

Form K

Factoring to Solve Quadratic Equations

Use the Zero-Product Property to solve each equation.

1. $(n + 3)(n - 2) = 0$

2. $(4a + 2)(a - 6) = 0$

3. $(5y - 3)(2y + 1) = 0$

4. $(3k - 2)(6k + 8) = 0$

5. $x(x - 3) = 0$

6. $2v(3v + 4) = 0$

Solve by factoring.

7. $t^2 + 3t - 18 = 0$

8. $j^2 - 17j + 72 = 0$

9. $2c^2 + 9c + 4 = 0$

10. $8k^2 - 2k - 3 = 0$

11. $m^2 + 6m = -5$

12. $y^2 + 3y = 28$

13. $2z^2 + z = 6$

14. $15a^2 - a = 6$

Use the Zero-Product Property to solve each equation. Write your solution in roster form.

15. $x^2 - 10x + 24 = 0$

16. $d^2 + 3d - 10 = 0$

17. The volume of a storage tub shaped like a rectangular prism is 24 ft^3. The height of the tub is 3 feet. The width is w feet and the length is $w + 2$ feet. Use the formula $V = lwh$ to find the value of w.

18. The area of a parking lot is 2475 ft^2. The rectangular parking lot has dimensions such that the length is 10 feet longer than the width. What are the dimensions of the parking lot?

9-4 Practice (continued)

Form K

Factoring to Solve Quadratic Equations

Write each equation in standard form. Then solve.

19. $3x^2 - x - 7 = 2x^2 + 5$

20. $x^2 - 4x - 2 = -9x + 4$

Find the value of *x* as it relates to each rectangle or triangle.

21. Area = 15 m^2

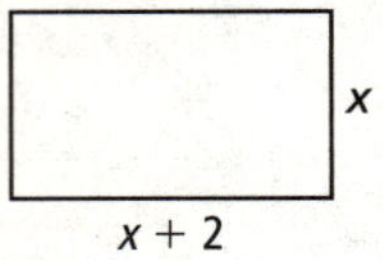

22. Area = 408 in^2

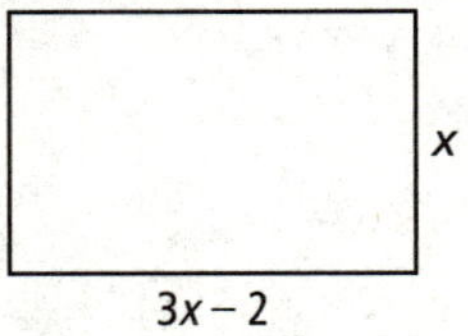

23. Area = 36 ft^2

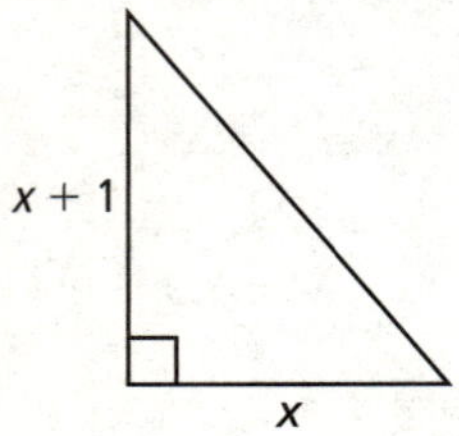

24. Area = 600 cm^2

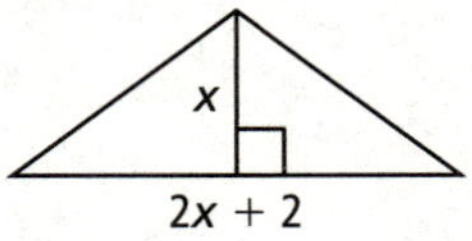

25. Reasoning For each equation, find k and the value of any missing solutions.

a. $x^2 - kx - 15 = 0$ where -3 is one solution of the equation.

b. $x^2 - 10x = k$ where 12 is one solution of the equation.

26. Writing Explain how you solve an equation by using the Zero-Product Property.

Name ______________________ Class ____________ Date ____________

9-4 Standardized Test Prep

Factoring to Solve Quadratic Equations

Gridded Response

Solve each exercise and enter your answer on the grid provided.

1. What is the positive solution of $3x^2 - 10x - 8 = 0$?

2. A triangular-shaped wall has a base of $2x + 4$ and a height of $x + 3$. The area of the triangle is 56 in.^{2}. What is the value of x?

3. The product of two consecutive integers, n and $n + 1$, is 42. What is the positive integer that satisfies the situation?

4. One more rectangular-shaped piece of metal siding needs to be cut to cover the exterior of a pole barn. The area of the piece is 30 ft^2. The length is 1 less than 3 times the width. How wide should the metal piece be? Round to the nearest hundredth of a foot.

5. What solution do $2x^2 - 31x + 21 = 0$ and $2x^2 + 9x - 56 = 0$ have in common? Round your answer to the nearest tenth if necessary.

1. 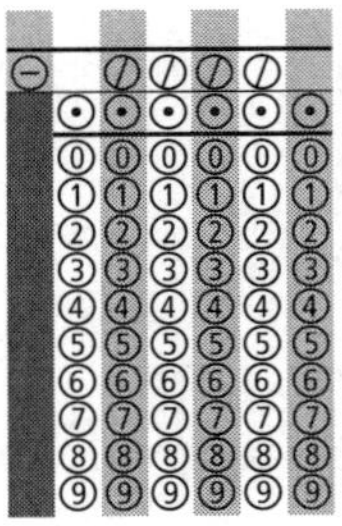

2. 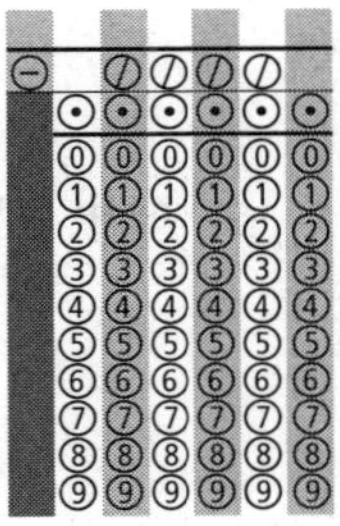

3. 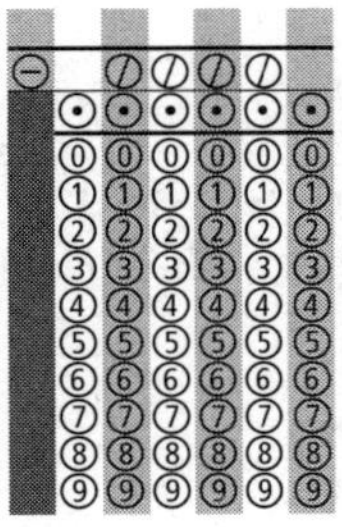

4. 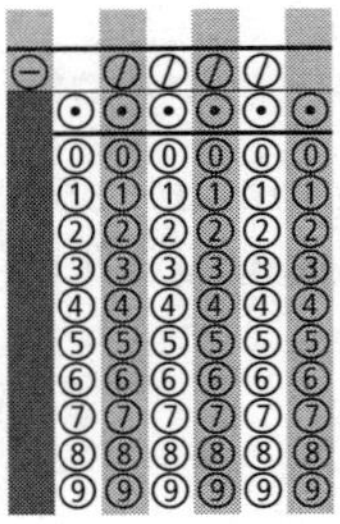

5. 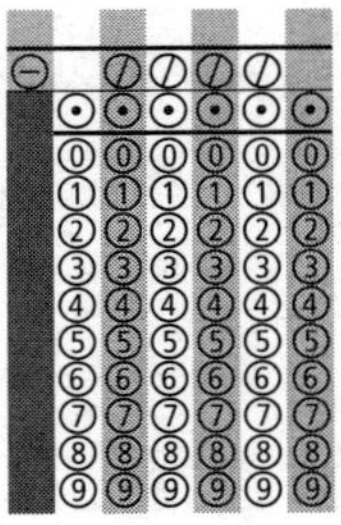

Name ______________________ Class ______________ Date ______________

9-5 Think About a Plan

Completing the Square

Landscaping A school is fencing in a rectangular area for a playground. It plans to enclose the playground using fencing on three sides, as shown at the right. The school has budgeted enough money for 75 ft of fencing material and would like to make a playground with an area of 600 ft^2.

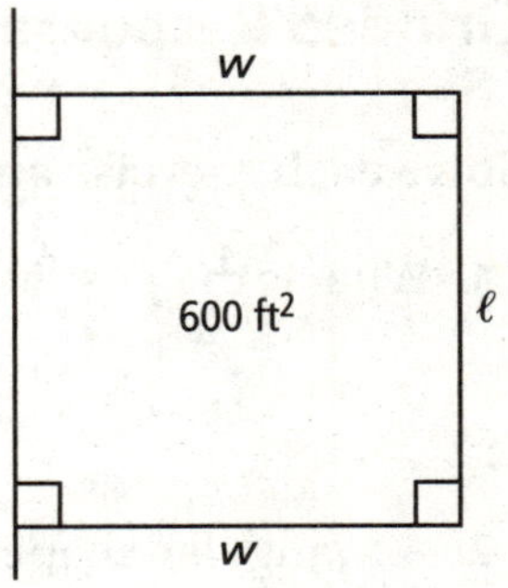

a. Let w represent the width of the playground. Write an expression in terms of w for the length of the playground.

b. Write and solve an equation to find the width w. Round to the nearest tenth of a foot.

c. What should the length of the playground be?

What do you know?

1. Let w represent the width of the playground. Write an expression in terms of w for the length of the playground.

   $w + w + l =$ [ ] feet

   $l =$

2. Write an equation for the area of the playground.

   $w \cdot l =$ [ ] ft^2

What do you need to solve the problem?

3. Substitute the expression for l from Step 1 in the equation from Step 2.

How do you solve the problem?

4. Solve the equation in Step 3 to find the width w. Round to the nearest tenth of a foot. What should the length l of the playground be?

Name ______________________ Class ____________ Date ____________

9-5 Practice

Form K

Completing the Square

Find the value of c such that each expression is a perfect-square trinomial.

1. $z^2 + 2z + c$

2. $h^2 + 14h + c$

3. $p^2 - 11p + c$

4. $n^2 + 26n + c$

Solve each equation by completing the square. If necessary, round to the nearest hundredth.

5. $t^2 - 17t = -52$

6. $m^2 + 6m = 7$

7. $f^2 + 3f = 88$

8. $z^2 + 9z = 36$

9. $a^2 + 13a = 12$

10. $g^2 + 5g + 4 = 0$

11. $d^2 + 7d + 9 = 0$

12. $b^2 - 5b - 10 = 0$

Solve each equation by completing the square. If necessary, round to the nearest hundredth.

13. $6n^2 + 9n = 12$

14. $2t^2 - 4t = 1$

15. $3v^2 + 9v + 5 = 0$

16. $4c^2 - 8c = 1$

9-5 Practice (continued) Form K

Completing the Square

17. The rectangle shown at the right has an area of 663 in^2. What is the value of x?

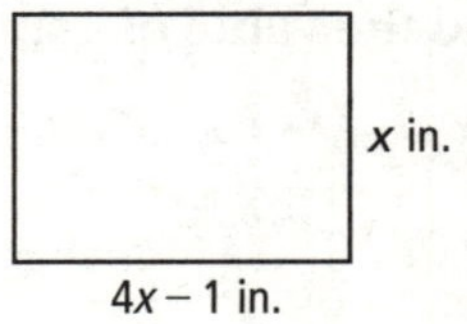

18. What are all of the values of b that will make $x^2 + bx + 64$ a perfect square?

19. What are all of the values of b that will make $x^2 + bx + 144$ a perfect square?

20. The product of two consecutive positive even integers is 168. What are the integers?

21. Writing Discuss how you could use graphing, factoring, and completing the square for solving the quadratic equation $x^2 + 3x - 2 = 0$.

22. The height of a triangle is $6x$ cm and the base is $(3x + 10)$ cm. The area of the triangle is 816 cm^2. What are the dimensions of the base and height of the triangle?

23. Writing Does completing the square always give a solution for a quadratic equation that cannot be factored? Explain.

24. Reasoning How do the solutions of the equation $x^2 - 6x + 9 = 16$ compare to the solutions of $x^2 - 6x + 9 = 25$? Explain how you can determine the relationship without solving both equations.

9-5 Standardized Test Prep

Completing the Square

Multiple Choice

For Exercises 1–6, choose the correct letter.

1. What is the value of n such that the expression $x^2 + 11x + n$ is a perfect square trinomial?

   A. 11 **B.** 25 **C.** 30.25 **D.** 36

2. What is a solution of $x^2 + 6x = -5$?

   F. $x = -6$ **G.** $x = -1$ **H.** $x = 1$ **I.** $x = 6$

3. Which of the following is a solution of $x^2 + 4x - 1 = 0$? If necessary, round to the nearest hundredth.

   A. $x = -0.24$ **B.** $x = -4.24$ **C.** $x = 4.24$ **D.** no solution

4. Which of the following is a solution of $x^2 + 14x + 112 = 0$? If necessary, round to the nearest hundredth.

   F. $x = -0.24$ **G.** $x = -4.24$ **H.** $x = 4.24$ **I.** no solution

5. The rectangular poster shown at the right has an area of 5400 cm^2. What is the value of w?

   A. −45 cm **C.** 60 cm

   B. 45 cm **D.** 90 cm

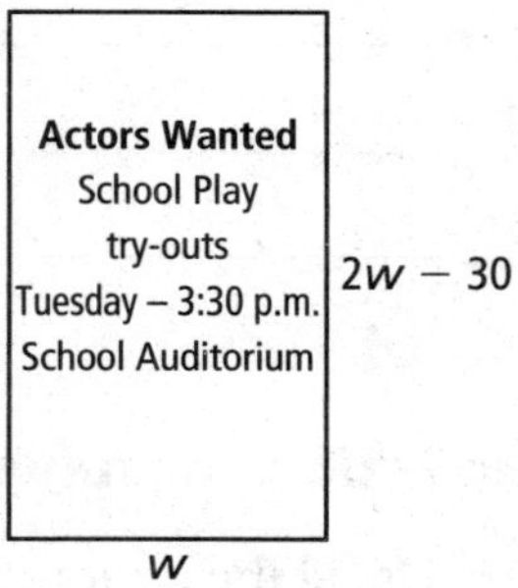

6. A box shaped like a rectangular prism has a height of 17 in. and a volume of 2720 $in.^3$. The length is 4 inches greater than twice the width. What is the width of the box?

   F. −10 in. **H.** 20 in.

   G. 8 in. **I.** 40 in.

Short Response

7. The area of a rectangular television screen is 3456 $in.^2$. The width of the screen is 24 inches longer than the length. What is a quadratic equation that represents the area of the screen? What are the dimensions of the screen?

Name ______________________ Class ____________ Date ____________

9-6 Think About a Plan

The Quadratic Formula and the Discriminant

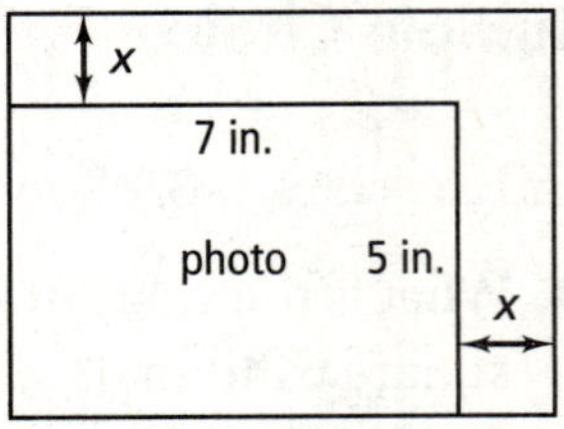

Sports Your school wants to take out an ad in the paper congratulating the basketball team on a successful season, as shown at the right. The area of the photo will be half the area of the entire ad. How wide will the border be?

What do you know?

1. What are the dimensions of the photo and the ad? Let w = the width of the photo and l = the length of the photo.

____

____

What do you need to solve the problem?

2. What quadratic equation can you write that best describes the relationship between the area of the photo and the area of the ad?

____

____

____

How do you solve the problem?

3. Using the quadratic formula, how will you be able to solve for x, the width of the border? What is the width of the border?

____

____

____

Name ______________________ Class ____________ Date ____________

9-6 Practice

Form K

The Quadratic Formula and the Discriminant

Use the quadratic formula to solve each equation.

1. $3z^2 + z - 4 = 0$

2. $2d^2 + 9d = 5$

3. $2y^2 + 12y + 10 = 0$

4. $2t^2 - 5t - 12 = 0$

5. $3c^2 - 13c + 4 = 0$

6. $15b^2 + 22b + 8 = 0$

Use the quadratic formula to solve each equation. Round answers to the nearest hundredth.

7. $y^2 - 4y - 4 = 0$

8. $3r^2 + 5r = 1$

9. $h^2 + 12h = -16$

10. $5v^2 + 3v = 1$

11. A football is passed through the air and caught at ground level for a touchdown. The height h of the ball in feet is given by $h = -d^2 + 12d + 6$, where d is the distance in feet the ball travels horizontally. How far from the player passing the ball will the ball be caught?

Which method(s) would you choose to solve each equation? Justify your reasoning.

12. $a^2 + 3a - 11 = 0$

13. $9d^2 - 100 = 0$

14. $6h^2 - 11h - 3 = 0$

15. $n^2 - n - 6 = 0$

9-6 Practice (continued)

Form K

The Quadratic Formula and the Discriminant

Find the number of real-number solutions of each equation.

16. $x^2 - 10x + 9 = 0$

17. $-5x^2 - 2x - 14 = 0$

18. $x^2 + 10x + 25 = 0$

19. $x^2 - 4x = 0$

Use the quadratic formula to solve each equation. If necessary, round answers to the nearest hundredth.

20. $4r^2 - 100 = 0$

21. $a^2 - 2a = 99$

22. $7g^2 - 2g - 10 = 0$

23. $15k^2 - 7k = 2$

Find the value of the discriminant and the number of real-number solutions of each equation.

24. $x^2 + 7x + 5 = 0$

25. $x^2 + 4x + 10 = 0$

26. $-3x^2 + 9x - 2 = 0$

27. $5x^2 + 11x + 8 = 0$

28. The daily production of a company is modeled by the function $p = -w^2 + 75w - 1200$. The daily production, p, is dependent on the number of workers, w, present. If the break-even point is when $p = 0$, what are the least and greatest number of workers the company must have present each day in order to break even?

29. Reasoning The equation $3x^2 + bx + 3 = 0$ has one real solution. What must be true about b?

Name ______________________ Class ____________ Date ____________

9-6 Standardized Test Prep

The Quadratic Formula and the Discriminant

Multiple Choice

For Exercises 1–6, choose the correct letter.

1. Which expression gives the solutions of $-5 + 2x^2 = -6x$?

A. $\dfrac{2 \pm \sqrt{4 - (4)(6)(-5)}}{12}$

B. $\dfrac{-5 \pm \sqrt{25 - (4)(2)(6)}}{-10}$

C. $\dfrac{-6 \pm \sqrt{36 - (4)(2)(-5)}}{4}$

D. $\dfrac{6 \pm \sqrt{36 - (4)(2)(5)}}{4}$

2. What are the approximate solutions of $2x^2 - x + 10 = 0$?

F. $-2, 2.5$ **G.** $-1.97, 2.47$ **H.** $-2.5, 2$ **I.** no solution

3. What are the approximate solutions of $7x^2 + 4x - 9 = 0$?

A. $-1.42, 0.85$

B. $-1.5, 0.88$

C. $-0.88, 1.5$

D. no solution

4. Which method is the best method for solving the equation $8x^2 - 13x + 3 = 0$?

F. square roots

G. factoring

H. graphing

I. quadratic formula

5. How many solutions are there for $5x^2 + 7x - 4 = 0$?

A. 0 **B.** 1 **C.** 2 **D.** 3

6. The perimeter of a rectangle is 54 cm. The area of the same rectangle is $176\ \text{cm}^2$. What are the dimensions of the rectangle?

F. 11 cm by 16 cm

G. 8 cm by 22 cm

H. 5.5 cm by 32 cm

I. 4 cm by 44 cm

Short Response

7. The flight of a baseball that has been hit when it was 4 feet off the ground is modeled by the function $h = -16t^2 + 75t + 4$ where h is the height of the baseball in feet after t seconds. Rounding to the nearest hundredth, how long will it take before the ball lands on the ground? Show your work.

Name ______________________ Class ____________ Date ____________

9-7 Think About a Plan

Linear, Quadratic, and Exponential Models

Zoology A conservation organization collected the data on the number of frogs in a local wetlands. Which kind of function best models the data? Write an equation to model the data.

Year	Number of Frogs
0	120
1	101
2	86
3	72
4	60

What do you know?

1. Let $x =$ year and $y =$ number of frogs. Graph the points in the table.

2. How will graphing the points in the table help you determine which function best models the data?

____

What do you need to solve the problem?

3. How will finding the differences or ratios between the data points help you determine which function best models the data?

____

____

How do you solve the problem?

4. Write an equation that best models the data.

Name ______________________________ Class ______________ Date ______________

9-7 Practice

Form K

Linear, Quadratic, and Exponential Models

Graph each set of points. Which model is most appropriate for each set?

1. (−3, −1), (−2, 0), (−1, 1), (0, 2), (1, 3)

2. (0, 3), (1, 1), (2, 0), (3, 1)

3. (−2, −0.25), (−1, −0.5), (0, −1), (1, −2)

4. (−4, 0), (−2, 2), (0, 3), (2, 2), (4, 0)

5. (−6, 6), (−4, 4), (−2, 2), (0, 0)

6. (−2, 0.25), (−1, 0.5), (0, 1), (1, 2)

Which type of function best models the data in each table? Use differences or ratios.

7.

x	*y*
0	0
1	−2
2	−8
3	−18
4	−32

8.

x	*y*
0	1
1	−3
2	−9
3	−27
4	−81

9. Which type of function best models the ordered pairs (−1, 1), (0, −2), (1, 1), and (2, 10)? Use differences or ratios.

10. Which type of function best models the ordered pairs (−1, 2.5), (0, 1), (1, −0.5), and (2, −2)? Use differences or ratios.

9-7 Practice (continued) — Form K

Linear, Quadratic, and Exponential Models

Which type of function best models the data in each table? Write an equation to model the data.

11.

x	y
0	−2
1	−4
2	−8
3	−16
4	−32

12.

x	y
0	−2
1	−5
2	−8
3	−11
4	−14

13.

x	y
0	1
1	1.5
2	3
3	5.5
4	9

14.

x	y
−2	12
−1	6
0	3
1	1.5
2	0.75

Which type of function best models the data in each ordered pair? Write an equation to model the data.

15. $(-1, 4), (0, 5), (1, 4), (2, 1), (3, -4)$

16. $(-2, -36), (-1, -12), (0, -4), (1, -\frac{4}{3}), (2, -\frac{4}{9})$

17. $(0, -6), (4, -5), (6, -4.5), (8, -4), (12, -3)$

18. $(-1, -6), (0, 1), (2, -3), (3, -10), (4, -21)$

Name ______________________ Class ____________ Date ____________

9-7 Standardized Test Prep

Linear, Quadratic, and Exponential Models

Multiple Choice

For Exercises 1–4, choose the correct letter.

1. Which kind of function best models the set of data points $(-1, 22)$, $(0, 6)$, $(1, -10)$, $(2, -26)$, $(3, -42)$?

A. linear **B.** quadratic **C.** exponential **D.** none of the above

2. Which kind of function best models the set of data points $(-3, 18)$, $(-2, 6)$, $(-1, 2)$, $(0, 11)$, $(1, 27)$?

F. linear **G.** quadratic **H.** exponential **I.** none of the above

3. What function can be used to model data pairs that have a common ratio?

A. linear **B.** quadratic **C.** exponential **D.** none of the above

4. The attendances at the high school basketball games seemed to be affected by the success of the team. The graph at the right models the attendance over the first half of the season. Which function would also represent the data shown in the graph where a represents the attendance and g represents the number of games the team has won?

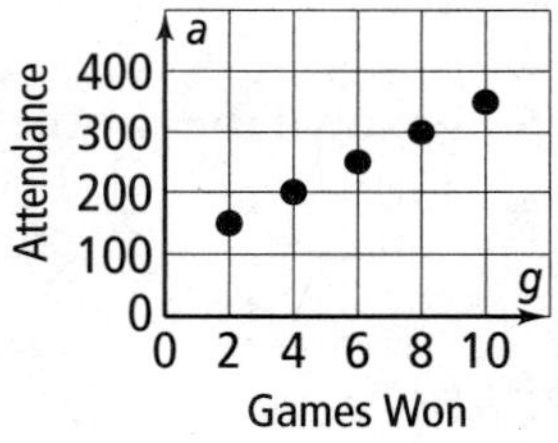

F. $a = 25(3)^g$

G. $a = 25g + 100$

H. $a = 25g^2 + 100$

I. $a = -25g^2 + 100$

Short Response

5v. The data in the table shows the population growth of a city since the year 2000. What kind of function models the data? How do you know?

Year	Population
0	5275
1	10,550
2	21,100
3	42,200
4	84,400

Name ______________________________ Class ____________ Date ____________

10-1 Think About a Plan

The Pythagorean Theorem

Construction A construction worker is cutting along the diagonal of a rectangular board 15 ft long and 8 ft wide. What will be the length of the cut?

KNOW

1. The board measures ☐ ft long by ☐ ft wide.

2. The board is in the shape of a ____________, which has 4 ____________ angles.

3. A diagonal cut divides the board into 2 equal ____________ triangles.

4. The Pythagorean Theorem states ______________________________.

NEED

5. To solve the problem I need to find ______________________________

______________________________.

PLAN

6. What drawing can you make to show what you are given and what you are trying to find?

7. What equation can you use to find the length of the cut?

8. Solve the equation.

9. Is the solution reasonable? Explain.

____

____

____

Name ______________________ Class ____________ Date ____________

10-1 Practice

Form K

The Pythagorean Theorem

Use the triangle at the right. Find the missing side length. If necessary, round to the nearest tenth.

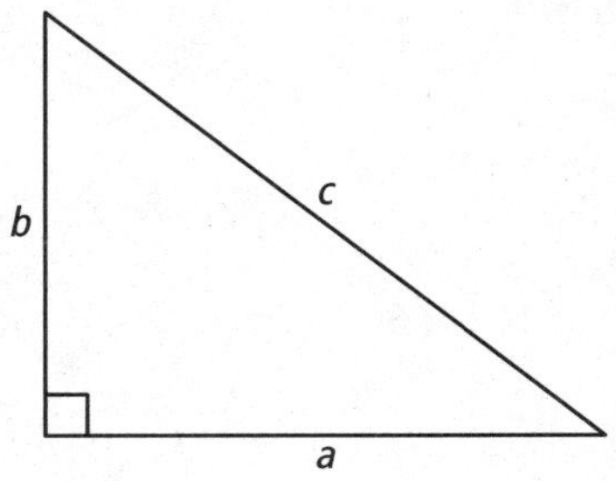

1. $a = 16, b = 12$

2. $a = 0.8, b = 0.6$

3. $a = 15, c = 20$

4. $b = 18, c = 30$

5. $a = 72, c = 98$

6. $b = 32, c = 44$

7. A hiker goes six miles east and then turns south. If the hiker finishes 7.2 miles from the starting point, how far south did the hiker go?

8. A teacher is cutting along the diagonal of a rectangular piece of construction paper for a bulletin board which is 11 inches long and 8.5 inches wide. What will be the length of the cut?

Determine whether the given lengths can be side lengths of a right triangle.

9. 15 m, 20 m, 25 m

10. 22 ft, 24 ft, 30 ft

11. 38 yd, 72 yd, 80 yd

12. 46.5 cm, 62 cm, 77.5 cm

13. A roofer is gathering information for purchasing supplies for the roof shown at the right. Using the dimensions shown, what is the length x of the roof from the top to the lower edge? If necessary, round to the nearest tenth.

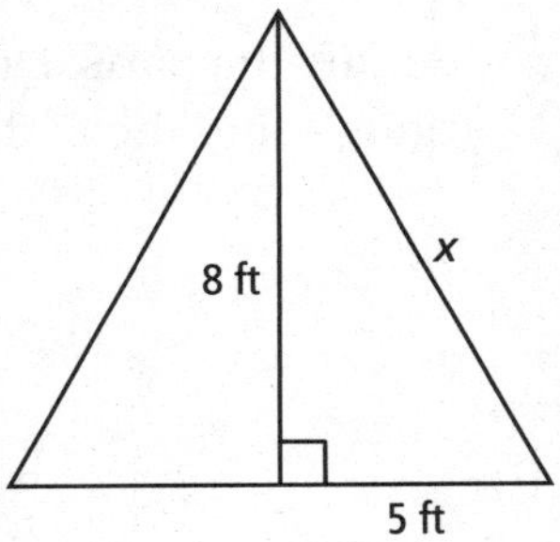

Name ________________ Class ________ Date ________

10-1 Practice (continued)

Form K

The Pythagorean Theorem

Any set of three positive integers that satisfies the equation $a^2 + b^2 = c^2$ is a *Pythagorean triple*. Determine whether each set of numbers is a Pythagorean triple.

14. 5, 9, 11

15. $\sqrt{3}, \sqrt{4}, \sqrt{5}$

16. 8, 10, 6

17. $\sqrt{5}, \sqrt{8}, \sqrt{13}$

Find each missing side length.

18.

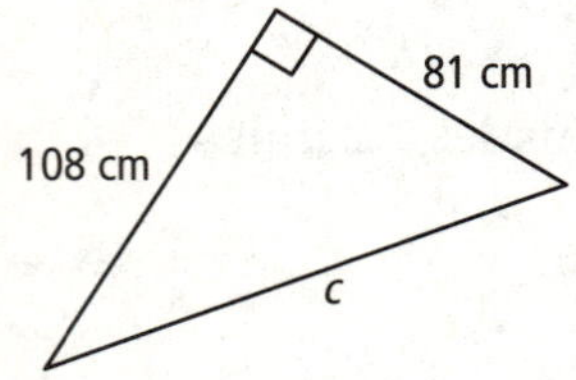

19.

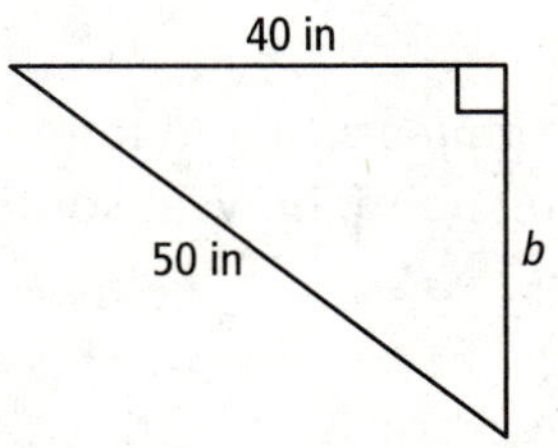

20. A rectangular box is 9 in. wide, 11 in. tall, and 20 in. long. What is the diameter of the smallest circular opening through which the box will fit? If necessary, round to the nearest tenth of a centimeter.

21. Find the height of a pyramid whose square base measures 30 yd on each side and whose slant height is 45 yd. If necessary, round to the nearest tenth of a yard.

22. Open-Ended Write the lengths of the sides of a right triangle with one leg whose length is 75 cm.

23. Writing State the various parts of a right triangle. Explain how you can identify the parts. Describe the relationship between each part of the right triangle and the Pythagorean Theorem.

Name ______________________ Class ____________ Date ____________

10-1 Standardized Test Prep

The Pythagorean Theorem

Multiple Choice

For Exercises 1–6, choose the correct letter.

1. What is the length of the missing side?

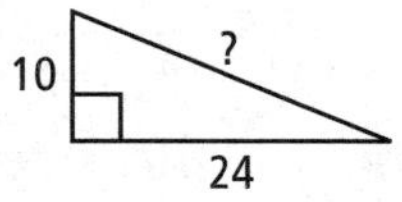

A. 21.8 **C.** 28
B. 26 **D.** 34

2. What is the length of the missing side?

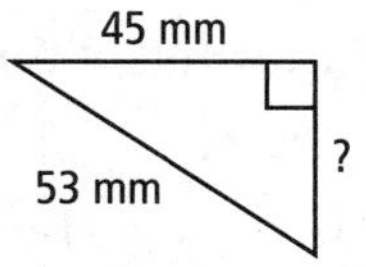

F. 16 mm **H.** 42 mm
G. 28 mm **I.** 69.5 mm

3. Which set of lengths could be the side lengths of a right triangle?

A. 20 cm, 22 cm, 29 cm **C.** 7 km, 24 km, 28 km
B. 10 ft, 12 ft, 15 ft **D.** 13 in., 84 in., 85 in.

4. A right triangle has a side length that measures 4 m and a hypotenuse that measures 8.5 m. What is the measure of the other side of the triangle?

F. 7.5 m **G.** 8.1 m **H.** 9.4 m **I.** 9.8 m

5. How long is the diagonal of a 12 ft-by-16 ft rectangular garden?

A. 6 ft **B.** 14 ft **C.** 18 ft **D.** 20 ft

6. You want to divide a square piece of paper into two equivalent triangles. If the square measures 20 cm on each side, what will the third side of each triangle measure?

F. 8.9 cm **G.** 20 cm **H.** 28.3 cm **I.** 40 cm

Short Response

7. Joe is cutting three risers for a set of stairs. Each riser is a right triangle with legs $7\frac{1}{2}$ in. and 10 in.

a. What equation could you use to find the length of the third side of a riser?

____

b. How long will the staircase measure when the 3 risers are installed?

Explain. ______________________________

____

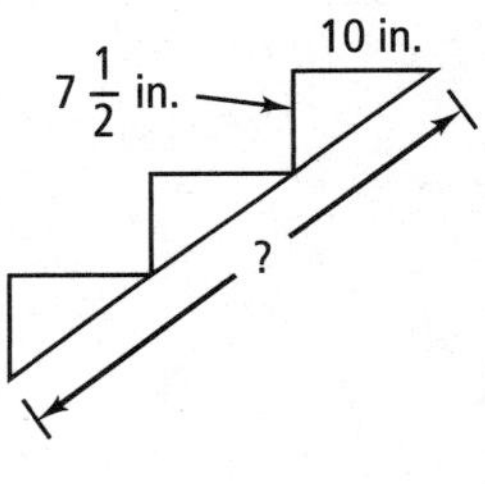

Name ______________________ Class __________ Date __________

10-2 Think About a Plan

Simplifying Radicals

Sports The bases in a softball diamond are located at the corners of a 3600 ft^2 square. How far is a throw from second base to home plate?

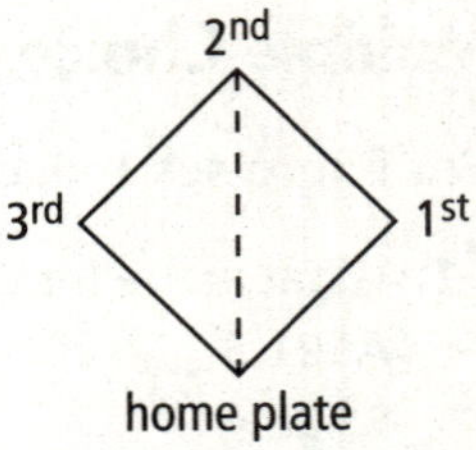

Understanding the Problem

1. What is the area of the softball diamond? ______________________

2. Where are second base and home plate located? ______________________

3. What is the problem asking you to determine? ______________________

____

Planning the Solution

4. What equation can be used to determine the side length of the softball diamond? ______________________

5. What equation can be used to determine the length of the throw from second base to home plate? ______________

6. How many steps will it take to solve this problem?

Getting an Answer

7. What is the first step in finding the solution? What is the solution of the first step? What is the second step in finding the solution? What is the solution?

Name ______________________ Class ____________ Date ____________

10-2 Practice

Form K

Simplifying Radicals

Simplify each radical expression.

1. $\sqrt{196}$

2. $\sqrt{28}$

3. $-\sqrt{275}$

4. $3\sqrt{12}$

5. $-5\sqrt{128}$

6. $9a\sqrt{243}$

7. $\sqrt{324x^2}$

8. $3\sqrt{27m^4n}$

9. $-2\sqrt{147a^2b^4}$

Simplify each product.

10. $\sqrt{12} \cdot \sqrt{20}$

11. $2\sqrt{18} \cdot \sqrt{75}$

12. $\frac{1}{2}\sqrt{72} \cdot 3\sqrt{48}$

13. $10\sqrt{20} \cdot (-9\sqrt{27})$

14. $\sqrt{24a} \cdot \sqrt{32b}$

15. $\sqrt{15x} \cdot \sqrt{20xy}$

16. $3\sqrt{50f^2g^3} \cdot \sqrt{63fg}$

17. $\sqrt{xy^7z^2} \cdot \sqrt{x^2yz^3}$

18. $4\sqrt{15hk^2} \cdot (-8\sqrt{5hk})$

19. A carpenter is building rectangular walls for a room addition. The width of a section of wall is two times the height h. Each section has a brace that connects two opposite corners of the section. What is a simplified expression for the length of a brace?

20. A walking path is shaped like a rectangle with a width 7 times its length l. What is a simplified expression for the distance between opposite corners of the walking path?

Name ______________________ Class ____________ Date ____________

10-2 Practice (continued)

Form K

Simplifying Radicals

Simplify each radical expression.

21. $\sqrt{\frac{36}{25}}$

22. $\frac{1}{\sqrt{7}}$

23. $-5\sqrt{\frac{121}{361}}$

24. $\frac{\sqrt{6}}{\sqrt{3y}}$

Explain why each radical expression is or is not in simplified form.

25. $\frac{\sqrt{12n}}{n}$

26. $\frac{5}{\sqrt{5}}$

27. $5\sqrt{2}$

28. $12\sqrt{24}$

Simplify each radical expression.

29. $\frac{\sqrt{s^3}}{\sqrt{t^3}}$

30. $\frac{\sqrt{120}}{\sqrt{6}}$

31. $\frac{-5\sqrt{3}}{\sqrt{12}}$

32. $\sqrt{\frac{5x}{49x^2}}$

33. Writing Describe when it is necessary to rationalize the denominator. Explain how you do this. Provide an example to demonstrate.

Name ______________________ Class ____________ Date ____________

10-2 Standardized Test Prep

Simplifying Radicals

Multiple Choice

For Exercises 1–5, choose the correct letter.

1. What is the simplified form of $\sqrt{140}$?

   A. $4\sqrt{35}$ B. $10\sqrt{14}$ C. $2\sqrt{70}$ D. $2\sqrt{35}$

2. What is the simplified form of $\sqrt{48n^9}$?

   F. $4n^3\sqrt{3}$ G. $4n^4\sqrt{3n}$ H. $3n\sqrt{4n^8}$ I. $4\sqrt{3n^9}$

3. What is the simplified form of $3\sqrt{5c} \cdot \sqrt{15c^3}$?

   A. $15c^2\sqrt{3}$ B. $6c^2\sqrt{5}$ C. $5c^2\sqrt{3}$ D. $12c^4\sqrt{5}$

4. Which radical expression is in simplified form?

   F. $\frac{11y}{\sqrt{3}}$ G. $\frac{\sqrt{6}}{5y}$ H. $\frac{\sqrt{17}}{\sqrt{4}}$ I. $\sqrt{\frac{25}{81}}$

5. A gardener is mowing a 20 yd-by-40 yd rectangular pasture using a diagonal pattern. He mows from one corner of the pasture to the corner diagonally opposite. What is the length of this pass with the mower? Give your answer in simplified form.

   A. $10\sqrt{20}$ B. $20\sqrt{2}$ C. $400\sqrt{5}$ D. $20\sqrt{5}$

Short Response

6. Suppose the height of the freight elevator in your building is half its width w when the doors are all the way open.

   a. What is an expression for the maximum side length of a sheet of metal that will fit through the elevator doors?

   ____

   b. If the height of the elevator is 3 meters, what is the maximum length that will fit through the doors?

   ____

Name ______________________ Class ____________ Date ____________

10-3 Think About a Plan

Operations with Radical Expressions

Chemistry The ratio of the diffusion rates of two gases is given by the formula $\frac{r_1}{r_2} = \frac{\sqrt{m_2}}{\sqrt{m_1}}$, where m_1 and m_2 are the masses of the molecules of the gases. Find $\frac{r_1}{r_2}$ if $m_1 = 12$ units and $m_2 = 30$ units. Write your answer in simplified radical form.

Understanding the Problem

1. How many gases are involved in the problem? ______________________

2. What variables represent the masses of the molecules of the two gases? ____________

3. What are the masses (in units) of the molecules of the two gases? ____________

Planning the Solution

4. What ratio can you simplify to find the ratio $\frac{r_1}{r_2}$? ______________________

5. What values can you substitute for m_1 and m_2? ______________________

6. How can you simplify the radical expression that results when you substitute values for m_1 and m_2? ______________________

Getting an Answer

7. Simplify the radical expression. What is the ratio of diffusion rates between the two gases?

____

8. Is diffusion faster or slower for the molecule with less mass? ____________

9. Is the solution reasonable? Explain. ______________________

____

Name ______________________ Class ____________ Date ____________

10-3 Practice

Form K

Operations with Radical Expressions

Simplify each sum or difference.

1. $11\sqrt{7} - 4\sqrt{7}$

2. $5\sqrt{5} + \sqrt{5}$

3. $9\sqrt{10} - 8\sqrt{10}$

4. $8\sqrt{2} - \sqrt{98}$

5. $\sqrt{245} + 2\sqrt{320}$

6. $2\sqrt{54} - 3\sqrt{96}$

Simplify each product.

7. $\sqrt{3}(\sqrt{5} + \sqrt{3})$

8. $-\sqrt{8}(2 - 3\sqrt{6})$

9. $2\sqrt{10}(\sqrt{5} - 4\sqrt{10})$

10. $(3\sqrt{3} - 2\sqrt{2})^2$

11. $(\sqrt{3} + \sqrt{6})(\sqrt{3} - \sqrt{6})$

12. $(2\sqrt{2} + \sqrt{5})(2\sqrt{2} - \sqrt{5})$

13. An area rug is shaped like a golden rectangle. Its length is 8 ft. What is the rug's width? Write your answer in simplified radical form and rounded to the nearest tenth of a foot.

14. A car fits onto a golden rectangle with a length of 12 ft. What is the car's width? Write your answer in simplified radical form and rounded to the nearest tenth of a foot.

Name ______________________ Class ____________ Date ____________

10-3 Practice (continued) *Form K*

Operations with Radical Expressions

Simplify each quotient.

15. $\frac{3}{\sqrt{5} - 1}$

16. $\frac{7}{\sqrt{2} - \sqrt{3}}$

17. $\frac{-1}{9 - \sqrt{3}}$

18. $\frac{-3}{\sqrt{2} + \sqrt{5}}$

Find the exact solution for each equation. Find the approximate solution to the nearest tenth.

19. $\frac{3\sqrt{3}}{\sqrt{1} + 1} = \frac{x}{\sqrt{3}}$

20. $\frac{5}{1 - \sqrt{2}} = \frac{1 + \sqrt{2}}{x}$

21. $\frac{4 - \sqrt{5}}{4 + \sqrt{5}} = \frac{x}{2}$

22. $\frac{x}{3 - \sqrt{2}} = \frac{2 + \sqrt{2}}{5}$

Simplify each expression.

23. $\sqrt{108} + \sqrt{147}$

24. $2\sqrt{3}(6 + 2\sqrt{6})$

25. $(\sqrt{2} + \sqrt{3})^2$

26. $5\sqrt{96} - 8\sqrt{150}$

27. Writing Are $\sqrt{2}$ and $\sqrt{32}$ like radicals? Can their sum be simplified? Explain.

Name ______________________ Class ____________ Date ____________

10-3 Standardized Test Prep

Operations with Radical Expressions

Multiple Choice

For Exercises 1–6, choose the correct letter.

1. What is the simplified form of $8\sqrt{5} + 5\sqrt{5}$?

   A. $3\sqrt{5}$ B. $13\sqrt{5}$ C. $40\sqrt{5}$ D. 200

2. What is the simplified form of $\sqrt{2} - 11\sqrt{2}$?

   F. $-10\sqrt{2}$ G. $-11\sqrt{2}$ H. $-12\sqrt{2}$ I. -22

3. What is the simplified form of $4\sqrt{3} - \sqrt{27}$?

   A. $-5\sqrt{3}$ B. $-7\sqrt{3}$ C. $\sqrt{3}$ D. $-\sqrt{9}$

4. What is the simplified form of $\sqrt{8}(\sqrt{5} + 4)$?

   F. $16\sqrt{10}$ G. $2\sqrt{10} + 4\sqrt{2}$ H. $4\sqrt{10} + 4\sqrt{2}$ I. $2\sqrt{10} + 8\sqrt{2}$

5. What is the simplified form of $\frac{40}{\sqrt{11} + \sqrt{7}}$?

   A. $10\sqrt{11} - 10\sqrt{7}$ B. $\frac{20\sqrt{11} - 20\sqrt{7}}{9}$ C. $30\sqrt{2}$ D. $10\sqrt{11} + 10\sqrt{7}$

6. A golden rectangle is 32 cm long. The ratio of length to width is $(1 + \sqrt{5}) : 2$. What is the width of the rectangle in simplest radical form?

   F. $16\sqrt{5} + 16$ G. $8\sqrt{5} - 8$ H. $16\sqrt{5} - 16$ I. $\frac{32\sqrt{5} - 32}{3}$

Short Response

7. The diagram to the right shows the design of the 12-in. quilt block that a quilter is sewing.

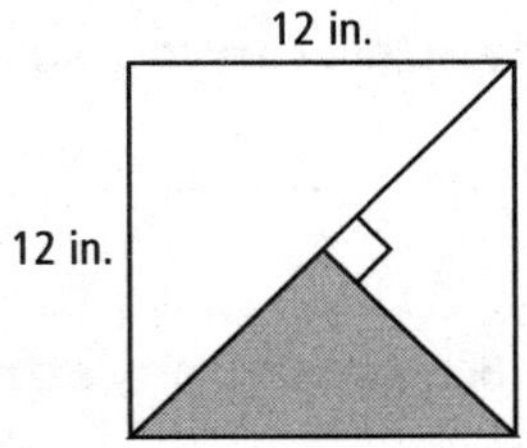

   a. What are the dimensions of each triangle in the quilt block? Give your answers as simplified radicals.

   ____

   b. What are the dimensions of each triangle to the nearest tenth of an inch?

   ____

Name ______________________ Class ____________ Date ____________

10-4 Think About a Plan

Solving Radical Equations

Packaging The radius r of a cylindrical can with volume V and height h is given by $r = \sqrt{\frac{V}{\pi h}}$. What is the height of a can with a radius of 2 in. and a volume of 75 in.^{3}?

KNOW

1. What equation can you use to find the height of a cylindrical can? ____________

2. What known values will you substitute into the equation? ____________

3. What is the meaning of the symbol π? ____________

NEED

4. Which variable represents the height of the can? ____________

PLAN

5. What equation do you get after substituting the known values? ____________

6. Can you solve this equation by squaring both sides? ____________

7. How can you isolate the remaining variable? ____________

____

8. Are there any extraneous solutions? If so, what are they? ____________

9. What is the height of the can? ____________

10. Is the solution reasonable? Explain. ____________

____

10-4 Practice
Form K

Solving Radical Equations

Solve each radical equation. Check your solution.

1. $\sqrt{y} + 6 = 12$

2. $\sqrt{4n} - 6 = 0$

3. $\sqrt{3k + 3} = 6$

4. $\sqrt{4p - 8} = 8$

5. $\sqrt{5t + 1} = 9$

6. $\sqrt{\frac{x^2}{8}} = 12$

7. $\sqrt{\frac{3m}{2}} = 3$

8. $\sqrt{\frac{a^2}{4}} = 8$

9. The motion of a pendulum can be modeled by $t = 2\sqrt{\frac{l}{3.3}}$, where t is the time in seconds for one complete swing and l is the length of the pendulum in feet. If the pendulum takes 2 seconds to complete one swing, how long is the pendulum? Round to the nearest hundredth of an foot.

10. The length r of the radius of a sphere is given by $r = \sqrt{\frac{SA}{4\pi}}$, where SA represents the sphere's surface area. If a sphere has a surface area of 276 cm^2, what is the length of its radius? Use $\pi = 3.14$. Round to the nearest hundredth of a centimeter.

11. The distance d in feet that it takes an automobile to stop if it is traveling S miles per hour is given by $S = 21d$. Find the distance it would take an automobile traveling 45 miles per hour to stop. Round your answer to the nearest tenth of a foot.

10-4 Practice (continued)

Form K

Solving Radical Equations

Solve each radical equation. Check your solution.

12. $\sqrt{5p + 1} = \sqrt{2p + 7}$

13. $\sqrt{n + 3} = \sqrt{11 - n}$

14. $\sqrt{t^2 + 3} = \sqrt{4t}$

15. $\sqrt{2b^2 + 6} = \sqrt{5b}$

16. $10 = \sqrt{8q + 36}$

17. $\frac{z}{2} = \sqrt{z - 5}$

Solve each radical equation. Check your solution. If there is no solution, write *no solution*.

18. $x = \sqrt{-x + 20}$

19. $g = \sqrt{g + 2}$

20. $h = \sqrt{-13h - 42}$

21. $w = \sqrt{7w + 18}$

22. Writing What is an extraneous solution? How do you determine if a solution is extraneous?

23. Open-Ended Write a radical equation that has two solutions. Solve the equation. Check both solutions. Show your work.

10-4 Standardized Test Prep

Solving Radical Equations

Multiple Choice

For Exercises 1–6, choose the correct letter.

1. What is the solution of the radical equation $\sqrt{t} + 9 = 16$?

   A. 5 B. 7 C. 25 D. 49

2. What is the solution of $\sqrt{6g - 23} = \sqrt{12 - g}$?

   F. 5 G. 7 H. 11 I. 35

3. What are the solutions of $\sqrt{d^2 - 11} = 5$?

   A. 4, −4 B. 5, −5 C. 5, 6 D. 6, −6

4. Which is the extraneous solution of $-x = \sqrt{2x + 15}$?

   F. −5 G. −3 H. 3 I. 5

5. The pendulum of a cuckoo clock completes one full swing every *t* seconds. The variable *t* is determined by the function $t = 2\sqrt{\frac{l}{3.3}}$ where *l* is the length in meters of the pendulum. Each swing takes 0.5 seconds. How many centimeters long is the pendulum?

   A. 20.625 cm B. 41.25 cm C. 82.5 cm D. 330 cm

6. A company invests $15,000 in an account that compounds interest annually. After two years, the account is worth $16,099.44. Use the function $A = P(1 + r)^2$, where *r* is the annual interest rate, *P* is the principal, and *A* is the amount of money after *t* years. What is the interest rate of the account?

   F. 1.04% G. 3.6% H. 5.4% I. 7.3%

Extended Response

7. The radius of Earth is about 6378 kilometers. The escape velocity V_e is determined by the function $V_e = \sqrt{2gR}$ where *g* is acceleration due to gravity in m/s^2 and *R* is the radius of Earth in meters. If *g* for Earth is 9.8 m/s^2, what is the escape velocity of Earth? Show your work.

Name ______________________ Class ____________ Date ____________

11-1 Think About a Plan

Simplifying Rational Expressions

a. Construction To keep heating costs down for a building, architects want the ratio of surface area to volume to be as small as possible. What is an expression for the ratio of surface area to volume for each shape?

i. square prism

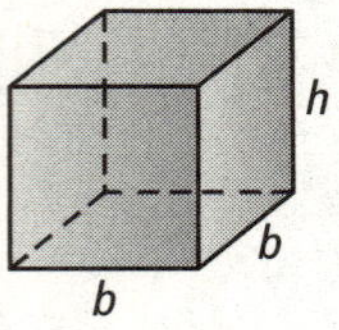

ii. cylinder

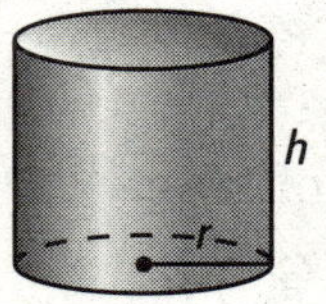

b. Find the ratio for each figure when $b = 12$ ft, $h = 18$ ft, and $r = 6$ ft.

Understanding the Problem

1. What is a ratio? ______________________

2. What are the other two forms of a ratio from 2 to 4? ______________________

3. What are the formulas for the surface area of a square prism and of a cylinder? What are the formulas for the volume of a square prism and of a cylinder?

____

____

Planning the Solution

4. What is the difference between surface area and volume? ______________________

5. What is the ratio of the surface area to the volume for the square prism?

6. What is the ratio of the surface area to the volume for the cylinder?

Getting an Answer

7. Use the ratio in Exercise 5 to find the ratio for the square prism with the given measurements.

____

8. Use the ratio in Step 6 to find the ratio for the cylinder with the given measurements. How does your answer compare to your answer for Exercise 7? ______________________

Name ______________________ Class ____________ Date ____________

11-1 Practice

Form K

Simplifying Rational Expressions

Simplify each expression. State any excluded values.

1. $\frac{3n - 15}{12}$

2. $\frac{12t^8}{36t^6}$

3. $\frac{y + 2}{y^2 - 4}$

4. $\frac{15a - 50}{10a + 35}$

5. $\frac{q^2 - 16}{7q^2 + 28q}$

6. $\frac{5x^2 + x - 6}{x^2 - 1}$

7. $\frac{m^3 + 9m}{6m^2 - 3m}$

8. $\frac{9z^2 - 36}{12z + 24}$

9. The length of a rectangle is $8n + 24$ and the width is $12n + 28$. What is the ratio of its length to its width? Simplify your answer.

10. The area of a rectangle is $x^2 + 6x - 16$. Its width is $x - 2$. What is a simplified expression for its length?

11. **Writing** Describe how you determine what values should be excluded when simplifying a rational expression. Explain why this must be done.

12. Are the given factors opposites? Explain.

 a. $5x - 2; 2 - 5x$

 b $-t + 10; t + 10$

 c. $102 + 11d; -102 - 11d$

11-1 Practice (continued) Form K

Simplifying Rational Expressions

13. A mother is packing away winter clothes into two rectangular tubs. Both hold the same volume of clothes. The first tub has a length of $2b + 5$, a width of $b - 3$, and a height of $4b$. The second tub has a width of $4b^2 + 20b$ and a length of $b - 3$. What is a simplified expression for the height of the second tub? Show your work.

Simplify each expression. State any excluded values.

14. $\dfrac{x^2 - 121}{3x^2 - 9x}$

15. $\dfrac{v^3w^3}{v^2w^3}$

16. $\dfrac{5x^2 - 41x + 42}{x^2 - 49}$

17. $\dfrac{2t^4 + t^3 - 28t^2}{t^2 + 4t}$

18. $\dfrac{9m^2 - 32m - 65}{m^2 - 25}$

19. $\dfrac{8a^2 - 12a - 36}{a^2 - 9}$

20. Writing Is $\dfrac{x^2 - 81}{x - 9}$ the same as $x + 9$? Explain.

21. Reasoning Is $y = 4$ an acceptable value for the expression $\dfrac{3y^2 - 10y - 8}{y^2 - 16}$? Explain.

Name ______________________ Class ____________ Date ____________

11-1 Standardized Test Prep

Simplifying Rational Expressions

Multiple Choice

For Exercises 1–4, choose the correct letter.

1. What is the simplified form of $\frac{x^4 - 81}{x + 3}$?

A. $x^3 - 3x^2 + 9x - 27$

B. $(x^2 + 9)(x^2 - 9)$

C. $x^3 + 3x^2 + 9x + 27$

D. $x^3 + 3x^2 - 9x - 27$

2. What is the simplified form of $\frac{(x^2yz)^2(xy^2z^2)}{(xyz)^2}$?

F. $\frac{(xyz)^2(xyz)}{x}$

G. $\frac{1}{(xyz)^2}$

H. $x^3y^2z^2$

I. x^4y^4z

3. What is the excluded value of the rational expression $\frac{2x + 6}{4x - 8}$?

A. -3

B. -2

C. 0

D. 2

4. What is the simplified form of $\frac{x^2 - 25}{x^2 - 3x - 10}$?

F. $\frac{x - 3}{x - 5}$

G. $\frac{(x - 5)(x + 5)}{(x + 5)(x - 3)}$

H. $\frac{x + 5}{x + 2}$

I. $\frac{x - 5}{x + 2}$

Short Response

5. When an object is free falling, the equation is $d = 16t^2$ where d is the distance in feet and t is the time in seconds. What happens to the distance d as t increases from 0 to 20? Draw the graph. Plot points for values of t between 0 and 20. ($d = 16t^2$ is a quadratic equation. You can substitute $y = 16x^2$ to graph the equation.)

Name ______________________ Class ____________ Date ____________

11-2 Think About a Plan

Multiplying and Dividing Rational Expressions

Auto Loans You want to purchase a car that costs $18,000. The car dealership offers two different 48-month financing plans. The first plan offers 0% interest for 4 yr. The second plan offers a $2000 discount, but you must finance the rest of the purchase price at an interest rate of 7.9% for 4 yr. For which financing plan will your total cost be less? How much less will it be?

Know

1. The car costs ____________.

2. There are 2 different ____________-month plans.

3. The purchase price for Plan 1 is ____________.

4. The interest rate for Plan 1 is ____________.

5. The purchase price for Plan 2 is ____________.

6. The interest rate for Plan 2 is ____________.

Need

7. To solve the problems for the two plans, you need the ________________.

Plan

8. Write the formula to be used by the 2 plans. ______________________________

9. Set up the 2 formulas, 1 for each plan. ______________________________

10. What is the total cost for Plan 1? What is the total cost for Plan 2?

11. For which financing plan will the total cost be less and how much less?

____

Name ______________________ Class ____________ Date ____________

11-2 Practice

Form K

Multiplying and Dividing Rational Expressions

Multiply.

1. $\frac{5n^2}{3n^2} \cdot \frac{3}{n}$

2. $\frac{t}{t-3} \cdot \frac{t+1}{t+2}$

3. $\frac{3a-9}{3a-6} \cdot \frac{a}{a^2-9}$

4. $\frac{18q-36}{2q} \cdot \frac{4q^2}{54q-18}$

5. $\frac{m^2-m-20}{m^2-4m} \cdot \frac{2m^2}{m^2-25}$

6. $\frac{8v}{6v^2+22v-8} \cdot \frac{3v-1}{4v^2}$

7. $\frac{z^2}{z^2+5z-6} \cdot \frac{2z^2-7z+5}{6z^2-15z}$

8. $(3x^2+7x+4) \cdot \frac{x^2-4x}{9x^2-16x}$

9. Which of the following is the reciprocal of $x^2 - 2x - 63$?

   a. $\frac{1}{(x+7)(x-9)}$

   b. $(x+7)(x-9)$

   c. $\frac{1}{x-9}$

Find the reciprocal of each expression.

10. $x^2 - 2x - 15$

11. $\frac{6p^2}{7p^2-12}$

Name ______________________ Class ____________ Date ____________

11-2 Practice (continued)

Form K

Multiplying and Dividing Rational Expressions

Divide.

12. $\frac{6f-6}{3f-8} \div \frac{6f-6}{f+9}$

13. $\frac{12m-20}{27m} \div \frac{3m-5}{9m}$

14. $\frac{18c-27}{9t^2-16} \div \frac{2c-3}{3t+4}$

15. $\frac{2x^2-23x+56}{10x+6} \div \frac{x-8}{5x+3}$

Simplify each complex fraction.

16. $\dfrac{\frac{1}{x-3}}{\frac{3}{x-3}}$

17. $\dfrac{\frac{m}{n}+2}{\frac{m}{n}+5}$

18. A shipping box has a base area of $4x^2 + 52x + 168$ and a height of $\frac{x}{4x+28}$. What is the volume of the box?

19. Karl drives for $(x^2 - 100)$ hours at a rate of $\frac{1}{5x-50}$ miles per hour. How far does Karl drive?

20. Open-Ended Write two rational expressions whose product is 1.

Name ______________________ Class ____________ Date ____________

11-2 Standardized Test Prep

Multiplying and Dividing Rational Expressions

Multiple Choice

For Exercises 1–3, choose the correct letter.

1. What is the quotient $\frac{x^2 - 16}{2x^2 - 9x + 4} \div \frac{2x^2 + 14x + 24}{4x + 4}$?

A. $\frac{1}{x + 3}$ B. $\frac{2x + 2}{x + 3}$ C. $\frac{2x + 2}{2x^2 + 5x - 3}$ D. $\frac{2(x + 1)}{2x^2 - 5x - 3}$

2. What is the simplified form for the product $\frac{x + 1}{x^2 - 25} \cdot \frac{x + 5}{x^2 + 8x + 7}$?

F. $\frac{x + 1}{(x + 5)(x + 7)}$ H. $\frac{1}{(x - 5)(x + 7)}$

G. $\frac{1}{(x + 5)(x + 7)}$ I. $\frac{1}{(x - 5)(x - 7)}$

3. What are the coordinates of the x-intercepts of the graph of $y = 2x^2 + 6x - 20$?

A. $(-5, 0), (2, 0)$ B. $(5, 0), (-2, 0)$ C. $(-4, 0), (10, 0)$ D. $(4, 0) (-10, 0)$

Short Response

4. A football is kicked with an upward velocity of $25\frac{\text{ft}}{\text{s}}$ from a starting height of 0.5 ft. How long does the ball stay in the air if no one catches it? Use the formula $h = -16^2 + vt + c$, where h is the ball's height at time t, v is the initial upward velocity, and c is the starting height. What is the height when the time is 1 second? How does the height change as the time increases? What happens at 5 seconds?

Name ______________________ Class ____________ Date ____________

11-3 Think About a Plan

Dividing Polynomials

Geometry The volume of the rectangular prism shown at the right is $m^3 + 8m^2 + 19m + 12$. What is the area of the base of the prism?

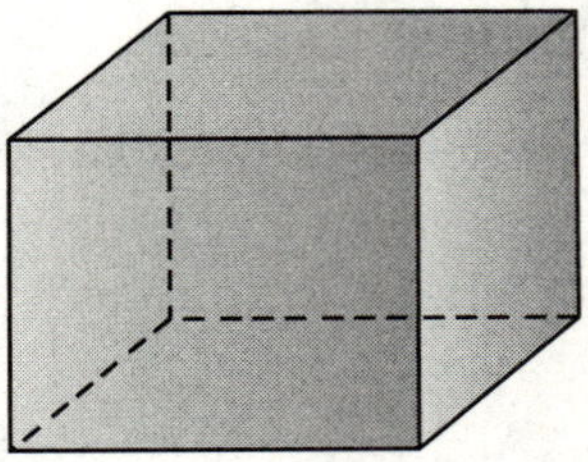

Understanding the Problem

1. What is a rectangular prism?

____

2. What is the literal formula for the volume of a rectangular prism?

____

3. What is the formula for the volume of the rectangular prism shown?

____

Planning the Solution

4. Using the given information from Step 3, what is the area of the base of the rectangle equal to?

____

Getting an Answer

5. Divide $(m^3 + 8m^2 + 19m + 12)$ by $(m + 3)$ to find the area of the base of the prism.

____

6. What does $m^2 + 5m + 4$ equal?

____

Name ______________________ Class ____________ Date ____________

11-3 Practice

Form K

Dividing Polynomials

Divide.

1. $(y^2 - 2y) \div y$

2. $(a^4 + 7a^3 - 3a^2) \div a^2$

3. $(5g^5 - 15g^3) \div 5g^3$

4. $(6t^2 + 8t + 10) \div 2t$

5. $(2q^5 - 12q^3 + 9q^2) \div 6q^2$

6. $(9k^4 - 12k^3) \div 2k^3$

7. $(-18w^4 + 48w^3 - 24w^2) \div 6w^2$

8. $(-4n^6 - 52n^4 + 36n^2) \div (-4n^3)$

9. $(n^2 + 9n + 20) \div (n + 4)$

10. $(y^2 + 6y + 5) \div (y + 5)$

11. $(h^2 - 5h - 14) \div (h + 2)$

12. $(3d^2 - 12d - 96) \div (d - 8)$

13. $(2m^2 - 5m - 3) \div (2m + 1)$

14. $(6r^2 + 43r - 40) \div (6r - 5)$

15. $(5c^2 - 125) \div (c + 5)$

16. $(k^2 - 36) \div (k - 6)$

17. Find the height of a trapezoid if the area of the trapezoid is $4x^3 - 2x^2$, the length of one base is $3x + 1$, and the length of the other base is $x - 3$. (*Hint*: The height of a trapezoid equals $\frac{2 \cdot \text{Area}}{\text{Base}_1 + \text{Base}_2}$.)

11-3 Practice (continued)

Form K

Dividing Polynomials

Divide.

18. $(9x^2 + 59x - 28) \div (9x - 4)$

19. $(11v^2 + 21v - 2) \div (v + 2)$

20. $(2p^2 + 3p - 44) \div (p - 4)$

21. $(10j^2 + 93j - 70) \div (10j - 7)$

22. $(6a^2 + 7a - 3) \div (3a - 1)$

23. $(10h^2 - 15h + 5) \div (2h - 1)$

24. The area of a rectangle is $x^2 - 2x - 15$ and the length of the rectangle is to $x + 3$.

a. Find the width of the rectangle.

b. Find the area of the rectangle if the width is 6 ft.

25. Reasoning If $x - 2$ is a factor of $x^2 + 3x + k$, what is the value of k?

26. Open-Ended Write a monomial and a trinomial such that the monomial is a factor of the trinomial. Explain how you know that the monomial is a factor of the trinomial.

Name ______________________ Class ____________ Date ____________

11-3 Standardized Test Prep

Dividing Polynomials

Multiple Choice

For Exercises 1–4, choose the correct letter.

1. What is the remainder of $(x^3 - 6x^2 - 9x + 3) \div (x - 3)$?

   A. -51 B. $\frac{-51}{x - 3}$ C. $\frac{-17}{x}$ D. $\frac{-17}{x - 3}$

2. If the area of a rectangle is $x^2 - 9$, can the length be $x - 1$?

   F. Yes; it divides perfectly.
   G. No; the length would be larger.
   H. Yes; but the width will have a remainder.
   I. No; the measurements of the rectangle must multiply and divide evenly.

3. If a line passes through the points (2, 0) and (−2, −3), what is the y-intercept of the line?

   A. $\frac{-3}{2}$ B. $\frac{3}{2}$ C. $\frac{3}{4}$ D. $\frac{-3}{4}$

4. What coordinates satisfy the equation of the line $y = -\frac{7}{8}x + 2$?

   F. $(-8, 11)$ G. $\left(-4, \frac{11}{2}\right)$ H. both F and G I. $\left(4, \frac{11}{2}\right)$

Short Response

5. What are the factors of the expression $x^2 + 12x - 64$? What numbers would you change to make it a perfect square? Explain.

Name ______________________ Class ____________ Date ____________

11-4 Think About a Plan

Adding and Subtracting Rational Expressions

Rowing A rowing team practices rowing 2 mi upstream and 2 mi downstream. The team can row downstream 25% faster than they can row upstream.

a. Let *u* represent the team's rate rowing upstream. Write and simplify an expression involving *u* for the total amount of time they spend rowing.

b. Let *d* represent the team's rate rowing downstream. Write and simplify an expression involving *d* for the total amount of time they spend rowing.

c. Reasoning Do the expressions you wrote in parts (a) and (b) represent the same time? Explain.

Know

1. What is the distance the team rows upstream? ____________________

2. What is the distance the team rows downstream? ____________________

3. How much faster does the team row downstream? ____________________

Need

4. What is the formula for time written in terms of the distance *d* and the rate *r*? ____________________

5. Write expressions for the time rowing upstream and the time rowing downstream by substituting values for the distance and variables for the rate in the formula in Exercise 4.

a. Time rowing upstream = ____________________

b. Time rowing downstream = ____________________

Plan

6. Write an equation that relates to *u* and *d*.

____

7. Rewrite the expressions you wrote in Exercise 6 in terms of *u*.

a. ____________________

b. ____________________

8. Do the expressions you wrote in Exercise 7 represent the same time? Why or why not?

____

____

Name ______________________ Class ____________ Date ____________

11-4 Practice

Form K

Adding and Subtracting Rational Expressions

Add or subtract.

1. $\frac{2}{n} + \frac{2}{n}$

2. $\frac{8}{7p} + \frac{19}{7p}$

3. $\frac{x-3}{x} - \frac{x+3}{x}$

4. $\frac{1}{2-b} + \frac{b}{b-2}$

5. $\frac{4}{d} - \frac{2d}{2}$

6. $\frac{2k}{7} - \frac{7}{5k}$

Find the LCD of each pair of expressions.

7. $\frac{1}{5}, \frac{2}{g}$

8. $\frac{2}{3m^2n}, \frac{7}{mn^2}$

9. $\frac{6}{x-3}, \frac{1}{x+4}$

10. $\frac{2y}{y^2+1}, \frac{y^2}{3}$

11. **Writing** Explain how you can find the LCD when the denominators are different.

12. What do you need to do to the numerators when using the LCD to add or subtract the rational expressions? Explain.

Name ______________________________ Class ____________ Date ____________

11-4 Practice (continued)

Form K

Adding and Subtracting Rational Expressions

Add or subtract.

13. $\frac{2}{m} + \frac{5}{n}$

14. $\frac{3}{t + 3} + 5$

15. $1 + \frac{x}{y}$

16. $\frac{a}{b} + \frac{2}{c(b - 2)}$

17. $\frac{2.2}{2n} - \frac{8.8}{3n}$

18. $\frac{\frac{3 + 2}{w}}{10 - 7}$

19. What is the perimeter of a rectangular area rug that is $\frac{3 + p}{3}$ ft long and $\frac{4p - 6}{5}$ ft wide?

20. Jennifer rode her bike to the store at a rate of 15 mi/h. She rode back home at a rate of 10 mi/h. How far is it to the store if the round trip takes 1 hour?

21. Writing Why would you change a rational expression with a denominator of $x^2 - 6x + 8$ to $(x - 2)(x - 4)$ when adding or subtracting rational expressions?

22. Open-Ended Write a problem that uses addition of rational expressions in which you need to find an LCD. Simplify the expression.

Name ____________ Class ________ Date ________

11-4 Standardized Test Prep

Adding and Subtracting Rational Expressions

Multiple Choice

For Exercises 1–5, choose the correct letter.

1. What is the difference $\frac{5x - 2}{4x} - \frac{x - 2}{4x}$?

   A. 1 B. $\frac{x - 1}{x}$ C. 0 D. $\frac{3}{2}$

2. What is the sum $\frac{1}{2b} + \frac{b}{2}$?

   F. $\frac{b + 1}{2b + 2}$ G. 2b H. $\frac{1}{4}$ I. $\frac{b^2 + 1}{2b}$

3. What is the sum $\frac{1}{g + 2} + \frac{3}{g + 1}$?

   A. $\frac{3}{g + 3}$ B. $\frac{g + 3}{(g + 1)(g + 2)}$ C. $\frac{4g + 7}{(g + 1)(g + 2)}$ D. $\frac{2g + 3}{(g + 1)(g + 2)}$

4. What is the difference $\frac{r + 2}{r + 4} - \frac{3}{r + 1}$?

   F. $\frac{-1}{r + 3}$ G. $\frac{r^2 - 1}{(r + 1)(r + 4)}$ H. $\frac{r^2 - 10}{(r + 1)(r + 4)}$ I. $\frac{r^2 + 14}{(r + 1)(r + 4)}$

5. What is the sum $\frac{a - 1}{abc^3} + \frac{3 - b}{abc^3}$?

   A. $\frac{a - b - 3}{abc^3}$ B. $\frac{a - b + 2}{abc^3}$ C. $\frac{a - 4 + b}{abc^3}$ D. $\frac{-3}{c^3}$

Short Response

6. Elena went on a 6-mile walk. She completed the first half of the walk 1 mi/h faster than usual and the second half of the walk 2 mi/h slower than the first half.
   a. If it took her 7.2h to complete the walk, what is her usual rate?
   b. What is the formula necessary to solve this problem?

Name ______________________ Class __________ Date __________

11-5 Think About a Plan

Solving Rational Equations

Running You take 94 min to complete a 10-mi race. Your average speed during the first half of the race is 2 mi/h greater than your average speed during the second half of the race. What is your average speed during the first half of the race?

Understanding the Problem

1. What is the distance of the first half of the race? ______________________

2. What is the distance of the second half of the race? ______________________

3. What is the total time it takes to complete the race? ______________________

Planning the Solution

4. Rewrite the distance formula $d = rt$ for time t in terms of distance d and rate r. ______________________

5. Use your answer to Exercise 4 to write an expression for the time it takes to run each part of the race.

   a. Time for first half of race = ______________

   b. Time for second half of race = ______________

6. Compare the units of the given time it takes to complete the race with the units of the description of the average speed. Write the time so that it matches the units in the rates.

   ____

Getting an Answer

7. Write an equation for the total time it takes to complete the race. Solve the equation.What is the rate for the first half of the race?

   ____

Name ______________________ Class ____________ Date ____________

11-5 Practice

Form K

Solving Rational Equations

Solve each equation. Check your solutions. If there is no solution, write *no solution.*

1. $\frac{3}{3+a} + 5 = \frac{8}{3+a}$

2. $\frac{6}{x-4} - 2 = \frac{8}{x-4}$

3. $\frac{7}{h-5} + \frac{1}{2} = \frac{6}{h-5}$

4. $\frac{9}{f+9} + 4 = \frac{f}{f+9}$

5. $\frac{8}{x+1} - 10 = \frac{4}{x} - 10$

6. $\frac{x}{x-1} + \frac{2}{x+1} = 1$

7. $\frac{5}{z-2} = \frac{3}{2+z}$

8. $\frac{t}{t+1} = \frac{4}{t+1}$

9. It takes Frank about 45 minutes to mow a yard and Paul about 38 minutes to mow a yard. How much time does it take them to mow a yard together?

10. Sam can wash 8 cars in 1 hour. Shelly can wash 6 cars in 1 hour. How much time does it take them to wash 70 cars if they work together?

Solve each equation. Check your solutions. If there is no solution, write *no solution.*

11. $\frac{1}{v} = \frac{2}{v^2} + \frac{1}{9}$

12. $\frac{1}{n-1} + \frac{n}{n+3} = \frac{4}{n^2 + 2n - 3}$

13. $1 + \frac{4}{3k+12} = \frac{2k}{k+4}$

14. $\frac{2x}{3x^2 - 4x - 4} + \frac{3+x}{2x-4} = \frac{-x}{3x+2}$

11-5 Practice (continued) — Form K

Solving Rational Equations

15. It takes Jeremy 4 hours to clean an auditorium, Cheryl 5 hours, and Gerald 8 hours. If all three of them work together, how long will it take them to clean the auditorium?

16. Shannon and Bruce are library workers. It takes Shannon 75 minutes to shelve a cart of books. It takes Bruce $3x$ min to shelve a cart of books. If they work on shelving a cart of books together, it will take them 30 min to complete it.

a. Write an equation for this problem.

b. Solve for x.

c. How long does it take Bruce to shelve a cart of books?

17. Error Analysis A student solved the rational equation $\frac{9x}{x(x+3)} - \frac{12x}{6x} = 6\left(\frac{1}{2}\right)$ and found $x = 1.2$. What was her mistake?

18. Open-Ended Write a rational equation that has $x = 2$ as a solution.

Solve each equation. Check your solutions.

19. $\frac{2}{t-1} = \frac{3}{t+1}$

20. $\frac{1}{x^2 - 25} - \frac{3}{x+5} = \frac{5}{x-5}$

Name ____________________ Class __________ Date __________

11-5 Standardized Test Prep

Solving Rational Equations

Multiple Choice

For Exercises 1–4, choose the correct letter.

1. What is the excluded value of the equation $y = \frac{2}{x-1} + 1$?

   A. -1 B. 0 C. 1 D. 2

2. A bus trip along the coast takes one route going, for a total of 1024 miles, and another route returning, for a total of 896 miles. If the bus travels at a constant speed of 65 mi/h, how far did the bus travel per second on the return trip?

   F. 0.07 mi/s G. 13.8 mi/s H. 896 mi/s I. 0.0181 mi/s

3. What is the LCD for the equation $\frac{6-x}{2x^2y} - \frac{2x}{3xy^2} = \frac{x}{x^2y^2}$?

   A. $6x^2y^2$ B. x^2y^2 C. $12x^2y^2$ D. $6xy$

4. What is the excluded value of the rational expression? Include all possible solutions.

$$y = \frac{1}{x^2 + 2x - 24}$$

   F. 0, 24 G. 6, -4 H. 4, 6 I. 4, -6

Short Response

5. Every morning Diane runs 6 miles in about an hour. What is her rate in feet per second? What equations would you use to solve? Explain and show your work.

Name ________________________ Class ____________ Date ____________

12-1 Think About a Plan

Organizing Data Using Matrices

Politics The results of an election for mayor are shown below. The town will hold a runoff election between the top two candidates if no one receives more than 50% of the votes. Should the town hold a runoff? If so, which candidates should be in the runoff? Explain your reasoning.

Votes by Precinct

	Precinct			
Candidate	**1**	**2**	**3**	**4**
Greene	373	285	479	415
Jackson	941	871	114	97
Voigt	146	183	728	682

Understanding the Problem

1. What does each column in the table represent?

2. What does each row in the table represent?

Planning the Solution

3. How will you find how many total votes each candidate received?

4. How will you find how many total votes were cast?

5. How will you find the percentage of votes for each candidate?

Getting an Answer

6. How many votes did each candidate receive?

7. What percent of the votes did each candidate receive?

8. Did any candidate receive more than 50% of the total votes?

9. Who are the top two candidates?

10. Should the town hold a runoff between the top two candidates?

Name ______________________ Class ____________ Date ____________

12-1 Practice

Form K

Organizing Data Using Matrices

Find each sum or difference.

1. $\begin{bmatrix} 4 & 7 \\ -1 & -2 \end{bmatrix} + \begin{bmatrix} -4 & 1 \\ -2 & 3 \end{bmatrix}$

2. $\begin{bmatrix} -9 & -3 \\ 4 & 6 \end{bmatrix} + \begin{bmatrix} -4 & 2 \\ -1 & 3 \end{bmatrix}$

3. $\begin{bmatrix} 5 & 7 \\ -3 & 3 \\ -4 & 0 \end{bmatrix} - \begin{bmatrix} -8 & 1 \\ 2 & 2 \\ 0 & -5 \end{bmatrix}$

4. $\begin{bmatrix} -2 & -1 \\ 0 & 2 \\ -6 & 4 \end{bmatrix} - \begin{bmatrix} 2 & -1.1 \\ -1 & -2 \\ -7 & 2.5 \end{bmatrix}$

5. $\begin{bmatrix} 4 & -2 & 3 \\ -1 & 2.2 & -0.1 \\ 1.5 & 6 & -1.8 \end{bmatrix} + \begin{bmatrix} 3.1 & 2 & 1.5 \\ 2.5 & 4 & -3 \\ 1 & -5 & 2 \end{bmatrix}$

6. $\begin{bmatrix} 2 & 8 & -3 \\ -1 & 3.6 & 5 \\ 0.5 & 4.2 & 1.8 \end{bmatrix} - \begin{bmatrix} 2.2 & 3.5 & -1.1 \\ -2.7 & 1.2 & 3 \\ 1 & -2 & 1 \end{bmatrix}$

Find each product.

7. $5\begin{bmatrix} 4 & -3 \\ 0 & 1 \end{bmatrix}$

8. $-2\begin{bmatrix} -2 & 1 \\ 4 & -3 \end{bmatrix}$

9. $6\begin{bmatrix} 3 & -5 \\ 1 & -9 \end{bmatrix}$

10. $-1\begin{bmatrix} -8 & 0 \\ 10 & -4 \end{bmatrix}$

11. $0\begin{bmatrix} 0 & -8 \\ 5 & 12 \end{bmatrix}$

12. $-4\begin{bmatrix} 1 & 5 \\ -1 & -4 \end{bmatrix}$

13. $0.5\begin{bmatrix} -6 & 4.2 \\ 12 & 1 \\ -3 & 0 \end{bmatrix}$

14. $-1.1\begin{bmatrix} -2 & 0 \\ -1 & -1.1 \\ 4 & 8 \end{bmatrix}$

12-1 Practice (continued)

Form K

Organizing Data Using Matrices

15. The number of books each girl read during the months of June and July during two different summers is shown below. Which girl showed the greatest improvement, in number of books read in July, from 2009 to 2010? Find the answer using matrices.

Books Read During 2009

	June	July
Anne	7	5
Soraya	4	6
Tiffany	10	9
Willow	13	13

Books Read During 2010

	June	July
Anne	8	12
Soraya	4	7
Tiffany	11	8
Willow	9	15

16. Pre-test and test scores for four algebra students on two different tests are shown below. Which student showed the greatest improvement from the pre-test to the test on the second test? Find the answer using matrices.

Pre–Test

	Test 1	Test 2
Jeremiah	87	85
Shasta	75	81
Jerud	85	83
Zack	71	78

Test

	Test 1	Test 2
Jeremiah	91	89
Shasta	81	82
Jerud	92	81
Zack	67	87

Simplify each expression. (*Hint*: Multiply before adding or subtracting.)

17. $\begin{bmatrix} 3 & -1 \\ 3 & 1 \end{bmatrix} + 2\begin{bmatrix} 1 & 4 \\ 0 & -1 \end{bmatrix}$

18. $-1\begin{bmatrix} 3 & -4 \\ 2 & -1 \end{bmatrix} - \begin{bmatrix} 2 & 0 \\ -2 & -3 \end{bmatrix}$

19. $\begin{bmatrix} -2 & -8 \\ 5 & 0 \end{bmatrix} - 3\begin{bmatrix} -1 & 5 \\ -2 & 0 \end{bmatrix}$

20. $-6\begin{bmatrix} 2 & -2 \\ 0 & -0.5 \end{bmatrix} - \begin{bmatrix} 5 & -9 \\ -3 & 2 \end{bmatrix}$

21. $5\begin{bmatrix} -1 & -2 \\ 1 & 1 \\ -3 & 3 \end{bmatrix} - 2\begin{bmatrix} -2 & 4 \\ 0 & -1 \\ 1 & -3 \end{bmatrix}$

22. $-3\begin{bmatrix} 8 & -4 \\ -1 & 0 \\ 0 & 2 \end{bmatrix} + 2\begin{bmatrix} 0 & -3 \\ 2 & -5 \\ 3 & -1 \end{bmatrix}$

Name ____________________ Class __________ Date __________

12-1 Standardized Test Prep

Organizing Data Using Matrices

Multiple Choice

For Exercises 1–5, choose the correct letter.

1. What is the sum of $\begin{bmatrix} 3 & -2 \\ 4 & -3 \end{bmatrix} + \begin{bmatrix} -5 & -4 \\ 3 & -2 \end{bmatrix}$?

   A. $\begin{bmatrix} -8 & 2 \\ 1 & 6 \end{bmatrix}$ B. $\begin{bmatrix} -2 & 2 \\ 7 & -1 \end{bmatrix}$ C. $\begin{bmatrix} 2 & 6 \\ -7 & 5 \end{bmatrix}$ D. $\begin{bmatrix} -2 & -6 \\ 7 & -5 \end{bmatrix}$

2. What is the difference of $\begin{bmatrix} 3 & -2 \\ 4 & -3 \end{bmatrix} - \begin{bmatrix} 2 & -5 \\ 7 & 12 \end{bmatrix}$?

   F. $\begin{bmatrix} -3 & 3 \\ -1 & 7 \end{bmatrix}$ G. $\begin{bmatrix} 1 & 3 \\ -3 & 15 \end{bmatrix}$ H. $\begin{bmatrix} -3 & -3 \\ 3 & 15 \end{bmatrix}$ I. $\begin{bmatrix} -1 & 3 \\ 3 & -15 \end{bmatrix}$

3. Which matrix is equal to $-6\begin{bmatrix} 2 & -7 \\ -3 & 4 \end{bmatrix}$?

   A. $\begin{bmatrix} -4 & -13 \\ -9 & -2 \end{bmatrix}$ B. $\begin{bmatrix} -8 & 1 \\ -3 & -10 \end{bmatrix}$ C. $\begin{bmatrix} -12 & 42 \\ 18 & -24 \end{bmatrix}$ D. $\begin{bmatrix} 12 & -42 \\ -18 & 24 \end{bmatrix}$

4. What is the value of x in the equation $2\begin{bmatrix} -6 & 9 \\ -3 & 1 \end{bmatrix} - \begin{bmatrix} -4 & -6 \\ -5 & 3 \end{bmatrix} = \begin{bmatrix} -8 & x \\ -1 & -1 \end{bmatrix}$?

   F. -24 G. -12 H. 12 I. 24

5. What is the value of x in the equation $-x\begin{bmatrix} 5 & 12 \\ -2 & -3 \end{bmatrix} = \begin{bmatrix} -35 & -84 \\ 14 & 21 \end{bmatrix}$?

   A. -40 B. -7 C. 7 D. 16

Short Response

6. The table at the right shows the sales of cell phones and televisions at an electronics store on Fridays, Saturdays, and Sundays of June and July. On which day did the store sell the most televisions during these two months? Find the answer using matrices.

June

	Cell Phones	TVs
Fri	127	114
Sat	138	146
Sun	98	106

July

	Cell Phones	TVs
Fri	112	117
Sat	122	152
Sun	101	92

Name ______________________ Class ____________ Date ____________

12-2 Think About a Plan

Frequency and Histograms

Error Analysis A student made the frequency table at the right using the data below. Describe and correct the error.

40 21 28 53 24 48 50 55 42 29 22 52 43 26 44

Interval	Frequency
20–29	6
40–49	5
50–59	4

Understanding the Problem

1. What does the first column represent? What errors might someone make in the first column?

2. What does the second column represent? What errors might someone make in the second column?

Planning the Solution

3. What is the minimum data value? What is the maximum?

4. What size interval would you choose to check the student's work?

5. How many intervals of that size are needed?

Getting an Answer

6. What error did the student make?

7. What change will you make to correct the student's frequency table?

Name ______________________ Class ____________ Date ____________

12-2 Practice

Form K

Frequency and Histograms

Use the data to make a frequency table.

1. strikeouts per game: 10 5 1 7 6 7 5 3 9 8 4 6 6 8 2

2. weight (kg): 27 19 21 31 29 24 18 19 30 25 26 20 18 27

Use the data to make a histogram.

3. number of lawns mowed:
12 15 10 22 7 12 18 14 9 11 5 14 19

4. price per foot of rope:
\$3 \$7 \$5 \$9 \$10 \$7 \$12
\$8 \$4 \$6 \$5 \$7 \$7 \$12

Tell whether each histogram is *uniform, symmetric,* or *skewed.*

5.

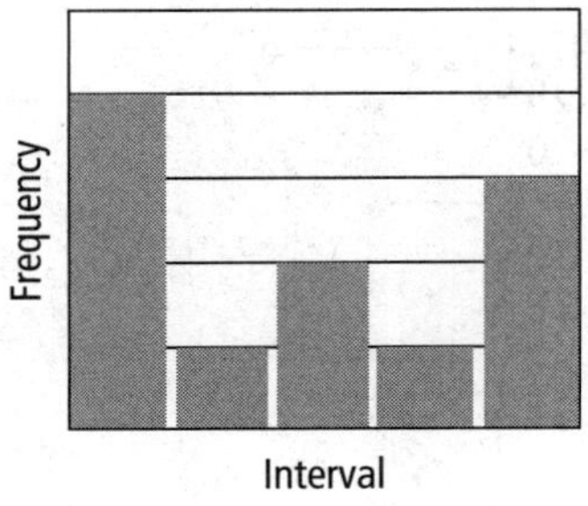

6.

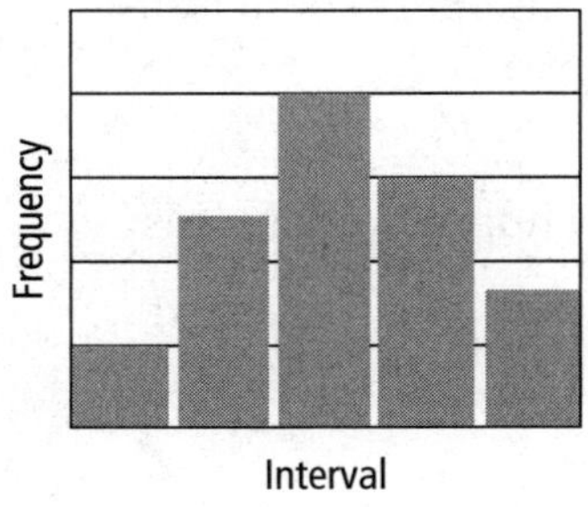

12-2 Practice (continued) — Form K

Frequency and Histograms

Use the data to make a cumulative frequency table.

7. minutes used per month:
675 815 747 508 642 588 821 818 689 590 777

8. weight (lb):
3.5 2.75 1.1 5.25 6.1 2.4 1.8 4.2 3.15 5.25 3.9 2.5

9. Rainfall amounts, in centimeters, are listed below. Make a histogram of the data that uses intervals of 2.

12 6 9 6 2 10 7 12 3
3 4 5 2 11 8 6 3 7

The histogram below shows the amount of money that 100 shoppers spent on groceries this week.

10. Which interval represents the greatest number of shoppers?

11. How many shoppers spent more than $175?

12. How many shoppers spent less than $126?

Money Spent on Groceries

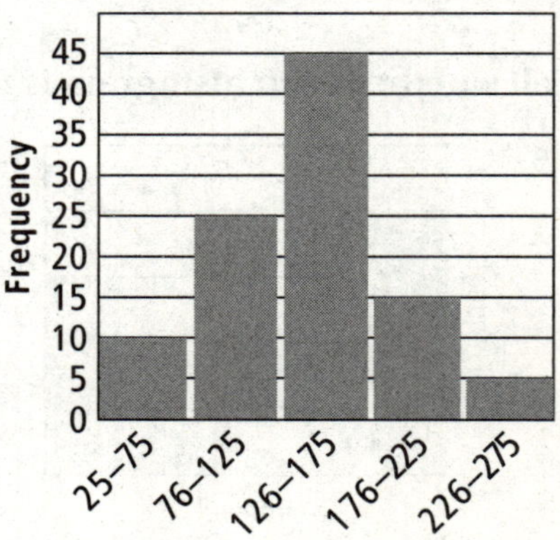

Name ______________________ Class ____________ Date ____________

12-2 Standardized Test Prep

Frequency and Histograms

Multiple Choice

For Exercises 1–3, choose the correct letter.

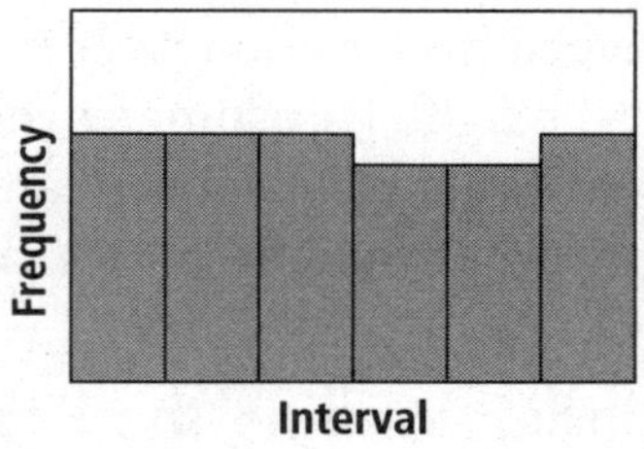

1. What is the shape of the histogram at the right?

A. symmetric   **C.** skewed
B. proportional   **D.** uniform

2. A student rolled two 6-sided number cubes several times. The numbers below are the sums of the numbers she rolled. Which histogram represents the data?

7 11 2 6 7 9 12 3 7 4 8 3 5 10 7 8 11 5 4 12

F.
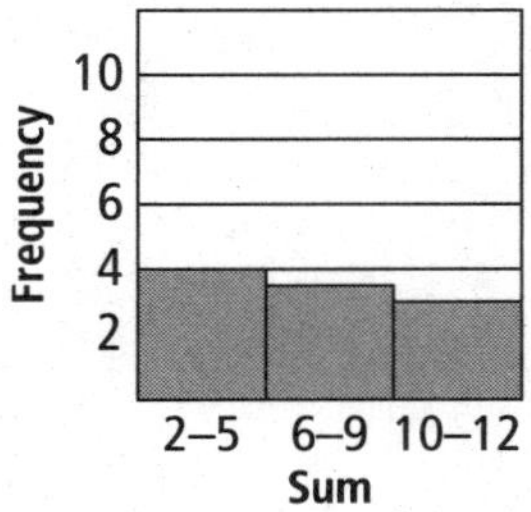

H.
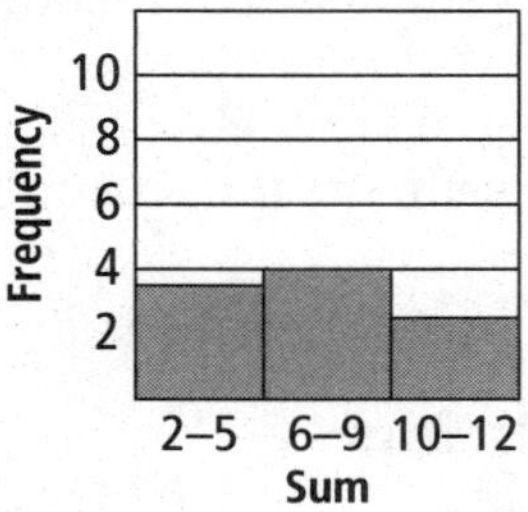

G.
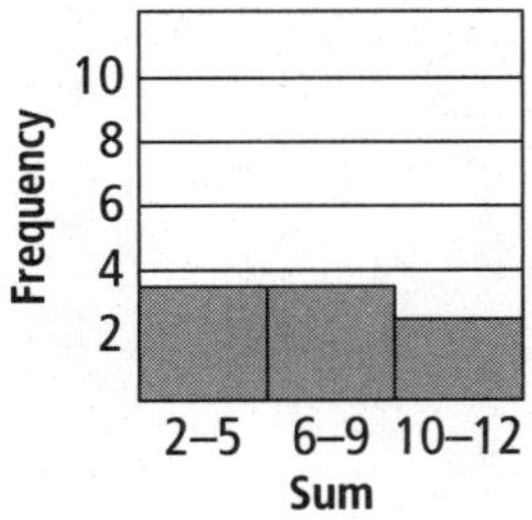

I.
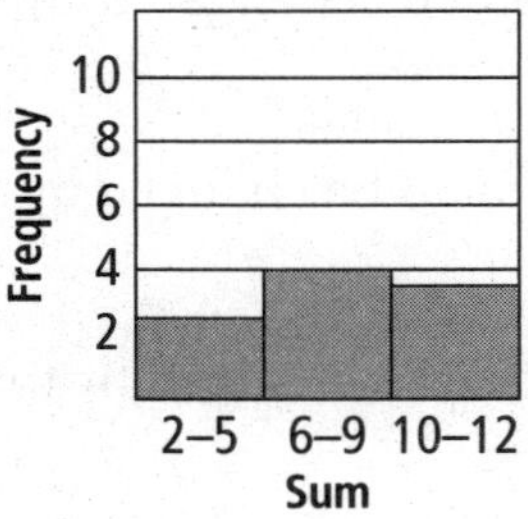

Short Response

3. The number of emails a friend received each day over the last 20 days is shown below. What is a cumulative frequency table that represents the data? What number of days did she receive 19 or fewer emails in a day?

15 22 18 9 32 35 14 10 34 45 21 25 6 12 7 14 16 20 5 37

Name ______________________ Class ____________ Date ____________

12-3 Think About a Plan

Measures of Central Tendency and Dispersion

Wildlife Management A wildlife manager measured and tagged twelve adult male crocodiles. The data he collected are at the right. He estimates the crocodiles will grow 0.1 m each year. What will be the mean, median, mode, and range of the crocodiles' lengths after 4 yr?

Crocodile Lengths (m)			
2.4	2.5	2.5	2.3
2.8	2.4	2.3	2.4
2.1	2.2	2.5	2.7

Understanding the Problem

1. What do the data in the table represent?

2. How would you estimate the crocodiles' lengths after 1 year?

3. How would you estimate the crocodiles' lengths after 4 years?

Planning the Solution

4. How will the mean be changed by the crocodiles' growth?

5. How will the median be changed by the crocodiles' growth?

6. How will the mode be changed by the crocodiles' growth?

7. How will the range be changed by the crocodiles' growth?

Getting an Answer

8. What is the mean of the crocodiles' lengths after 4 years?

9. What is the median of the crocodiles' lengths after 4 years?

10. What is the mode of the crocodiles' lengths after 4 years?

11. What is the range of the crocodiles' lengths after 4 years?

Name ______________________ Class ____________ Date ____________

12-3 Practice

Form K

Measures of Central Tendency and Dispersion

Find the mean, median, and mode of each data set. Which measure of central tendency best describes the data?

1. price per item:
   \$12 \$8 \$15 \$20 \$15

2. average rate (rev/sec):
   75 81 79 68 79

3. distance from the park (km):
   2.2 3 4.1 3.5 3 2.5

4. extra points kicked:
   3 5 3 2 4

Find the value of *x* so that the data set has the given mean.

5. 14, 10, 17, 9, x; mean 14

6. 101, 92, 76, 88, x; mean 93

7. 2.5, 6.1, 7.8, 3.7, x; mean 5.04

8. 22.6, 32.9, 29.7, 19.8, x; mean 26.5

9. 0.9, 1.6, 3.4, 0.5, x; mean 1.4

10. 77, 100, 92, 84, x; mean 88

11. One runner's times in the first six races of the year were 18.5, 18.2, 19, 18.75, 19.1, and 19 minutes. Another runner's times were 17.2, 18, 17.5, 18.75, 19, and 18.2 minutes. What are the range and mean of each runner's scores? Use your results to compare the runners' skills.

Find the range and mean of each data set. Use your results to compare the two data sets.

12. Set A: 17 13 21 10 14
    Set B: 12 16 15 11 13

13. Set C: 5.6 4.8 3.7 7.1 9.2
    Set D: 10 5.2 3.8 2.9 6.8

14. The lengths of some pieces of lumber are 6 ft, 12 ft, 9 ft, 11 ft, and 8 ft. What are the mean, median, mode, and range of the lengths?

12-3 Practice (continued)

Form K

Measures of Central Tendency and Dispersion

Find the mean, median, mode, and range of each data set after you perform the given operation on each data value.

15. 8, 12, 10, 7, 4, 7; subtract 1

16. 37, 32, 35, 41, 48, 36; add 3

17. 16.2, 16.7, 16.1, 16, 16.9, 16; add 3.5

18. 19, 12, 15, 14, 21, 9; divide by 3

19. 7.5, 14.2, 11.8, 19.6, 4.8, 11.8; multiply by 2

20. 2.1, 3.2, 4.5, 4.2, 3.2, 5.6; add −2

21. The lengths of George's last five road trips were 6 hr, 4 hr, 8 hr, 12 hr, and 10 hr. Jenny's last five trips were 6 hr, 9 hr, 2 hr, 15 hr, and 4 hr. Find the mean, median, mode, and range of George's trips and Jenny's trips. Use your results to compare each person's travels.

22. The goalkeeper had 7 saves, 4 saves, 9 saves, 12 saves, 2 saves, 7 saves, and 5 saves in the first seven games of the season. How many saves must the goalkeeper make in the next game to achieve an average of 8 saves per game?

23. Over six months, a phone bill averaged $35 per month. The bills for the first five months were $32, $35, $48, $29, and $31. What was the phone bill in the sixth month? Find the median, mode, and range of the six electric bills.

Name ______________________ Class ____________ Date ____________

12-3 Standardized Test Prep

Measures of Central Tendency and Dispersion

Multiple Choice

For Exercises 1–5, choose the correct letter.

1. What is the mean of the data set 23, 36, 42, 33, 27, 32, 42, 28, 18, and 39?

A. 23 **B.** 32 **C.** 35 **D.** 42

2. Six line segments were drawn at equal intervals across a sketch of Jackson Pond. Using the lengths of the line segments, what is the mean width of Jackson Pond?

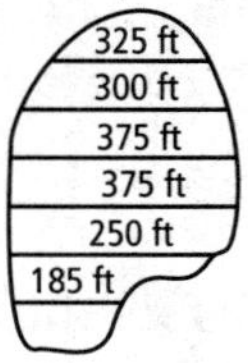

F. 190 ft **H.** 301.67 ft

G. 300 ft **I.** 375 ft

3. What is the range of the data set 125, 236, 185, 125, 201, and 155?

A. 62.5 **B.** 111 **C.** 125 **D.** 171.17

4. A world-class sprinter is the coach of a high school track team. There are 52 members of the track team. The coach times everyone on the team, including himself, running the 100-meter race. Which measure will be the most greatly affected by the inclusion of the coach's time?

F. mean **G.** median **H.** mode **I.** range

5. What is the mode of the data set 87, 78, 42, 97, 78, 92, 78, 48, 87, 94, and 59?

A. 55 **B.** 76.36 **C.** 78 **D.** 87

Short Response

6. The table at the right shows the number of wins a baseball team had in its first five seasons. What is the mean number of wins the team had per season? What is the median number of wins the team had per season?

Season	Wins
1	68
2	89
3	76
4	59
5	93

Name ______________________ Class ____________ Date ____________

12-4 Think About a Plan

Box-and-Whisker Plots

Basketball The heights of the players on a basketball team are 74 in., 79 in., 71.5 in., 81 in., 73 in., 76 in., 78 in., 71 in., 72 in., and 73.5 in. When the 76-in.-tall player is replaced, the percentile rank of the 73.5-in.-tall player becomes 60. Write an inequality that represents the possible heights of the replacement player.

1. How many players are there?

2. Before the replacement is made, how many players are less than or equal to 73.5 in. tall?

3. Before the replacement is made, what is the percentile rank of the 73.5-inch player? Show your work.

4. If the 76-inch player is replaced with a player less than or equal to 73.5 in. tall, how does that affect the percentile rank of the 73.5-inch tall player?

____

____

____

5. If the 76-inch player is replaced with a player greater than 73.5 in. tall, how does that affect the percentile rank of the 73.5-inch tall player?

____

____

____

6. Write an inequality that represents the height of the replacement player if the percentile rank of the 73.5-inch player becomes 60?

Name _______________________ Class ___________ Date ___________

12-4 Practice

Form K

Box-and-Whisker Plots

Find the minimum, first quartile, median, third quartile, and maximum of each data set.

1. 99 88 77 85 62 93 71

2. 22 19 32 35 28 25 33 24 27

3. 45.5 52.7 41 49.8 59 72.1 51.7 53.2

4. 7 7 11 14 15 13 19 17

5. 175 198 225 179 182 185 201 215

6. 42 58 18 37 51 49 32 61 99 45

Make a box-and-whisker plot to represent each set of data.

7. fair attendance: 2515 2725 2972 3125 3195 3250 3555

8. fundraiser revenue: $195 $275 $295 $185 $210 $115 $340 $285 $195

9. swimmers practicing: 17 22 19 17 25 9 14

10. games won: 97 55 78 86 77 68 92 81

11. admission prices: $14 $17 $10 $12.50 $19.50 $25 $15 $9 $11.50

12. height (in.): 66 58 80 72 65 70 62 66 59 60

12-4 Practice (continued) *Form K*

Box-and-Whisker Plots

13. Of 350 runners competing in a race, 50 run the race in less than or equal to 20 minutes. What is the percentile rank of the runners who finish in under 20 minutes?

14. Of 50 babies born, 5 weigh more than 10 pounds. What is the percentile rank of a baby that weighs 10 pounds?

15. Ten students earned the following scores on a test: 92, 73, 81, 90, 79, 66, 94, 83, 61, and 99. Which score has a percentile rank of 90? Which score has a percentile rank of 10?

Make box-and-whisker plots to compare the data sets.

16. Earned commission:
Dale's: $150 $125 $145 $175 $105 $100 $200 $180
Juanita's: $155 $185 $215 $205 $170 $165 $195 $200

17. Weekly cars sold:
Kathy's: 5 8 3 12 7 11 9 4 8
Samuel's: 9 2 5 10 9 7 7 6 10

18. Video length (min):
Training 1: 78 62 45 65 50 59 67 62 51 70
Training 2: 60 67 50 58 62 71 69 54 60 64

Name ______________________ Class ____________ Date ____________

12-4 Standardized Test Prep

Box-and-Whisker Plots

Gridded Response

Solve each exercise and enter your answer on the grid provided.

1. During the eight-game regular season, a running back ran the football for 125, 82, 105, 155, 98, 68, 111, and 95 yards. What is the third quartile of the data set?

2. During the last two weeks of work, a salesperson has sold 14, 22, 31, 7, 14, 15, 34, 42, 10, and 17 items each day. What is the first quartile of the data set?

3. This year, a toy drive for a charity lasted 15 days. The charity received 55, 63, 44, 110, 99, 67, 88, 75, 53, 47, 64, 76, 92, 56, and 110 toys on the days of the drive. What is the median of the data?

4. Using the box-and-whisker plot shown below, what is the interquartile range of the data?

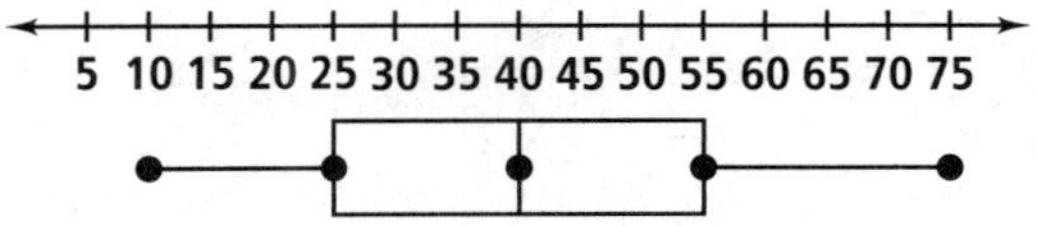

5. Of the 32 students in the class, 12 stand 5 feet 5 inches or are shorter. What is the percentile rank of a student who is 5 feet 5 inches tall?

1.
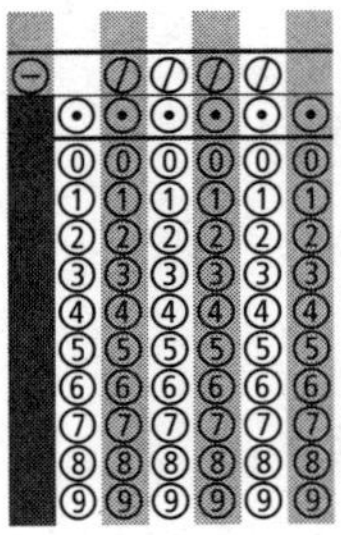

2.
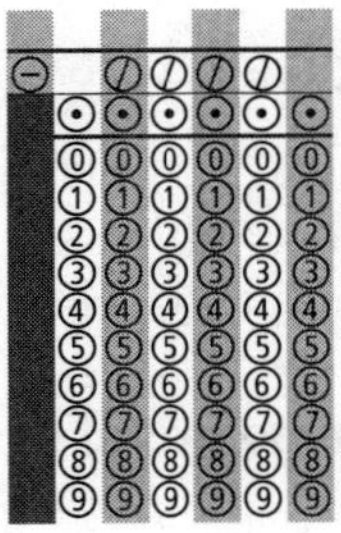

3.
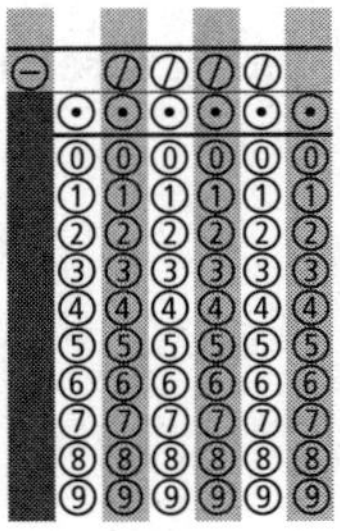

4.
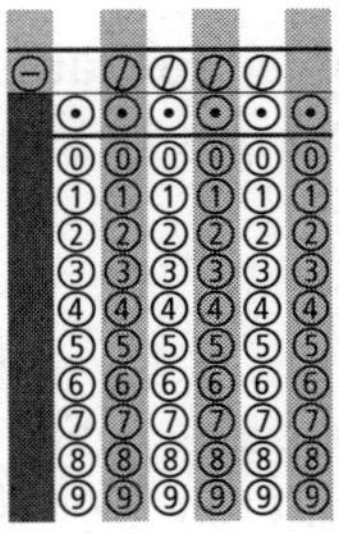

5.
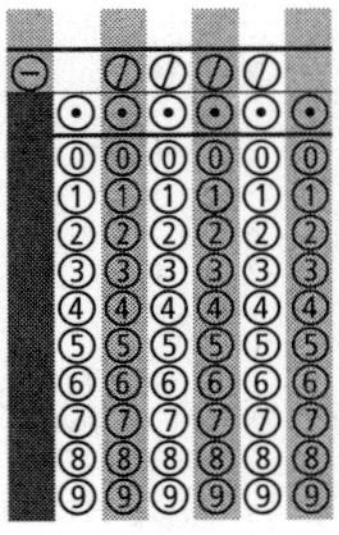

Name ____________________ Class __________ Date __________

12-5 Think About a Plan

Samples and Surveys

Travel A travel agent wants to determine whether a trip to France is a popular vacation for young adults. How could each factor described below cause bias in the survey results?

a. The agent interviews people at an international airport.

b. The agent asks, "Would you prefer to vacation in France or Italy?"

c. Of the people interviewed, 86% took a French class in high school.

1. What reasons might a person have for being at an international airport? How might those reasons cause bias in the survey results?

2. Name three locations for the agent's survey that are less likely to cause bias in the survey results.

3. How many different answers can the agent expect to his question, "Would you prefer to vacation in France or Italy?" How might the set of potential answers cause bias in the survey results?

4. Write three questions for the agent's survey that are less likely to cause bias in the survey results.

5. How might someone's familiarity with a foreign language create bias in a survey about travel to a foreign country?

6. How could the travel agent reduce bias caused by the potential customers' familiarity with French?

Name ______________________ Class ____________ Date ____________

12-5 Practice

Form K

Samples and Surveys

Determine whether each data set is *qualitative* or *quantitative*.

1. price of milk

2. car sales

3. favorite ice cream

4. age at retirement

5. miles per hour

6. lucky number

Determine whether each data set is *univariate* or *bivariate*.

7. height and weight of your friends

8. age of your fish

9. how many sports your friends play

10. distances driven

11. number of points scored

12. width and depth of patio

Determine whether the sampling method is *random*, *systematic*, or *stratified*. Tell whether the method will produce a good sample.

13. A counselor surveys students whose names are drawn out of a bag.

14. A teacher separates the students into boys and girls and randomly selects two students from each group to survey.

Determine whether each question is biased. Explain your answer.

15. Would you rather listen to boring classical music or upbeat pop music?

16. What is your favorite movie?

12-5 Practice (continued) *Form K*

Samples and Surveys

17. You want to find out how much households in your city spend on utilities each month. You ask every tenth person at a local restaurant. How might this create a bias in your results?

18. You want to find out how much time students in your school spend watching television each week. You ask every tenth student in your Advanced Biology class. How might this create a bias in your results?

19. A pizza parlor owner wants to determine whether a new topping, spicy Italian sausage, would be popular with his customers. How could each factor below create bias in the survey results?

a. The owner interviews customers outside the library.

b. The owner interviews his adult customers.

c. The owner asks, "Which would you prefer: pepperoni or spicy Italian sausage?"

In each situation, identify the population and sample. Tell whether each sample is a *random*, *systematic*, or *stratified* sample.

20. At an office supply store, every fourth customer is asked to complete a survey.

21. You ask a random selection of three girls and three boys in your Algebra class what their favorite movie is.

Classify the data as *qualitative* or *quantitative*, and as *univariate* or *bivariate*.

22. age and height of people at the park

23. favorite sports and favorite hobbies of students in the high school

24. weight of wildlife captured, tagged, and released

Name ______________________ Class ____________ Date ____________

12-5 Standardized Test Prep

Samples and Surveys

Multiple Choice

For Exercises 1–6, choose the correct letter.

1. When statisticians collect information to find characteristics of a large group of people, they survey part of the group. What is the part of the group called?

A. specimen **B.** part **C.** population **D.** sample

2. You want to find out what the favorite hot lunch in the school cafeteria is among the high school students. At an assembly for the whole school, you decide to survey all students who are sitting on the end of their rows in the auditorium. What type of survey are you conducting?

F. biased **G.** random **H.** systematic **I.** stratified

3. A survey is being conducted to determine the favorite movies for various ages. Which of the following best describes this survey?

A. qualitative and univariate
B. qualitative and bivariate
C. quantitative and univariate
D. quantitative and bivariate

4. A town wants to know the number of cell phones in each household. The town divides the population up by neighborhood and surveys a random number of households in each. What type of survey is this?

F. biased **G.** random **H.** systematic **I.** stratified

5. In order to find out what the best restaurant in town is, you call 25 of your friends at random. What type of survey is this?

A. stratified **B.** systematic **C.** biased **D.** unbiased

6. A store would like to understand what is important to their customers. They randomly select every 50th customer to survey. What type of survey is this?

F. biased **G.** random **H.** systematic **I.** stratified

Short Response

7. A pollster is trying to determine who the people in the state think will be the best candidate for senate. Her staff calls 1000 people in the 4 major cities of the state. Will this plan give a good sample? Explain.

Name ______________________ Class ______________ Date ______________

12-6 Think About a Plan

Permutations and Combinations

Media The call signs of radio and television stations in the United States generally begin with the letter W east of the Mississippi River and the letter K west of the Mississippi. Repetition of letters is allowed.

a. How many different call signs are possible if each station uses a W or K followed by 3 letters?

b. How many different call signs are possible if each station uses a W or K followed by 4 letters?

1. How many different call signs are possible if a station uses a W followed by 3 letters? Use the formula for permutations.

2. How many different call signs are possible if a station uses K followed by 3 letters? Compare this answer to the one above.

3. How would you combine your answers above to determine how many different call signs are possible if each station uses a W or K followed by 3 letters?

4. How many different call signs are possible if each station uses a W or K followed by 3 letters?

5. How many different call signs are possible if a station uses a W followed by 4 letters? Use the formula for permutations.

6. How many different call signs are possible if each station uses a W or K followed by 4 letters?

Name ______________________ Class ____________ Date ____________

12-6 Practice

Form K

Permutations and Combinations

1. A four-character secret code can begin with any two of the five vowels and end with any four numerals, from 0 to 9.
   a. How many possible choices are there for each of the first two characters? For each of the last four characters?
   b. How many different six-character license plate numbers are possible?

2. The baseball coach is selecting from 9 starters who will be the first three batters. How many different batter lineups can the coach consider for the first three up?

3. There are 5 books to be arranged on the bookshelf. How many different ways can the books be arranged on the bookshelf?

Find the value of each expression.

4. ${}_4P_2$
5. ${}_6P_4$
6. ${}_7P_3$
7. ${}_9P_3$
8. ${}_{10}P_2$
9. ${}_5P_4$
10. ${}_3P_2$
11. ${}_{13}P_3$

12. There are 60 songs on your music player. In how many different ways can you arrange 5 songs to listen to while exercising?

Find the value of each expression.

13. ${}_3C_1$
14. ${}_7C_5$
15. ${}_4C_3$
16. ${}_8C_4$
17. ${}_9C_5$
18. ${}_7C_6$
19. ${}_6C_2$
20. ${}_9C_3$

Name ______________________________ Class ______________ Date ______________

12-6 Practice (continued)

Form K

Permutations and Combinations

21. There are 20 marbles in a bag. Each marble has a different design or color. How many ways can you draw 8 marbles from the jar?

Explain whether each situation is a combination problem or a permutation problem.

22. Your friends borrowed 5 different movies from the library. In how many different orders can they watch the movies?

23. There are 100 comic books to choose from at the local hobby store. How many different sets of 10 comic books could you choose to buy?

24. An ATM machine requires a 4-digit PIN. The digits in the PIN can be selected from the digits 0 through 9 and can be reused. How many possible PINs are there?

25. You have 10 pictures to arrange in the scrapbook. How many different ways can you arrange 6 of the pictures on a single page?

26. A basketball coach chooses his 5 starters from 12 players. How many different groups of starters are there?

Find the value of each expression.

27. ${}_{18}P_2$ **28.** ${}_{18}C_2$ **29.** ${}_{8}C_5$ **30.** ${}_{8}P_5$

Name ______________________ Class ____________ Date ____________

12-6 Standardized Test Prep

Permutations and Combinations

Multiple Choice

For Exercises 1–7, choose the correct letter.

1. What is the value of ${}_5P_3$?

A. 20 **B.** 40 **C.** 60 **D.** 120

2. What is the value of ${}_{10}C_6$?

F. 210 **G.** 5040 **H.** 151,200 **I.** 3,628,800

3. There are 12 people on the basketball team. How many different 5-person starting lineups can be chosen?

A. 120 **B.** 792 **C.** 95,040 **D.** 3,991,680

4. The manager of a baseball team has 15 players to choose from for his 9-person batting order. How many different ways can he arrange the players in the lineup?

F. 5005 **G.** 362,880 **H.** 3,603,600 **I.** 1,816,214,400

5. For a road trip, a friend is going to place 5 CDs into her CD player. She has 9 CDs to choose from. How many different selections of CDs can she make?

A. 126 **B.** 3024 **C.** 15,120 **D.** 362,880

6. There are 8 students on the ballot who are running for student council. Four students will be selected for the council. How many different groups of students can be selected for the council?

F. 24 **G.** 70 **H.** 1680 **I.** 40,320

7. A website requires a 4-digit numerical password in which the digits cannot repeat. How many possible passwords are there?

A. 24 **B.** 5040 **C.** 151,200 **D.** 3,628,800

Short Response

8. A restaurant serves 4 different sandwiches, 3 different sides, and 3 different beverages for lunch. How many possible meals are there? Show your work.

Name ______________________ Class ____________ Date ____________

12-7 Think About a Plan

Theoretical and Experimental Probability

Transportation Out of 80 workers surveyed at a company, 17 walk to work.

a. What is the experimental probability that a randomly selected worker at that company walks to work?

b. Predict about how many of the 3600 workers at the company walk to work.

Understanding the Problem

1. Write a fraction that represents the probability that a randomly selected worker at the company walks to work.

$$P(\text{walks to work}) = \frac{\text{number surveyed who walk to work}}{\text{total number surveyed}} = \frac{\square}{\square}$$

Planning the Solution

2. Let w represent the number of workers who walk to work. Write an equation that could be used to predict the total number of workers who walk to work.

$$w = \frac{\square}{\square} \times \boxed{}$$

Getting an Answer

3. Solve the equation.

4. Is your answer reasonable? Explain.

____

____

5. The experimental probability is ____________, and I predict that approximately ____________ workers walk to work.

Name ______________________ Class ____________ Date ____________

12-7 Practice

Form K

Theoretical and Experimental Probability

You spin a spinner that has 8 equal-sized sections numbered 1 to 8. Find each probability.

1. $P(7)$

2. $P(\text{odd number})$

3. $P(\text{not } 2)$

4. $P(\text{less than } 6)$

5. $P(\text{multiple of } 2)$

6. $P(\text{less than } 9)$

7. You roll a number cube. What is the probability that you will roll a number greater than 4?

8. The probability drawing a purple marble is $\frac{3}{5}$. What is the probability that the marble drawn will not be purple?

You choose a marble at random from a bag containing 5 yellow marbles, 3 black marbles, and 6 orange marbles. Find the odds.

9. odds in favor of yellow

10. odds in favor of orange

11. odds against black

12. odds against orange

13. You roll a number cube. What are the odds that you will roll a number less than 6?

12-7 Practice (continued)

Form K

Theoretical and Experimental Probability

One hundred randomly selected students at East High School were asked to name their favorite subject. The results are as follows: Art: 12, Math: 20, English: 35, Social Studies: 33. Find the experimental probability that a student selected at random makes the given response.

14. *P*(Art)

15. *P*(Math)

16. *P*(English)

17. *P*(Social Studies)

18. A soccer player predicts that the probability of her team winning the match is 64%. What is the probability that her team will not win?

19. Pasco usually makes 3 out of every 4 of his extra point kicks. What is the probability that he will miss his next kick?

20. There are 700 students at Washington High School. You survey 75 randomly selected students and find that 60 plan to go to college after graduation. How many students are likely to go to college after graduation?

21. The Acme Production Company randomly selects its products and checks for defects. If 2 of the 90 selected products are defective, how many defective products would you expect in the 2000 products manufactured?

Name ______________________ Class ____________ Date ____________

12-7 Standardized Test Prep

Theoretical and Experimental Probability

Multiple Choice

For Exercises 1–5, choose the correct letter.

1. A letter from the word *MISSISSIPPI* is selected at random. What is the probability that the letter is *I*?

A. $\frac{2}{11}$ **B.** $\frac{1}{5}$ **C.** $\frac{4}{11}$ **D.** $\frac{2}{5}$

2. You spin a spinner that has 8 equal-sized sections numbered 1 to 8. Which event is least likely to occur?

F. The number is even.
G. The number is greater than 3.
H. The number is less than 3.
I. The number is a multiple of 5.

3. You toss a number cube. What are the odds against getting a number less than 3?

A. 2 : 1 **B.** 1 : 2 **C.** 3 : 1 **D.** 1 : 3

4. A meteorologist says that the probability of snow today is 45%. What is the probability that it will *not* snow?

F. $\frac{2}{11}$ **G.** $\frac{9}{20}$ **H.** $\frac{11}{20}$ **I.** $\frac{9}{11}$

5. What is the probability that a number picked from the set $\{-4, -3, -2, -1, 0, 1, 2, 3, 4, 5\}$ will be a solution of $2x + 5 > 1$?

A. 20% **B.** 30% **C.** 70% **D.** 80%

Short Response

6. A pizza restaurant is having a contest. The restaurant advertises that one out of every 25 customers will win a small pizza.

a. What is the probability that a customer will win?

b. If the restaurant has 275 customers on Monday, how many winners would you expect?

Name ______________________ Class ____________ Date ____________

12-8 Think About a Plan

Probability of Compound Events

Phone Poll A pollster conducts a survey by phone. The probability that a call does not result in a person taking this survey is 85%. What is the probability that a pollster makes 4 calls and none result in a person taking the survey?

Understanding the Problem

1. What is the probability that the first call results in the person not taking the survey?

2. What is the probability that the second call results in the person not taking the survey?

3. Are the first and second calls *independent* or *dependent* events?

4. How could you find the probability that the first two calls result in neither person taking the survey?

Planning the Solution

5. Write an expression for the probability that none of the 4 calls result in a person taking the survey.

Getting an Answer

6. Evaluate the expression you wrote in Exercise 5.

7. Explain whether it is more likely that the 4 calls result in no one taking the survey or that at least one person takes the survey.

Name ______________________ Class ____________ Date ____________

12-8 Practice

Form K

Probability of Compound Events

You spin a spinner that has 8 equal-sized sections numbered 1 to 8. Find each probability.

1. $P(2 \text{ or } 4)$

2. $P(\text{odd or } 6)$

3. $P(\text{multiple of 2 or odd})$

4. $P(\text{odd or greater than } 3)$

5. $P(\text{even or less than } 4)$

6. $P(\text{multiple of 3 or multiple of 2})$

7. Open-Ended What is an example of a compound event composed of two mutually exclusive events when you spin a spinner numbered 1 to 8?

You roll a black number cube and a white number cube. Find each probability.

8. $P(\text{black 4 and white 4})$

9. $P(\text{black even and white even})$

10. P(black 3 or 4 and white 1 or 6)

11. $P(\text{black 1 and white odd})$

12. $P(\text{black even and white greater than 2})$

Name ________________________________ Class ______________ Date ______________

12-8 Practice (continued) *Form K*

Probability of Compound Events

13. The probability that Hannah will be late for dinner is $\frac{1}{2}$. What is the probability that she will be late for dinner two nights in a row?

You choose a tile at random from a bag containing 4 tiles with R, 2 tiles with S, and 3 tiles with T. You replace the tile and then choose again. Find each probability.

14. P(both S)

15. P(both T)

16. P(R then T)

17. P(T then S)

You choose a marble at random from a bag containing 3 yellow marbles, 8 red marbles, and 4 blue marbles. You pick a second marble without replacing the first. Find each probability.

18. P(red then blue)

19. P(both yellow)

20. P(yellow then blue)

21. P(both red)

22. The committee to plan the homecoming dance has 4 juniors and 6 seniors. To decide who will plan the decorations, the advisor puts the names of the students in a hat and randomly picks one name. Then the advisor picks another name without replacing the first. What is the probability that both students picked are seniors?

Name ______________________ Class ____________ Date ____________

12-8 Standardized Test Prep

Probability of Compound Events

Multiple Choice

For Exercises 1–5, choose the correct letter.

1. You spin a spinner that has 10 equal-sized sections numbered 1 to 10. Which compound event is most likely to occur?

A. a 2 or a 3
B. a 1 or a number greater than 8
C. an odd number or a 7
D. an even number or a 5

2. What type of compound event is represented by the roll of two number cubes?

F. dependent events
G. overlapping events
H. independent events
I. mutually exclusive events

3. You choose a marble at random from a bag containing 3 orange marbles, 4 green marbles, and 3 yellow marbles. You replace the marble and then pick a second marble. What is the probability that you will pick a green marble both times?

A. $\frac{6}{50}$ **B.** $\frac{2}{15}$ **C.** $\frac{4}{25}$ **D.** $\frac{8}{45}$

4. Seven of 28 domino tiles show the same number of dots on each side. These tiles are called *doubles*. You pick a domino tile at random. Then you pick another tile without replacing the first. What is the probability that both tiles are doubles?

F. $\frac{3}{56}$ **G.** $\frac{1}{18}$ **H.** $\frac{1}{16}$ **I.** $\frac{7}{648}$

5. There are 8 jellybeans in a bag. The probability of randomly picking two orange jellybeans without replacement is $\frac{3}{14}$. How many orange jellybeans are in the bag?

A. 3 orange jellybeans
B. 4 orange jellybeans
C. 5 orange jellybeans
D. 6 orange jellybeans

Extended Response

6. There are 20 marbles in a bag. The probability that you pick one red marble at random is $\frac{1}{5}$. What is the probability that you will pick two red marbles in a row if you do not replace the first? Explain.